Surviving Job Loss

Surviving Job Loss

Papermakers in Maine and Minnesota

Kenneth A. Root
Rosemarie J. Park

2016

W.E. Upjohn Institute for Employment Research
Kalamazoo, Michigan

Library of Congress Cataloging-in-Publication Data

Names: Root, Kenneth A., author. | Park, Rosemarie J., author.
Title: Surviving job loss : papermakers in Maine and Minnesota / Kenneth A. Root, Rosemarie J. Park.
Description: Kalamazoo, Mich. : W.E. Upjohn Institute for Employment Research, [2016] | Series: WE focus series | Description based on print version record and CIP data provided by publisher; resource not viewed.
Identifiers: LCCN 2016002251 (print) | LCCN 2015048918 (e-book) | ISBN 9780880995085 (e-book) | ISBN 0880995048 (e-book) | ISBN 9780880995078 (pbk. : alk. paper) | ISBN 0880995076 (pbk. : alk. paper)
Subjects: LCSH: Paper industry workers—United States—Case studies. | Plant shutdowns—United States—Case studies. | Unemployed—United States—Case studies. | Displaced workers—United States—Case studies. | Older people—Employment—United States—Case studies.
Classification: LCC HD8039.P332 (print) | LCC HD8039.P332 U676 (e-book) | DDC 331.13/78760974145—dc23
LC record available at http://lccn.loc.gov/2016002251

© 2016
W.E. Upjohn Institute for Employment Research
300 S. Westnedge Avenue
Kalamazoo, Michigan 49007-4686

Cover design by Alcorn Publication Design.
Index prepared by Diane Worden.
Printed in the United States of America.
Printed on recycled paper.

This book is dedicated to the memory of Steven A. Root.

Contents

Figures

Tables

Acknowledgments

For most people, getting a book idea to the finish line as a completed accomplishment is no easy task, and that is certainly the case for us. While book authors are (presumably) responsible for the bulk of the work, there are others involved in significant ways who remain anonymous. These "others," paid for their work as research assistants, proofreaders, or typesetters, are not formally acknowledged by name, yet their work is essential, and the project wouldn't be completed if not for their involvement.

One of the individuals who has been a major helper to the senior author has been his son, Steve. Over the years, Steve's task in numerous research projects was often to do the coding and setup work for computer analysis. Steve did the coding for this project, too, and he did it well. Then, at age 45, Steve died—an early death for sure—and we no longer have his very capable assistance, pleasant manner, personal warmth, and wonderful smile.

While this book focuses on two paper mills in Sartell, Minnesota, and Bucksport, Maine, we have benefited from the assistance of Christina Greenleaf, the rapid response and peer support coordinator for the Maine AFL-CIO, who, with the permission of Judy Pelletier from the Maine Department of Labor, served as our Maine contact. Our primary access to contacts with the situation in the Sartell, Minnesota, area involved Gerry Parzino, United Steelworkers (USW) staff representative for District 11, located in Minneapolis, and Don Reginek, who served as the USW Local 274 president at the time of the Sartell downsizing and mill closure. Certainly, William Craig at the University of Minnesota's Center for Urban and Regional Affairs was also instrumental in helping us initiate this project; he then helped us expand the project when the Sartell mill closure was announced. We happily recognize the contributions of Kevin Hollenbeck, Benjamin Jones, and Erika Jackson at the W.E. Upjohn Institute for Employment Research, who were significantly involved in getting this book to publication. Of course, Verso employees at both the Sartell and Bucksport paper mills who participated in this research similarly deserve our thanks and recognition; we greatly appreciate their assistance. We are hoping that this book will initiate a fresh focus on the paper industry, and in particular provide assistance to those paper workers confronted with job loss.

Many thanks to all who have provided assistance in helping us complete our research.

Kenneth A. Root
Rosemarie J. Park

1
Introduction

Our results show that a job loss at age 50 or above has substantial and long-lasting employment effects. Estimated entry rates suggest that a representative displaced worker in his or her 50s has a 70–75 percent chance of returning to work within two years of a job loss. Return rates for displaced workers in their 60s are substantially lower. These postdisplacement jobs are often short-lived, with displaced but reemployed workers facing significantly increased probabilities of exiting employment.
—Sewin Chan and Ann Huff Stevens (2001, p. 485)

Losing a job through no fault of one's own is a significant event that often poses difficulty for the job loser and for his or her family. Most of us work because we need the compensation provided by the tasks we do. But beyond that, we also work to be included in the social milieu—to have an economic identity connecting us to an employer, work colleagues, clients, customers, and our community. Without work, we are separated from our identity as a productive person, and if we go through an extended period of unemployment, we are likely to feel distant, isolated, detached, and unfulfilled (Young 2012).

For many displaced workers, there is an eagerness, even a desperation, to get back to work. The difficulty is that their personal skills may not be in demand, retraining in a different set of skills may be difficult to obtain, the economy may be in a recession (or recovering from one), and, as researchers have found, becoming fully integrated into the labor force after displacement can take time, perhaps two years or more (Silver, Shields, and Wilson 2005).

Our study of dislocated workers focuses on a comparison of downsized paper mill workers from a mill in Sartell, Minnesota, and another in Bucksport, Maine. Verso Corporation owned the two mills, which are now closed. A few months after the downsizing in Minnesota, the Sartell mill had an explosion and a fire, and the mill shut down for an assessment of damages. Ultimately, the company decided to close the

Sartell mill, so another 280 workers were then thrown out of work. Our comparison of downsizing impacts and opportunities is somewhat complex: initially the comparison operates between the Bucksport and Sartell workers, then between those downsized from Sartell and those terminated from Sartell in the closure, and finally, in terms of policy and programs, between displacement at U.S. paper mills (as reflected in Sartell and Bucksport) and at a Canadian paper mill in Nova Scotia that shut down at about the same time as the Sartell facility.

While a large number of paper mills have closed in the United States over the past 25 years, there has been only one study (Minchin 2006) that we are aware of that describes the impact of job loss on those in the paper industry. For that reason, Chapter 2 summarizes the recent past and current environment for the paper industry. Chapter 3 focuses on job loss at both the Bucksport and Sartell mills, along with follow-up data on those terminated from Sartell after the explosion and fire. Chapter 4 describes the response of those who lost their jobs. Chapter 5 covers the types of assistance provided to displaced workers generally, along with a comparison of the Maine and Minnesota state programs. While most of the mill workers were male, there were some who were female, and Chapter 6 focuses on these female production workers who lost their jobs. Chapter 7 covers cases where both husband and wife lost their jobs at the Sartell mill.

Chapter 8 evaluates how the community in which economic displacement occurs is relevant to the adjustment and opportunities for displaced workers. Chapter 9 describes how a Canadian mill that shut down provided support for the needs of its workers. In Chapter 10, we conclude our study with a look at the future for displaced workers and a discussion of how society can be more proactive in retaining good employees and assisting those who have been economically displaced. Chapter 11, which forms an epilogue to the book, updates the reader on recent developments involving Verso.

Even before the Great Recession, more than 15 percent of U.S. workers worried about losing their jobs. That percentage ranked sixth-highest out of 15 OECD countries (Anderson and Pontusson 2007). However, with the ongoing threat of job loss to workers even after the nation has largely recovered from the recession, job loss is likely to remain a significant concern for U.S. residents, not only in the paper industry but in almost all sectors of the economy.

2

The Study, Job Loss, and the Paper Industry

Corporate mergers and acquisitions [in pulp and paper mills] have become commonplace. For example, more than half of the mills in Upper Michigan have experienced an ownership change since 1990. The industry has become increasingly global, with most of the plants in Wisconsin and Upper Michigan owned by large multinational corporations. This means that local industries not only compete among themselves, but with plants in Europe, Asia, South America, and elsewhere. Expansion of pulp and paper capacity overseas, primarily in Asia and South America, has had major impacts on the paper industry.
—Bay-Lake Regional Planning Commission et al. (1999, p. ii)

In October 2011, the Verso Paper Company announced downsizings at its Sartell, Minnesota, and Bucksport, Maine, facilities, eliminating 169 and 151 workers, respectively, as it retired older paper machines. That was the bad news—until seven months later, when a 2012 Memorial Day explosion and fire killed one worker and injured several others at the Sartell facility. This ultimately prompted Verso to permanently close its Minnesota mill. Another 280 workers were now out of work. The job losses to downsized paper workers from the Verso mills in Maine and Minnesota and the termination of those from the shutdown of the Minnesota mill compose the database for our study. A brief summary of the paper industry frames the conditions of their displacement.

JOB LOSS IN THE PULP AND PAPER INDUSTRY

Our research centers on job loss among those who worked in the paper industry. In the case of the two Verso plants, the workers' displacement occurred on the heels of the Great Recession. This was a dif-

3

ficult time to be a papermaker without work—perhaps the most difficult time in recent history. Industry difficulties severely reduced the likelihood that terminated workers would have any option of being rehired in paper and pulp production. These difficulties included the following:

- The loss of foreign markets
- Stronger competition in Asia and South America from companies with newer, faster, more technologically sophisticated machines
- Stiffer competition among U.S. mills at a time of declining demand for paper products because of electronic conversion

To keep up with this competition, many companies have had to replace older paper machines with modern ones that have increased the width of the rolls of paper and the speed of production and require fewer workers to run them. Given these conditions, the chance that downsized workers would be able to transfer to another paper mill with the same employer or find a job at another paper company was remote.

Job loss in the paper industry is not new (Figure 2.1).[1] Companies have been shuttering mills for many years, and thousands of paper workers have become job losers. What *is* new is that the United States is not building new paper mills to replace those that become idled. Second, mergers and acquisitions have become commonplace to obtain market share, and once a mill has been acquired it is quickly evaluated to determine whether it should be shut down. And third, a reestablished balance point in world paper production and demand has yet to be determined. Given projections of a significant decline in paper demand in the coming years, it is likely that the next several years will see a continuing and pronounced job loss in the U.S. paper industry, both through workforce reductions as older machines are retired and through mill closures.

While there have been important displacement studies completed on various industries, the manufacture of paper is not among them. Meatpacking, autos, steel, defense, and textiles have been studied by numerous researchers and usually over a period of several years.[2] Nonetheless, numerous paper mills have been closed, as shown in Figure 2.1, and continue to be closed in the United States and Canada.[3] Perhaps one explanation for the lack of interest in paper and pulp mill job loss is the fact that most mills are typically located in rural areas and generally bypassed by media attention and awareness of the general population.

Figure 2.1 Pulp and Paper Mill Closures in the United States (1989–2010)

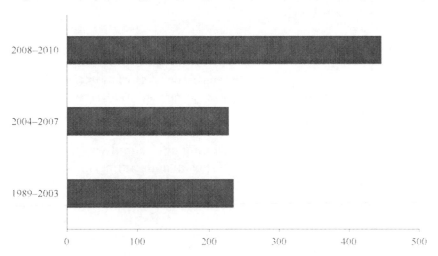

NOTE: While an exact count of pulp and paper mill closures is difficult to determine, over the past 25 years the Pulp and Paperworkers' Resource Council has followed mill curtailments and closures, noting job loss from temporary shutdowns, paper machine reductions, and sawmill closures. Figure 2.1 includes these types of mill changes.
SOURCE: Pulp and Paperworkers' Resource Council (2014).

Among major paper manufacturing states, the closure of paper mills or the reduction of employment levels has been of concern. Wisconsin, the leading U.S. paper producer, had 173 paper-related-industry plants in 1999, 121 (70 percent) of which were converters and 52 (30 percent) pulp and paper mills. In 1997–1998, several plants in Wisconsin and Upper Michigan either reduced their employment levels or closed. In Upper Michigan in 1999, there were 11 pulp and paper mills remaining after the closures. In Wisconsin, one seven-county area (the Fox River region) still had 23 pulp and paper mills. The Wisconsin and Upper Michigan study concluded that "the ability of communities to impact decisions regarding plant closings, layoffs, etc., is limited for pulp and paper mills due to their large size, the globally competitive market environment in which they operate, and the huge level of capital investment required to remain competitive" (Bay-Lake Regional Planning Commission et al. 1999, p. iii). Wisconsin took the lead among paper-producing states in 1950 and has not relinquished it since. The

American Forest and Paper Association ranked the state first in value of shipments for 2014 with $14.5 billion.[4]

A Brief History of U.S. Paper Production

According to the Maine Pulp and Paper Association (2013b), the first North American paper mill was started in 1690 at Wissahickon Creek, near Philadelphia. Other mills soon appeared, particularly in New York, Massachusetts, Pennsylvania, and Connecticut. Maine became involved in paper manufacturing after a mill was built on the Presumpscot River in the 1730s. Paper manufacturing in Maine was attractive because of its clean rivers and streams and the potential for power from harnessed water. The Maine forests were initially unimportant in paper production because at that time rags were used as raw material for paper production, and most paper mills were in populated areas, close to market outlets. According to Hunter (1955), early raw materials usable in paper production were straw, rags, waste paper, and manila stock, with most of these materials available in urban areas. Urban areas also could provide a supply of clean water and power. But once wood pulp became the core ingredient of paper, mill owners had to choose production sites that were either close to market outlets or near raw materials. Major early paper-producing states like Ohio, Indiana, Illinois, Connecticut, and New Jersey had limited forest resources, and in New York, Pennsylvania, Michigan, and Wisconsin, existing paper mills were not close to forests. The outcome was that paper mills close to market were shuttered as mills close to long-term, cheap supplies of wood were built. The same situation occurred with pulp mills, which had been located close to existing paper mills near the paper market. Hunter writes that more than 50 of the 135 pulp mills in existence in 1882 had closed by 1899, and "new large pulp and paper mills were being built in the forested counties of New York, New Hampshire, Maine, and Wisconsin, often on logging rivers" (p. 317).

The sawmill boom after 1900 created added competition for wood, particularly in the East, and lumber production moved to the Midwest region. As a result of eastern sawmill operations, pulpwood logs imported from Canada rose from 370,000 cords in 1899 to 740,000 in 1906 to 950,000 in 1911 (Hunter 1955). Change in the supply of wood was one factor in increasing the scale of production and the physical size of new paper and pulp mills. Poorly located or small paper operations, particularly those producing low-grade paper, were closed between 1882 and 1899. The development of large firms such as the International Paper Company (founded in 1898 in Corinth, New York) absorbed most of the newsprint mills in New York and New England, and from 1920 on, new mill sites were based on extensive forest surveys.

Technological changes in the paper industry advanced simultaneously, resulting in new, larger mills that boasted adaptable paper machines capable of producing different grades of paper, as well as pulp supplies that could be procured from pulp mills located elsewhere in the United States or purchased from Scandinavia or Canada. Imposing a tariff on all paper grades reduced competition from these same Scandinavian and Canadian mills (Hunter 1955). Without the protection of a tariff, some U.S. paper mills would have had to close.

In the 1850s, Samuel Dennis Warren purchased a small mill at Westbrook, Maine. By 1856, the S.D. Warren mill was the largest importer of rags in the world. A rag shortage and increasing demand for paper were the stimuli for finding alternative materials to create pulp. Both mechanical and chemical methods proved efficient for making paper from wood, and new mills started up. Wood pulp production in 1868 helped develop Maine's paper industry, and by 1875 the S.D. Warren mill had become the world's largest paper mill.

Further growth in the Maine paper industry occurred in the 1880s with the development of a sulfite chemical pulping process, such as created by the Penobscot Chemical Fiber Company, located in Old Town. Other Maine mills were started in Otis, Madison, Gardiner, Mechanic Falls, Poland, Canton, Waterville, Norway, South Paris, and Brunswick, although many of these mills have since closed. By 1890 there were 25 pulp mills in Maine, making Maine the leading producer of pulp. Paper production developed rapidly, and when the Great Northern Paper Company opened in 1900 it was the world's largest papermaker, producing 240 tons a day of newsprint. Early on, Maine trailed Massachusetts and New York among papermaking states, but Maine eventually rose to number one, only to lose that title to Wisconsin at midcentury.

Early expansion of the U.S. paper industry took place along three dimensions: 1) new mills were built, particularly in midwestern states like Wisconsin and Michigan, and eventually in southern states; 2) machine improvements allowed for wider paper rolls as well as faster operating speeds; and 3) technological advances allowed for increased production and maximum use of resources.

The new paper and pulp mills were often located in isolated towns. Indeed, as with other resource-based production (e.g., mining), the communities existed because of the availability of resources. Known as single-industry communities, they drew residents for employment opportunities, largely limited to the dominant resource-based industry. For paper and pulp mills, location was dependent on the combination of water and access to forests, while for mining operations the buried resource (coal or gold, for example) was the basic reason for settlement. Numerous paper mill communities have learned to survive after the closure of the mill, but not without enduring tough times, and the residents that remained have likewise had to make difficult adjustments.[5]

The Current Situation for Pulp and Paper

Competition among mills is intense within the United States, within North America, and, since the 1980s and 1990s, with Europe and more recently with Latin America. The Maine Pulp and Paper Association summarizes the current situation for paper production:

> New paper capacity is now shifting to Asia. While no new mills have been built in the U.S. for many years, many new mills are under construction in China, Korea, Indonesia, and across the globe. These new mills are larger and faster than those in the United States. In most cases, the cost of labor is much cheaper where the new mills are being built. As a result, pulp and paper prices continue to decline (Maine Pulp and Paper Association 2013b, p. 1).

For several years the U.S. paper industry has been undergoing rapid change in numerous areas—employment, ownership, production, acquisitions, mergers, and mill closures or downsizings. The intense competition in the U.S. paper industry forces companies to be strategic and adaptable, says one paper company spokesperson: "We are not going to make our plans public. But like the other major companies, we are looking at several projects and several options. There is always something in the hopper" (Christensen and Caves 1997, p. 57).

Eaton and Kriesky (1994) identify several challenges facing the industry, including foreign competition, environmental protections, mergers and acquisitions, and technological change and the labor force.

In the previous 20 years, they note, "one-third of the top 100 companies in the industry [worldwide] disappeared as independent entities, primarily through merger and acquisition" (p. 38). The impact of these acquisitions can be problematic: Champion's takeover of St. Regis came with an increased debt that led "to a reduction by half of the combined companies' workforce through layoffs and division sales" (p. 39).

Austin (2008) attributes the current pulp and paper industry difficulties to the weak U.S. economy, high-priced inputs, and low-priced imports. Others attribute it to the increasing production efficiency of fewer mills,[6] concurrent with an increasing dependence on electronic media, which has lessened the demand for paper (CPBIS 2012). Google's plan to digitize every book (Miller 2012) will likely reverberate, causing additional reductions in the printed page; as Opidee (2012) notes, industry predictions are for a 20 percent loss of magazine paper usage within five years, increasing to a 51 percent loss within 15 years. Rondon (2013) characterizes the battle between digital and print as being in flux: "The paper industry has suffered through volatility as digital mediums wrest readers from print. The aggregate effects of publishers slashing pages and mills shutting down swung prices wildly over the past several years." Opidee writes that "even though a drop in demand might ordinarily mean a drop in price, the paper industry has become increasingly unstable, and such a fall in demand might lead to additional mill consolidation and closures, as well as greater underutilization of machines—all of which, many publishers fear, could lead to dramatic price increases and severe paper shortages" (p. 10).

An important shift in the paper industry in Minnesota, and probably for the industry as a whole, is the process of creating pulp for clothing (Feyder 2012). The Sappi Fine Paper mill in Cloquet (acquired from Potlatch in 2002) recently announced that its $170 million conversion to make pulp for clothing has been successful (Belz 2013). The process, known as chemical cellulose or dissolving pulp, uses a mix of wood pulp with other materials to produce thread for making textiles. While chemical cellulose is a high-demand product, the Cloquet mill will continue to produce high-end paper using pulp from other mills.

Besides the Sappi mill's shift to focus on textiles, Belz (2013) notes that UPM-Kymmene, the Finnish company that purchased the Blandin paper mill in Grand Rapids, Minnesota, in 1997, is undertaking pilot projects working on alternatives made from wood. Other research on nanomaterials made from wood has been underway in Sweden and Japan, as well as at both the University of Maine and the University of Minnesota. New types of forest products are needed, and the paper industry in Minnesota needs a place from which to begin anew. Companies have closed well over 100 American mills since 2000, according to the Center for Paper Business and Industry Studies at Georgia Tech University. And Belz reports that 223,000 paper industry jobs have been lost since 2000, including at least 3,800 in Minnesota.

Today, mills are looking for alternative products, including engineered wood products. Resolute Forest Products CEO Richard Garneau notes demand for Resolute products dropped from 24 million tons in 2009 to 13 million tons in 2011. He cautions, "Don't expect that we're going to continue to do business as usual" (Marotte 2011).

Some mills have always been flexible in responding to production needs. One mill in Brainerd that produced newsprint closed for several months in the 1930s during the Depression. When it reopened, it began producing wallpaper. When the wallpaper market declined in the 1950s, the mill began producing fine-grade paper (*Brainerd Dispatch* 2002). Thorp et al. (2014) note that the industry has shown resilience by developing innovations such as sterilized packaging, chlorine-free bleaching, and high-energy, efficient chemical-recovery boilers.

NewPage Corporation, the owner of 16 paper mills, recently reorganized under Chapter 11 bankruptcy. NewPage has acknowledged that heavy debt, raw-material inflation, and a decline in coated paper demand have been major problems (Feyder 2012). A Sartell rumor circulating among production workers was that Verso had hoped to buy NewPage, but that did not happen. According to Wiercinski (2012), NewPage and Verso control about 45 percent of magazine and catalogue paper use.

In addition to the expansion of digital technology as it affects paper production by providing paperless forms of communication, the paper industry is being challenged by environmental regulations, particularly the issue of clean water. State and local regulations vary, but the demand for decreased effluents and improved water quality remain a challenge. Environmental remediation has become an important variable in plant-level efficiencies influencing industry competition (Giebelhaus and Usselman 2005). Liberty Diversified International had shown interest in purchasing the closed Wausau Paper mill in Brainerd but withdrew, citing environmental concerns (Associated Press 2013b).

One other change currently confronting the paper industry, at least in Minnesota, is changes in land use from forest to cultivation. A 1,500-acre forest tract in Cass County, Minnesota, is slated to be converted to potato production for McDonald's fast-food restaurants (Marcotty 2013). In addition, nearly 100 square miles of timberland presently owned by Potlatch Corporation is at risk as the company divests itself of its commercial forests in Minnesota. According to the *Brainerd Dispatch* (2002), Potlatch owned 350,000 acres of forest in 2002. When Ralph Nader's study group report on the pulp and paper industry in Maine appeared in 1974, seven giant corporations owned 6.5 million acres in the state, producing 90 percent of its paper (Osborn 1974, p. 2).

In a reversion to earlier days in the industry, some pulp and paper companies are testing whether the use of wheat and alfalfa straw is a viable alternative to hardwood pulp. Columbia Pulp, near Starbuck, Washington, was seeking 215,000 tons of straw per year for pulp production (McDonough 2014b). As an alternative to hardwood pulp, straw is cheaper to produce, has a similar fiber length, requires less water and fewer chemicals, and doesn't involve any odor-causing chemicals. Innovation is needed if most of the production units in the United States and Canada are to survive, since "Asia, particularly China and India, will account for more than half of global paper production and consumption by 2018" (CPBIS 2013b, p. 2).

In 2002, the leading paper companies in the United States, ranked by net sales, were International Paper, Georgia-Pacific, Weyerhaeuser, Kimberly-Clark, and Procter and Gamble Paper. That year, eight of the top 20 U.S. paper companies sustained a loss, including the top two, International Paper and Georgia-Pacific (Wikipedia 2014a).

Paper and pulp mills generally do not sell their product for direct consumer use. Most often, the paper rolls are sent to converter plants, which change rolled paper into products for a variety of uses, including home, office, educational, business, printing, or packaging use. Northrup (1969) notes that by the mid-1960s the South was the leading producer of pulp and paper (Table 2.1).

The Decline of Unions in the Industry

Paper is one of the most organized industries in the United States: 20 years ago, 96 percent of production workers in the industry belonged

Table 2.1 Wood Pulp, Paper, and Paperboard Production by Region, 1966 (000s of short tons)

Region	Wood pulp production	Paper and paperboard production
United States	36,640	47,189
South	22,376	20,708
New England	2,250	4,236
Middle Atlantic	1,159	5,586
North Central (Midwest)	3,517	9,921
West	7,339	6,739

NOTE: The regions listed consist of the following states:
South: Alabama, Arkansas, Delaware, Florida, Georgia, Kentucky, Louisiana, Maryland, Mississippi, North Carolina, Oklahoma, South Carolina, Tennessee, Texas, Virginia, West Virginia. According to Lupo and Bailey (2011), more than 70 percent of Alabama is in timberland, 64 percent of Georgia is in timber (24 million acres), and 62 percent of Mississippi is timbered (19 million acres).
New England: Connecticut, Maine, Massachusetts, New Hampshire, Rhode Island, Vermont.
Middle Atlantic: New Jersey, New York, Pennsylvania.
North Central (Midwest): Illinois, Indiana, Iowa, Kansas, Michigan, Minnesota, Missouri, Nebraska, North Dakota, Ohio, South Dakota, Wisconsin.
West: Alaska, Arizona, California, Colorado, Hawaii, Idaho, Montana, Nevada, New Mexico, Oregon, Utah, Washington, Wyoming.
SOURCE: Northrup (1969).

to a union (Eaton and Kriesky 1994). However, as a result of improvements in paper-making technology and the opening of nonunion mills, membership in the United Paperworkers International Union (UPIU) has declined somewhat.

The UPIU's strength was tested during a 76-day strike against the Boise Cascade mill in Rumford, Maine, in 1986, which ultimately cost 342 of the 1,200 union workers their jobs when replacement workers were hired (*New York Times* 1986). Many of those displaced had 30–40 years of experience. The focus of the strike was not wages but a corporate demand that workers fill other jobs when necessary. The union's position was that the changes would threaten job security and reduce union power. The union did not prevail, and the strike continued to affect the town—it divided some families, anger lingered against the company, and business in town was off.

Job security for U.S. workers has been an issue for both white-collar and blue-collar workers since the 1980s. Layoffs and staff reductions have increased, so many employees no longer expect to have job security (Brown 2006; Karren and Sherman 2012). In the third quarter of 2011 alone, nearly 184,500 U.S. workers lost their jobs in 1,226 mass layoffs (Gowan 2012). They experienced involuntary job loss through no fault of their own and were permanently separated from their employers even though they had strong attachments to their employers.

The Importance of Paper Mill Jobs

In 2001, U.S. paper mills employed nearly 115,000 workers, while pulp mills employed an additional 7,200 and paperboard mills yet another 48,770 (Wikipedia 2014a). According to the Wisconsin Paper Council, one of every 11 Wisconsin manufacturing jobs is tied to the paper and allied products industries, creating over $2 billion in wages annually. In Michigan's Upper Peninsula, hourly and weekly wages in the pulp and paper industry were the highest of any employment sector (Bay-Lake Regional Planning Commission et al. 1999).

While the Filter Materials mill in Waupaca, Wisconsin, employs only 75 people, the state's largest mill, Fort James Corporation (Green Bay), employs 3,500. There are 45 mills in Wisconsin that produce some type of paper product. These products include linerboard and paperboard (cardboard-like products), tissue products (including bathroom tissue, napkins, and paper towels), and paper (printing, writing, and specialty papers). In Wisconsin, linerboard and paperboard is primarily produced at 6 mills, tissue products at 9, and paper at 19. In Upper Michigan, two mills produce linerboard and paperboard, one produces tissue products, and six manufacture paper. Many of the Maine, Minnesota, and Wisconsin paper mills are older (Figure 2.2), while Upper Michigan mills are more recent (Bay-Lake Regional Planning Commission et al. 1999).

Minnesota data include only four operating mills, most of which are older: Sappi Fine Paper in Cloquet (built in 1898), Blandin Paper in Grand Rapids (1901), Boise Cascade in International Falls (1910), and NewPage in Duluth (1987). Recent Minnesota mill closures include Wausau Paper in Brainerd (built in 1917), IBT Consolidated in International Falls (1910), and the Verso Sartell mill (1905).

Figure 2.2 Date of Establishment of Pulp and Paper Mills in Maine, Wisconsin, Upper Michigan, and Minnesota

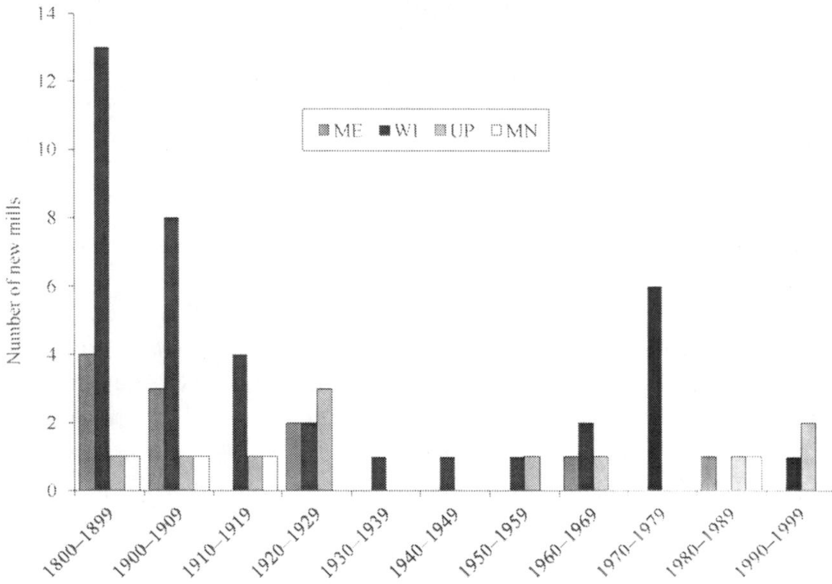

SOURCE: Bay-Lake Regional Planning Commission et al. (1999): Maine data provided by John Williams of the Maine Pulp and Paper Association.

Ownership Changes

For many paper companies, change in ownership through merger or acquisition has been part of the industrial history of paper manufacturing. The now-closed Verso Sartell Mill itself reflects these changes. The mill began as Watab Pulp and Paper, which bought its No. 1 paper machine in 1905, added a second paper machine in 1910, and produced newsprint until 1930. Converting to book and magazine papers in 1930 involved using recycled magazines and became the firm's core business until the end of World War II. At war's end, the company terminated its paper finishing (where paper is sheeted and cut to size), and from that time until closure, paper manufactured at Sartell was in roll form. St. Regis purchased Watab Pulp and Paper in 1946 and made many upgrades to the machines, including adding new steam turbine drives, supercalenders in 1960 for a high-gloss finish, and a No. 3 paper machine in 1982. St. Regis merged with Champion International in 1984, and in 2000, Champion was purchased by International Paper. In 2006, Verso Paper purchased the Coated and SC Papers Division of International Paper, which included the Sartell and Bucksport facilities as well as the Androscoggin Mill in Jay, Maine, and the Quinnesec Mill in Quinnesec, Michigan (Wikipedia 2014b).

Change in paper mill ownership is prevalent, even on an international basis. Within the past few years, these changes have been occurring at a frenetic pace. Paper companies merge to increase market share and reduce competition and because it is less expensive and faster to acquire an existing mill than to build a new plant (Bay-Lake Regional Planning Commission et al. 1999). In mergers and acquisitions, the dominant company often either closes or upgrades the least profitable operation in an effort to reduce duplication. For example, American Tissue purchased the Badger-Globe Mill in Neenah, Wisconsin, in 1996 and closed it in 1998.[7] Kimberly-Clark's purchase of Scott Paper in 1995 created job loss for workers in Marinette, Wisconsin, when two tissue-making machines were shut down in 1997 (Jensen 1999).

According to Pesendorfer (2003, p. 502), "about 40 percent of the 819 paper and paperboard plants operating in the United States between 1978 and 1992 were involved in at least one merger." During a concentrated period of industrial restructuring from August 1984 to July 1987, 31 mergers and acquisitions took place. Indeed, 1985–1987 is often referred to as a period of industrial restructuring in paper manufacturing. It was during this period that Champion International Corporation acquired St. Regis for $1.8 billion, Jefferson Smurfit bought Container Corporation for $1.2 billion, and International Paper acquired Hammermill for $1.1 billion.

Studying the Wisconsin and Upper Michigan paper industry, the Bay-Lake Regional Planning Commission et al. (1999) reported, "In looking at plant closures that have occurred in the study area, it is apparent that the plants which have closed were those with older, inefficient paper machines, and/or with physical plants which had not been adequately maintained. . . . If a parent company has consistently invested in new equipment, building upgrades, and new technology, it is less likely that that particular plant will be targeted for closure or cutbacks" (pp. 44–45).

A turnover in mill ownership does not necessarily mean that a downsizing or closure will occur immediately, as the 2001 shutdown of the Shasta Mill in Anderson, California, illustrates. The Shasta Mill operated on a 24-hour, seven-day-a-week basis, and the shutdown came as a shock to its over 400 employees. The mill was built by Kimberly-Clark in 1964 and sold in 1972 to Simpson-Lee Paper, which became Simpson Paper in 1977. Plainwell Group bought the mill in 1999 and closed it two years later. Explanations for the closure included

- a threefold increase in monthly utility costs in the months preceding the closure;

- competition from low-cost ("dumped") imported products; and

- the smaller width of the mill's two older paper machines, which required transferring some work to Texas.

No Worker Adjustment and Retraining Notification (WARN) Act notice was given, nor were employees given 60 days of pay, as provided for under WARN. Although a Shasta Paper Employee Buyout Association was formed to explore options to find a buyer, mill equipment was sold at auction in May of 2002, sealing the job loss. Federal TAA retraining funds (for workers displaced by import trade) did not become available until 2002, nearly a year after the mill closed (theshastamill.com 2015).

In describing the 1996 takeover of the St. Joe mill by Florida Coast Paper, Ziewitz and Wiaz (2004) see another ramification of change in ownership: they note that 45 percent of the St. Joe mill workforce was terminated, while pay was reduced for the remaining workers by $5,000 each. The mill shut down in August 1998, in what was described as a "temporary closure," but the closure became final a few months later.

The financial difficulties of pulp and paper mills have created some restructuring: after the Gold River, British Columbia, pulp mill lost $180 million over an eight-year period in the 1990s, Bowater acquired the mill from Montreal-based Avenor Inc. in July of 1998, suspended mill operations almost immediately, and closed the mill in February of 1999, terminating 380 employees (Neuwirth and Rosenberg 1998).

Two of the top 14 paper companies globally sustained heavy losses (Sappi Ltd. at $143 million and Resolute at $588 million), while five more companies showed a decline in net income from the previous year ranging from 1 to 18 percent (CPBIS 2013a).

Even though Resolute's (2014) newsprint production was 10 percent of worldwide output and 38 percent of North American output, the company still had to make financial adjustments. Restructuring included

- the indefinite idling of a paper machine at the Catawba mill;
- the indefinite idling of a paper machine at the Fort Francis mill;
- the closure of a high-gloss paper machine at the Laurentide mill, which displaced 111 workers (29 percent of the workforce); and
- the restart of the Dolbeau high-gloss paper machine.

Restructuring continued into 2014 at other Resolute mills, including, at the Fort Frances mill, the mothballing of the No. 5 paper machine, the idling of paper machine No. 7, and the shuttered pulp production (Hale 2014).

Restructuring has implications beyond displaced paper workers: other industries, such as suppliers of chemicals to the paper mills, follow suit with their own reductions and downsizings (Seewald and D'Amico 2009). Minerals Technologies Inc. (MTI) cut 340 employees as a result of reduced demand from several industries, including paper.

Recent newspaper headlines reflect continuing concerns over mill ownership changes. A *Minneapolis Star Tribune* story described Packaging Corporation of America's acquisition of Boise Paper: "Illinois-based Packaging Corporation of America (PCA) is best known for making boxboard and corrugated packaging products, while the smaller Boise makes copier paper, liner board and corrugated packaging products. But copier paper is the primary product for Boise's International Falls, Minnesota, plant, putting it at increased risk for cutbacks" (DePass 2013, p. D:1). In May 2013, Boise announced it would terminate 265 workers as it retired two paper machines and one coating machine at the International Falls mill. While the firm would retain 580 workers, it is uncertain whether PCA, as the new owner of Boise, will reduce the workforce further or close the plant entirely.

The loss of the Verso Sartell mill, the closure of Wausau Paper in Brainerd, and the sale of Boise to PCA have raised questions about the durability of the International Falls facility. These concerns follow on the heels of the 2014 closure of International Paper's Courtland, Alabama, mill, which affected 1,100 workers. International Paper chairman and CEO John Faraci said the Courtland mill closed because of declining demand since 1999 for uncoated freesheet paper products, especially as consumers embrace electronic alternatives.

EXAMPLES OF JOB LOSS AND RECENT MILL CLOSURES

It appears a given in the paper industry that when there is a change in mill ownership, economic displacement follows. For example, Potlatch sold its Brainerd mill, which employed 600 workers, to Missota Paper in 2003. In 2004, Missota sold out to Wausau Paper. Now the mill employs about 175 people, a net loss of 425 positions (Marohn 2012).

Mergers, sales, and acquisitions of pulp and paper facilities in recent years reflect internationalization, but numerous closures or downsizings are also characteristic of a mature industry. The consolidation in the United States and Canada has been intense. Some examples:

- Katahdin Paper Company in East Millinocket, Maine, was formerly a Great Northern Paper facility.

- Noranda acquired controlling interest in Fraser Paper (Madawaska, Maine) in 1974, became sole owner in 1985, and merged into Nexfors Fraser Papers in 1996. The mill eliminated 128 workers in 2007.

- In 1995, Sappi, a South African company, purchased the S.D. Warren mill in Westbrook, Maine, outsourcing most of the work and eliminating 90 percent of the local employees.

- The Oxford Paper Company of Rumford, Maine, was sold in 1967 to the Ethyl Corporation; the mill and woodlands located in Oxford were sold to Boise Cascade in 1976, which in turn sold them to Mead in 1996.

- The Hollingsworth and Whitney mill in Winslow, Maine, was purchased by the Scott Paper Company, which merged with Kimberly-Clark in 1995. The mill closed in 1997.

- Potlatch sold its Cloquet, Minnesota, plant to Sappi in 2002 and closed its Brainerd mill in 2002, terminating 660 workers.

- UPM Kymmene, a Finnish company, acquired Blandin Paper of Grand Rapids, Minnesota, in 1997, and shut down two of four production lines in 2003, terminating nearly 300 workers.[8]

- NewPage Paper purchased Stora Enso's Niagara, Wisconsin, mill site in 2007 for $2.5 billion and announced the mill's closure one month later. Within nine months, the mill was shuttered, leaving 320 workers jobless.

According to Robertson (2013), paper manufacturing in Minnesota has cut some 5,000 jobs since 2000, or about one-third of the Minnesota positions in the industry.

The paper industry has been in transition for many years and continues to undergo variable product demand, ownership change, international expansion, and reductions in paper machines. These factors have exacerbated downsizings and brought on permanent mill closures, creating displacement. Despite this, there has been little research on dislocation among paper mill workers. Rieland (2011) notes that 152 plants closed between 1998 and 2008, and the Center for Paper Business and Industry Studies says another 31 paper mills ceased operation between 2008 and 2012.

While mills have closed, many smaller, single-industry communities that were home to a paper mill have not pursued economic diversification. As a result of their dependence on mill employment for jobs and taxes, any downsizing or closure will pose serious problems for the community and those displaced from the industry.

Firms Close Plants under Variable Conditions

At least four factors influence plant closures (Townsend and Peck 1985):

1) Commercial influences related to specific market trends

2) Technological influences related to the productive capabilities

3) Organizational components—those influences that exist between different parts of corporations

4) Human relations factors—the relationships between management, unions, and local, regional, or national government

According to Schmenner's (1982) data, closing a facility is strictly an economic decision and could be determined based on a decline in sales, intense foreign competition, an obsolete product, a change in consumer tastes or interests, technological advances that make plant consolidations attractive, or a decline in the quality or quantity of raw materials. Unfavorable industry economics appear to be a more influential factor than production problems. Schmenner notes that in most situations, the company maintains the product but closes a particular plant, absorbing the operation into an existing facility (Table 2.2).[9]

Schmenner (1982) finds that the median age of plants closed was three years, and one-third of these plants had been in operation for six years or less when they were closed. The conversion of the Sappi paper mill in Cloquet, Minnesota, from paper pulp to cellulose pulp was viewed as advantageous because the pulp facility was only 12 years old and thus was seen as a relatively modern facility (Feyder 2012).

Mill communities are dependent upon the success of the mill, which they rely on for employment. For example, the Potlatch Pulp and Paper Division—with mills in Brainerd and Cloquet—had sales of more than $425 million and spent $154 million on payroll and benefits in these two communities. Mill owners created additional employment when they would modernize or expand operations—Potlatch spent $525 million in modernizing the Cloquet pulp mill from 1992 to 1999 (*Brainerd Dispatch* 2002).

While a mass layoff—a company layoff of 50 or more workers—shocks workers and the host community, research by the Federal Reserve Bank of Minneapolis acknowledges that in only a few counties (4 of 50) in the Minneapolis Fed's district was the county employment

Table 2.2 Disposition of a Plant's Former Operations

Disposition	% affected
Operations were absorbed by other company plants.	61
The company got out of the business.	24
The operations were relocated to a new plant.	12
The operations were subcontracted.	2
The operations were transferred out of the United States.	0
The government contract was completed.	1

SOURCE: Schmenner (1982).

affected negatively (Wirtz 2005). Explanations for the low impact of a mass layoff included the following:

- Mass layoffs are usually fewer than 200 workers, and they tend to occur in counties with a larger employment base.
- Large layoffs are often gradual, which could soften the impact at any one time.
- Sometimes employment options increase for other employers, reducing the out-migration and relocation of displaced workers.

Mayberry (2005) notes that paper mill construction in Quinnesec, Michigan (Champion International), and International Falls, Minnesota (Boise Cascade), which began in 1988 (involving 2,000–2,400 workers during peak months), increased the population. But in the early 1990s, when plant construction was complete and the workers left the area, the economy suffered, and per capita income dropped.

The Impact of the Recession

Figure 2.3 reflects the impact of the Great Recession on paper mill restructuring in the United States. Clearly there were a significant number of layoffs in the industry throughout the 10-year period depicted, but the height and width of the peak in January 2009 indicates a dramatic increase. In 2008, 146 industry layoffs occurred, and 241 took place the following year. In 2010–2012, the number of layoffs ranged from 69 to 95, roughly the same number that occurred from 2004 to 2007. Figure 2.4 further shows the impact of the recession on the number of mills that closed during the 2005–2014 period. While the number of operating paper mills continues to decline, the descent from 2006 to 2008 was less drastic than for the 2003–2006 era. However, from 2008 to 2012, the slope of the line in Figure 2.4 is noticeably steeper, reflecting that, on average, 160 mills closed each year during the 2009–2012 period.

"The immediate impact of a recession," say Grass and Hayter (1989, p. 241), "is to encourage a 'cost hunt' by reducing, at least temporarily, variable costs, notably employment levels." The impact of job loss in the paper industry, and in most other enterprises, shows that the recession has taken a heavy psychological toll. That impact hits displaced workers particularly hard, as they have difficulty adjusting

Figure 2.3 Layoff Events in U.S. Pulp and Paper Mills

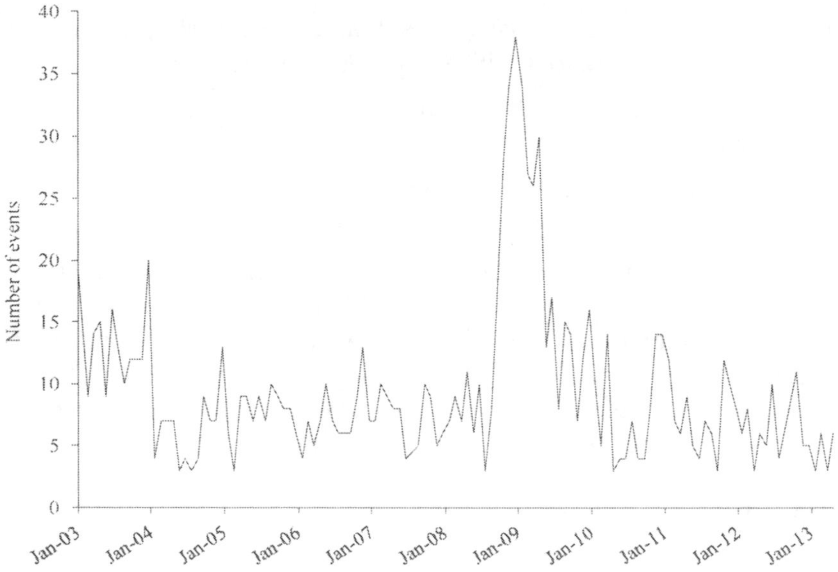

SOURCE: BLS (2015a).

to job loss both emotionally and financially. "Hospitals and counselors are straining under an increasing caseload as people suffering from job-related stresses seek help and often can't cover costs because they have lost jobs, income, or health insurance," the *Baltimore Sun* reported. "Employers are seeing a rising volume of requests to assistance programs that offer help resolving personal issues, including financial stress, as part of health benefits" (Sentementes 2010).

The *Sun* reporter interviewed Rita Preller, a clinical social worker in North Baltimore, who noted that her clients increasingly experience a high level of stress that is tied to the poor economy and their job—or their lack of a job. "This economy has forced them to deal with the fact they can't pay their bills," Preller is quoted as saying. "They feel like they can't do anything. They isolate. They withdraw. And the problem becomes worse" (Sentementes 2010, p. 2). Luo (2010) notes that Sullivan and von Wachter's (2009) research "examined death records and earnings data in Pennsylvania during the recession of the early 1980s

Figure 2.4 Ten-Year Decline in the Number of Existing Paper Mills, 2005–2014

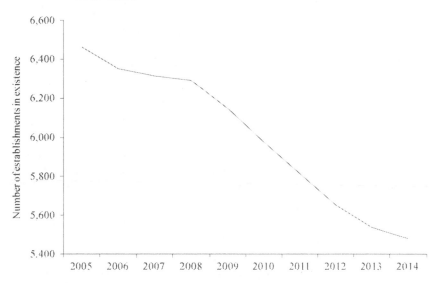

SOURCE: BLS (2015c).

and concluded that death rates among high-seniority male workers jumped by between 50 and 100 percent in the year after a job loss, depending on the worker's age" (p. 2).

Davis and von Wachter (2011) note that job displacement leads to significant earnings losses that have a lasting impact, including reduced job stability, worse health outcomes, and higher mortality. In the United States, the volume of job loss and unemployment is enormous, even independent of a recession. However, constant renewal and job re-allocation is achieved at a large capacity, so that many job loss events involve little financial loss or hardship. Still, Davis and von Wachter (p. 51) conclude that "high-tenure workers who lose jobs in mass-layoff events experience large and persistent earnings losses compared to otherwise similar workers who retain their jobs. . . . For high-tenure workers who experience job displacement in a recession, the losses amount to about three years of earnings at pre-displacement levels."

SUMMARY

The U.S. paper industry has a long and creative history, initially producing paper from rags in eastern urban settings. Once wood pulp became the basic raw material for paper production, paper mills were built closer to the source of materials rather than at the point of product distribution. Many of the early mills were isolated, locally owned industries, creating a community around the mill. Over time and up to the present, mill consolidation, and numerous mill closures, occurred. Today, a variety of issues, largely focusing on market demand, technological development, and environmental topics, have created an internationally intense competitive industrial sector.

Competition for market share, and perhaps even survival, has increased acquisitions and mergers within the paper and pulp industry. Some paper mills close, often leaving the community (and those displaced) without comparable industrial opportunities. Thus, the 2011 announcement by Verso to retire older mill machinery at Sartell and Bucksport might not have been unexpected, but the impact of reducing the operation by 169 workers at Sartell and 151 at Bucksport left those downsized with few employment opportunities locally or even more broadly, since transfer was not a viable option because of limited employment opportunities in the paper industry.

Within a few short months of the downsizing at the Minnesota mill, those who had survived that event were confronted with a shock on Memorial Day, when an explosion and fire temporarily closed the mill while an assessment of the damage was made. Two months after the fire, Sartell workers learned of the company's decision to immediately shut down the Sartell mill, throwing another 280 workers out of work. The Verso workers who had survived the downsizing were now left looking for replacement work after their downsized colleagues had had "first options" on local employment vacancies. Furthermore, a slow recovery from the Great Recession provided fewer opportunities for experienced long-term employees, most of whom were older workers.

Notes

1. In reality, a reduction in force at any particular company appears rather common, since Hewitt Associates (now Aon Hewitt, a subsidiary of the Aon Group) surveyed compensation managers about their organizations' involuntary workforce reductions more than 20 years ago and found that 90 percent of firms responding had gone through an involuntary reduction within the previous three years (Graffagna 1993).
2. Sociologists, labor economists, and others who study economic displacement have been selective in their focus on U.S. industries, which has resulted in a serious void when it comes to publications dealing with job loss in the paper industry.
3. Recent paper mill closures in Canada include the following: the 2012 Minas Basin Pulp and Power containerboard mill in Hantsport, Nova Scotia; the 2009 Fraser Papers pulp mill in Thurso, Quebec; the 2009 Tembec paper mill closure in Powerview–Pine Falls, Manitoba; the 2009 closure of production at the paper mill in Grand Falls–Windsor, New Brunswick; the 2008 closure of the AbitibiBowater mill in Dalhousie, New Brunswick; and the 2005 AbitibiBowater pulp and paper mill closure in Kenora, Ontario.
4. Earl Gustafson, vice president for energy, forestry, and human resources, Wisconsin Paper Council, e-mail message to author Kenneth Root, September 10, 2015.
5. Perhaps one of the most thoroughly studied single-industry dependence communities that has survived the boom-and-bust cycle of resource extraction is the town of Elliot Lake in Ontario, Canada (see Mawhiney and Pitblado [1999]).
6. For example, the Maine Pulp and Paper Association notes that Maine's paper production has consistently increased since 1990, making Maine the second-leading paper-making state by volume. Maine produced about four million tons of paper in 2000, and it produces more paper than any state other than Wisconsin (Maine Pulp and Paper Association 2013a).
7. Josh Dukelow, existing industry manager for the Fox Cities Regional Partnership, e-mail message to author Kenneth Root, March 4, 2014. http://www.hispanicbusiness.com/2014/3/3/resolute_forest_products_inc_-_10-k.htm.
8. Kent Koerbitz of UPM-Kymmene Corp., e-mail message to author Kenneth Root, March 3, 2014.
9. Schmenner's figures are based on 175 completed surveys, each representing a closed facility.

3

Job Loss at Verso

Job loss is a salient trigger event that sets off large changes in people's subjective well-being, on an order of magnitude greater than the effect of changes in family structure, home ownership, or parental status. Loss of work seems particularly hard to take.
—Cristobal Young (2012, p. 609)

On October 11, 2011, Verso announced that 175 employees would be terminated from its Sartell, Minnesota, plant. The reason for the downsizing was the anticipated December 14 shutdown of two paper-producing machines. Retiring two older machines at the Sartell mill meant an annual reduction of 103,000 tons of paper (*Sartell News-leader* 2011). Verso simultaneously announced the shutdown of the No. 2 paper machine at the mill in Bucksport, Maine, which was anticipated to reduce the Bucksport workforce by 125 employees, but which actually claimed 151. The Bucksport downsizing, effective October 23, would reduce annual production by another 90,000 tons. After the shutdown of these three paper machines, Verso would produce 925,000 tons of paper annually and would remain the second-largest producer of coated groundwood paper in North America (Business Wire 2011).

Both salaried personnel and hourly workers at each of the two Verso mills were downsized. Sartell production employees were United Steelworkers union members, and the 175 workers were given (legally, and by union contract) 60 days' notice prior to termination, while the displaced Maine employees were not given a Worker Adjustment and Retraining Notification (WARN) Act notice because 33 percent of the workforce was not affected.[1] Downsized Bucksport workers were members of one of the following unions: United Steelworkers, the International Brotherhood of Electrical Workers, the International Association of Machinists and Aerospace Workers, and the Office and Professional Employees International Union.

Most of the Bucksport workers were let go on October 23, with the balance terminated in November and December. For the majority

27

(69 percent) of those downsized at Sartell, their last day at work was December 14, 2011, while for those who were displaced after the fire, their work ended in 2012.

While there were not a large number of new hires at the Sartell mill in the last five years, there were nine men and one woman among our respondents who were downsized from the Sartell facility with five years or less of seniority. Among those who were displaced at the Sartell closure, one male had two years of seniority, but all others had at least 12 years of work experience. Seniority at Bucksport was different, in large part because the Bucksport mill employed temporary workers. Among the Bucksport respondents who were downsized, there were 13 employees who had one year or less of seniority, all of whom were temporary workers. Two of the temporary workers were women. An additional six downsized workers had two to five years of seniority at the Bucksport mill.

Not all mill workers lived in the town where the mill was located. Although Bucksport was home to several paper worker families, others lived in the smaller nearby communities of Ellsworth, Orrington, Brewer, and East Millinocket. Likewise, in Minnesota, several workers resided in Sartell proper, but a number also lived in St. Cloud, Rice, Sauk Rapids, St. Joseph, or other neighboring communities.

THE COMMUNITIES INVOLVED

Sartell, Minnesota

Sartell, straddling the Mississippi River, has 16,000 residents and, until 2012, was home to the Verso Paper Mill, which was then the city's largest employer. The city is far from the image of a single-industry community with a historical downtown area (most of the downtown buildings fell to the wrecking ball in the 1960s and 1980s to make way for the rerouting of U.S. Highway 10 and a new bridge over the Mississippi). Rather, it is a dispersed residential area with a limited commercial area consisting of a strip mall a mile west of the Mississippi River on a bluff 1,000 feet above the river. The paper mill, built in 1905, was located on the east side of the river, while the majority of the city is situated on the west side. Sartell is the most populous suburb of St. Cloud, and its business and residential areas stretch nearly continuously south and west to St. Cloud and east to Sauk Rapids.

An experienced paper mill manager, familiar with paper mill communities, told us that "Sartell is not a mill town." In part this is true because of its proximity to St. Cloud, and in part because the city has expanded and developed westward from the Mississippi River, away from the mill area on the east bank. Those familiar with paper mill production know that many mills are located in remote communities where the mill is the dominant employer. Characterizing Sartell as "not a mill town" puts the community in perspective.

Sartell was incorporated in 1907. It grew slowly during the first 50 years of its history. After the demolition of large chunks of the downtown for construction of the highway and the bridge, Sartell's close proximity to St. Cloud apparently minimized the need for local business expansion and simultaneously supported rapid population growth. From 1970 to 2010, the census figures for each 10 years rose by at least 55 percent over the previous decade (Table 3.1).

In 2012, Sartell's labor force was 57 percent of the 16,183 population base. While the mill had been the dominant city industry for over 100 years, the city's largest employer is currently DeZurik Valve Technologies, an industry built by a former Sartell mill employee (during Watab's ownership; see Table 3.2) who developed a segmented valve in 1928. The company has become a global leader in valve technologies.

Bucksport, Maine

Bucksport is a town of 5,000 founded in 1763 by Col. Jonathan Buck, who led a militia regiment in the Revolutionary War. Connected to Fort Knox and Bridge Observatory by a handsome suspension bridge,

Table 3.1 Sartell Population Growth, Bucksport Population Decline

Year	Sartell population	Bucksport population
2012	16,183 (est.)	2,818 (est.)
2010	15,878	2,885
2000	9,641	2,970
1990	5,393	2,989

SOURCE: U.S. Census Bureau (2015).

Table 3.2 Sartell Paper Mill History

Years	Owner
1905–1946	Watab Pulp and Paper
1946–1984	St. Regis Paper
1984–2000	Champion Paper
2000–2006	International Paper
2006–2012	Verso Paper (mill closed in 2012)

SOURCE: Authors' compilation.

Bucksport is home to the Verso pulp and paper mill, and several artists live in the surrounding area. Bucksport is only 35 miles from Bar Harbor, a tourist mecca. Locals have undertaken efforts to make Bucksport attractive to tourists, including constructing a mile-long walkway along the Penobscot River. Downtown Bucksport has a locally owned bookstore, a glass studio, other seasonal artistic outlets, and several restaurants. The Maine Employment Security Law was recently changed so that it now coincides with the law in Minnesota and 10 other states to pay benefits to part-time workers who have a history of part-time work (Thayer 2002).

The Verso Bucksport mill is a dominant employer in the community but not the largest—larger employers include a biotech research and development corporation and the Bucksport Regional Health Center. Still, visitors to the Bucksport mill are often impressed with its huge machinery, some five stories high. Some observe that work in such a large mill would be noisy, dirty, dangerous, and difficult.

Table 3.1 shows a slight population drop in Bucksport since 1990. In 2012 the labor force ranged from 2,316 in January to a high of 2,974 in August, with an average monthly labor force of 2,591. Table 3.3 shows the mill ownership changes throughout the years.

BACKGROUND TO THE PRESENT STUDY

After Verso's 2011 announcement that it would reduce production and downsize operations at two of its four mills, we determined that with support from the University of Minnesota's Center for Urban

Table 3.3 Bucksport Paper Mill History

Years	Owner
1930–1945	Maine Seaboard Paper
1945–1984	St. Regis Paper
1984–2000	Champion Paper
2000–2006	International Paper
2006–2012	Verso Paper

SOURCE: Authors' compilation.

and Regional Affairs (CURA), we could initiate a study to assess the impact of job loss on displaced paper workers. We had no direct access to worker rosters, but the Minnesota Department of Employment and Economic Development (DEED) staff agreed to take our sealed questionnaires and inserts and affix mailing address labels for salaried personnel at Sartell. The United Steelworkers District 11 office agreed to do likewise for union employees at Sartell, and the Maine AFL-CIO did this for both salaried and union workers in Bucksport, Maine.

All displaced workers (both salaried and union) in the downsizings at Bucksport and Sartell were asked to complete a generic questionnaire (see Appendix A). Each questionnaire was mailed with a cover letter requesting that the recipient participate in the survey and included a stamped, addressed return envelope along with a $10 bill. Displaced Sartell workers completed 96 questionnaires and Bucksport workers completed 67, for return rates of 56 and 44 percent.

The downsizing was catastrophic for many workers. The union workers downsized from Sartell were earning $24–$40 per hour and most, if not all, knew that finding another job that provided the same wage and benefit package would be difficult if not impossible. Some displaced Bucksport workers were temporary workers employed at reduced rates of $12.50 an hour (with no benefits), while those who were not temps had full benefits and made $30–$50 an hour. Sartell and Bucksport workers who survived the downsizing were pleased that their jobs were safe. Granted, there were others—workmates and in some instances relatives—that were now without work, but it could have been worse.

Explosion and Fire at the Sartell Mill

The 2012 Memorial Day explosion and fire that killed one worker and injured several others at the Sartell facility ultimately resulted in Verso deciding to permanently close the mill. The decision wasn't immediate; it took two months to evaluate the condition of the plant and the plausibility of continuing operations. Coming on top of the recent downsizing, the news was devastating: another 280 workers were now out of work. Sartell employees who had been relieved to have survived the downsizing were now about to be terminated, and they would be embarking on a job search after those displaced earlier had had first crack at available job openings locally.

Prior to the decision to close the Sartell mill, Minnesota officials—including Mark Phillips, commissioner of DEED, and Gov. Mark Dayton—toured the scarred mill. Greater St. Cloud Development Corporation CEO John Kramer argued for saving the mill: "Verso's impact to the state is dynamic—beyond the property taxes and the employees," he said. "They buy timber out of Bemidji. They have 27,000 acres of land near Alexandria. They make value-added products out of what we grow here and send them out of the state at much higher value. It has huge economic implications. . . . They're an economic engine we can't afford to let go" (Allenspach 2012, p. A:1).

In the fire investigation, damage evaluations brought both good and bad news: the paper machine was intact, but the fire had taken out the power plant. Given the reported damage, the slow recovery from the recession, increased competition from new paper mills in Asia, and increased consumer use of electronic forms of communication, the Verso decision to close the Sartell mill may have been a reasonably easy decision. Verso announced the closure on August 2, 2012.

Data Collection after the Sartell Mill Closure

A companion questionnaire (see Appendix B) to the one that had already been sent out to those downsized from the two Verso mills was now mailed to a random sample of 100 of the terminated Sartell workers in the first week of October. The 100 recipients were mailed a cover letter requesting their participation, a questionnaire (slightly revised from the first one), a stamped and addressed return envelope, and a $10 bill. While there were 280 salaried and union workers who were terminated after the fire, funding from CURA was available only to cover 100. The questionnaire was mailed from the DEED office, which had access to the names and addresses. Researchers only had access to the names and addresses of workers if that information was provided when the completed questionnaires were returned. From 100 questionnaires sent out, there were 66 returned.

Data analysis provided an overview of those displaced paper workers from both mills as well as those terminated in the Sartell closure:

- Displaced workers in our three samples averaged 55 years of age; the mean age of the Sartell displaced was 54.1, the mean age of the Bucksport displaced was 56.1, and the mean age of the Sartell workers terminated in the closure was 55.2 years. With a total of only 24 workers in all three samples under 45 years of age, our displaced paper mill workers are overwhelmingly older workers.[2]

- Women made up just over 12 percent of our samples and included 20 of the 27 women who worked at Sartell.

- Downsized Sartell workers averaged 25 years at their mill, while displaced Bucksport employees had 22 years of service, and those workers discharged from Sartell after the fire had 29 years of seniority at the mill.

- Many of the Bucksport workers lived in Bucksport or the nearby area, which combined had a 2010 population of almost 5,000. While some Sartell workers lived in small towns, others lived in the adjacent St. Cloud area, which has a population of 65,000.

Comparison of Our Data with State Dislocated Worker Data from Minnesota and Maine

While our samples of downsized Sartell and Bucksport workers are lower than desired, we are fortunate to have both Minnesota and Maine Dislocated Worker data from these two downsizings. Figure 3.1 provides the Minnesota DEED data on the age distribution of all the downsized Sartell workers. It peaks at around age 55, closely matching the mean ages from our sample of all three groups, given in the first bullet point of the previous section.

Figure 3.1 Age Distribution of Downsized Sartell Workers

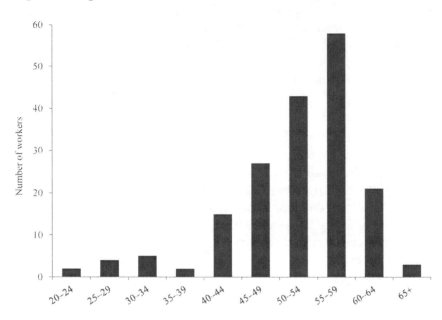

SOURCE: Minnesota DEED data of 180 workers.

Figure 3.2 reflects the age distribution of the Maine Dislocated Worker data, although these data are not taken from an exhaustive roster of all downsized employees, but rather from those who responded from the initial downsizing.

Issues Confronting Dislocated Paper Workers

One of the larger issues confronting displaced workers was that termination at the age of 50 or older is difficult to come back from. Research suggests that those beyond age 50 looking for work are hampered by many employers' view that they are too old to hire, too young to retire. Many of those let go at Verso had expected to retire from their paper mill employment, but job loss forced them to adjust their plans.

Displaced workers, particularly older ones, suggest that age discrimination is a force to be reckoned with and prevents them from being considered when a desired position has been advertised. Exactly

Figure 3.2 Age Distribution of Downsized Bucksport Workers

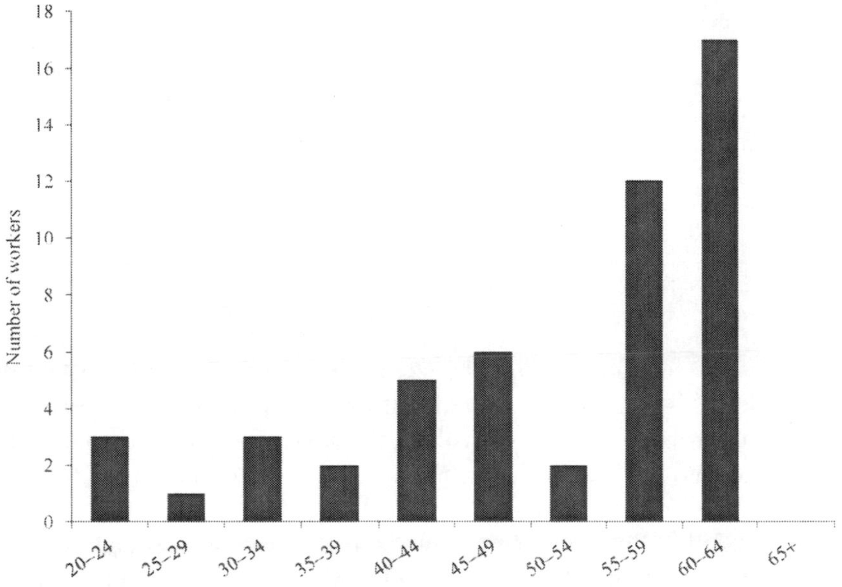

SOURCE: Maine data of 51 workers.

what the definition of "older" is remains obscure. For example, Rook, Dooley, and Catalano (1991a), in their study of coping skills and age, categorize "older" as being aged 60 and above. A government report titled "The Employment Problems of Older Workers" (USDOL 1971, p. 2) states, "Although age 65 is considered the beginning of old age for many purposes, the older worker generally is defined as those workers aged 45 or older." While several job loss researchers use age 45 as their boundary for "older" (Parnes, Gagen, and King 1981; Pursell and Torrence 1978; Root and Park 2009), others (Newman 1995; Rones and Herz 1992) go with 40 years of age, and Portis and Suys (1970) use 50. The cutoff points for age categories do make a difference, as Tables 3.4 and 3.5 illustrate.

A second issue confronting the displaced paper workers is that unpredictable unemployment has devastating effects on displaced individuals and their families, introducing stressors that one cannot pre-

Table 3.4 Distribution of Sartell and Bucksport Respondents Using Age Range Categories from Rook, Dooley, and Catalano, Including the Category of "Older" at Age 60+

Age range	Downsized Sartell workers	Downsized Bucksport workers	Displaced Sartell workers at the closure
18–34	4	4	1
35–59	63	28	51
60+	29	35	14
Total	96	67	66

SOURCE: Rook, Dooley, and Catalano (1991a).

pare for (Voydanoff 1983a). The stress can result in anxiety, psychophysiological distress, or lowered self-esteem. In addition to possible financial hardship, job loss involves the loss of the earner role and, for some who had a strong attachment to workmates and to their work tasks, a sense of grief and loss.

Attewell (1999, pp. 67–68) finds that job displacement differs according to marital status, the presence or absence of children, sex, race, and education. He writes, "People with less than a college education suffer higher rates of displacement than more educated workers; men are displaced in greater proportion than women; and younger workers lose jobs in higher numbers than older workers (although this is obscured when samples are limited to high-tenure workers)." Displaced single parents and workers with a high school diploma or less also had higher rates of long-term unemployment.

Table 3.5 Distribution of Sartell and Bucksport Respondents Using USDOL Age Range Categories, Including the Category of "Older" at Age 45+

Age range	Downsized Sartell workers	Downsized Bucksport workers	Displaced Sartell workers at the closure
23–45	11	9	4
45+	85	58	62
Total	96	67	66

SOURCE: USDOL (1971).

Family resources are important in responding to job loss, and how the family views unemployment will frame its immediate response. Additional resources include financial reserves, social support, adaptability, and cohesion (Voydanoff 1983b). How the family copes with the job loss is determined by how they utilize their resources and their behavioral response in maintaining or reachieving a balance in their family functioning. For some displaced workers, obtaining other work—even at less pay—is a significant component of adjustment; for others it might be continuing a job search for a position that is equally rewarding financially and remains stimulating and challenging, even though it requires relocation or temporary family separation.

In an earlier study, Root (1977) finds that most wives of dislocated workers perceived that a plant closing had been "generally good for their family." These families defined unemployment as an opportunity and had ample family resources, family cohesion, and the ability to make and adhere to a plan. The majority of displaced workers in a sample by Gabriel (2014) of a lockout report that they are better off now than before the lockout. While that sample initially suffered a financial setback, many have recovered financially, and they view their quality of life as "better." On the other hand, Young (2012), using data from the Panel Study of Income Dynamics, finds that unemployment functions as a "trigger event" that strips the displaced worker's identity as a productive person, a result that implies that employment equates with social quality. While unemployment insurance (UI) provides some help on the financial end, UI does not provide support for subjective feelings of self-worth.

The displaced paper workers from Bucksport and Sartell lost their jobs at a time when 82 percent of working Americans over age 50 said in an Associated Press–National Opinion Research Center (NORC) poll that it is at least somewhat likely they will work in retirement. In the same poll, one-third of those retired said they did not stop working by choice but felt they had no option and "were forced from a job because of their age" (Associated Press 2013a, p. 4). Allen (2014b) reports that nearly 19 percent of people 65 and older are still in the workforce, and that the number of these postretirement workers has steadily grown since the mid-1980s.

One of the core questions job loss researchers want to know the answer to is, "How do displaced workers fare after job loss?" For example, do older workers confronting job loss retire earlier than they had planned? At both mills, several workers were close to retirement age at the time of their displacement, so retirement, or even early retirement, was an option for them. Others were willing to be trained and eager to find full-time replacement work at comparable wages and benefits to what they had when working for Verso. Still others were confused or undecided about what they wanted to do, or could do, because most respondents, at either mill, indicated that they had anticipated working there until they retired.[3] For those not able to retire, they were much more likely to view their job loss as "generally bad." And in answer to our query on whether displaced older workers had taken early retirement, 80 of 115 (72 percent) workers aged 45 and older in our study replied affirmatively, although 40 of these, in response to a different question, said they had visited the workforce center to look for work, so their answers on retirement were inconsistent.

Cottell's (1974, p. 116) study of forest workers found there "was a relationship between the respondent's age and desire for a different job. . . . Men over the age of 35 were more commonly satisfied to remain in their current job while younger workers were more generally socially mobile, as was true for both unskilled and semi-skilled workers."

Tosti-Kharas (2012) raises the question of whether the well-being of displaced workers benefits or is harmed by postdisplacement organizational identification (that is, workers continuing to identify with the company that terminated them), and finds that for the white-collar workers in her sample (primarily from the financial services industry), having a continued organizational identification provided a valuable coping resource. Such a resource might include advice, references, and support during unemployment that could come from former coworkers or bosses, helping the displaced to cope with their involuntary job loss.

WHAT IMPACT HAS THE GREAT RECESSION HAD ON LOCATING NEW WORK?

A comparison of the impact of the Great Recession to other recent postwar recessions in the United States is shown in Figure 3.3. Job loss during the Great Recession is far greater than for any other recent

Figure 3.3 Indexed Job Loss in All Postwar Recessions

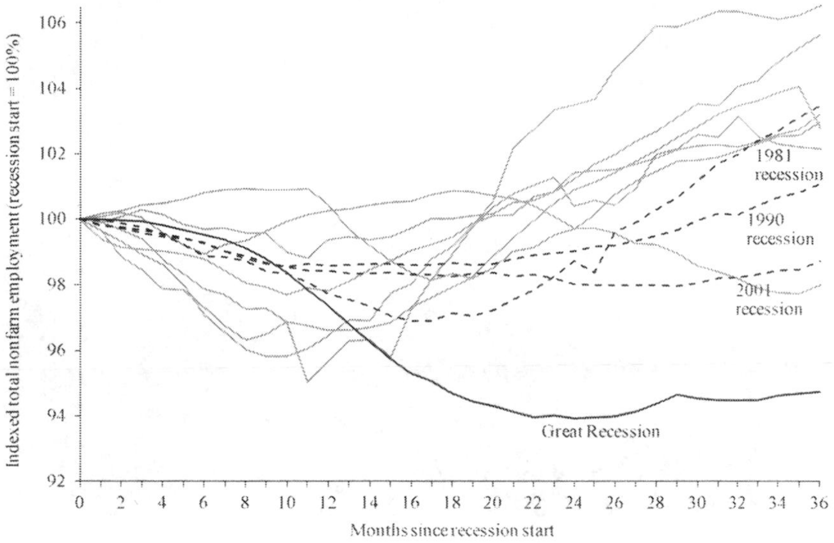

NOTE: Gray lines show recessions starting in 1948, 1953, 1960, 1969, 1973, and 1980.
SOURCE: Thiess (2011).

downturn, and the recovery is considerably slower than after other postwar recessions.

The impact of the Great Recession means that significant numbers of employees are only able to find part-time work (Figure 3.4). Some economists (e.g., Thiess [2011]) suggest that the underemployment rate might be a useful index because it takes into account not only those who are unemployed but those who are only able to find part-time work and those who have given up looking for work. Mui (2014) notes that in 2007 about 4.4 million people were part-time workers, but that in 2013 nearly 8 million people were part-time for economic reasons. (Part-time workers are those whose jobs average less than 35 hours per week.) One indication that part-time work may be one component of a polarized workforce pitting different age groups against each other is that the number of young people in part-time positions is dropping as their spots are being taken by adults of prime working age, those between ages 25 and 54.

Figure 3.4 Underemployment, 2000–2011

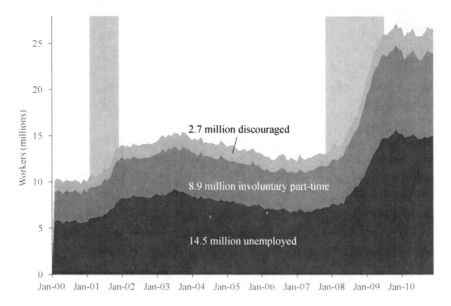

NOTE: Shaded vertical bands denote recession.
SOURCE: Thiess (2011).

As Figure 3.4 shows, the underemployed numbered more than 25 million in the United States in 2011, and the underemployment rate was nearly 17 percent. Individuals seeking work outnumbered job openings in every industrial sector (Thiess 2011). Figure 3.5 shows the severity of the recession: those who are long-term unemployed make up more than 44 percent of the unemployed. Thiess notes that the Great Recession has shattered records for long-term unemployment—defined as those who have been unemployed for six months or longer. Long-term unemployment can leave permanent scarring effects and eventually cause those who are unemployed to stop looking for work. Figure 3.6 provides another perspective on assessing the impact of the recession. This period (2007–2009) shows a sharp increase in the ratio of job seekers to job openings (cresting above 6.0), and a slower decline to 4.4 by September 2010. While downsizing and closures continue, Resolute's Calhoun, Tennessee, pulp and paper mill, which has been in operation

Figure 3.5 Long-Term Unemployment as a Share of the Unemployed

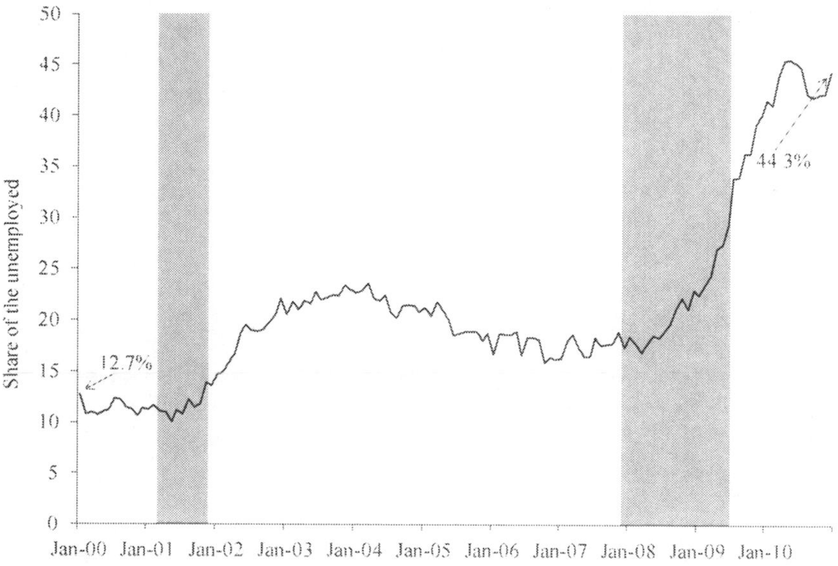

NOTE: Shaded vertical bands denote recession.
SOURCE: Thiess (2011).

since 1954, will get a $105 million upgrade by mid-2016 that will raise pulp capacity, cut costs, and improve versatility (CPBIS 2014a).

Using longitudinal data from both national and state-based studies, Burgard, Brand, and House (2007) find that involuntary job loss from either a closure or downsizing is associated with poorer self-rated health and more depressive symptoms. Studies, including Stephens (2003), have consistently reported that earnings losses follow job displacement. Davis and von Wachter's (2011) study notes that those displaced lose considerably more when the national unemployment rate is above 8 percent. And Farber (2011) finds that job losers in the Great Recession have been less successful at finding new full-time jobs, so that part-time work constitutes "new employment" for 20 percent of those displaced. Kletzer's (2000) research supports the assertion that as imports become more competitive, domestic industry displacement increases. An example is the considerable growth in the Chinese paper industry.

Figure 3.6   Job Seekers to Job Openings Ratio

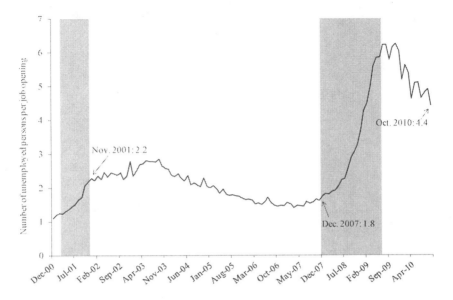

NOTE: Shaded vertical bands denote recession.
SOURCE: Thiess (2011).

Options for Dislocated Workers

The first topic we asked survey respondents about was what they were doing about work. Nine displaced Verso mill workers reported they were unable to work at present (presumably from physical limitations), 25 were in a training/education program, and 70 were looking for work, although there were differences in the timing of dislocation and which mill they had worked at, as shown in Table 3.6. Another 24 percent of our respondents were employed (23 percent of those downsized from Sartell, 24 percent downsized from Bucksport, and 26 percent of the Sartell workers displaced after the fire). Of those who were employed, 40 percent of the downsized Sartell respondents had their new job lined up by the time they were downsized; that was true for 33 percent of the Bucksport and terminated post-fire Sartell workers as well. Those who were downsized from Sartell did have 60 days between the downsizing announcement and the actual termination to

Table 3.6 Present Situation for Surveyed Dislocated Workers (%)

	Sartell downsized	Bucksport downsized	Sartell terminated at shutdown
Employed, full-time	23	24	26
Employed, part-time	4	16	3
Retired	15	40	0
Unable to work at present	5	4	2
In training/education program	14	7	11
Unemployed, looking for work	34	6	52
Unemployed, not looking	5	2	6
Total	100	99	100
N	95	67	65

NOTE: Totals may not sum to 100 because of rounding.
SOURCE: Authors' compilation.

look for work. Bucksport workers in the first cohort, terminated 11 days after the downsizing announcement, had no such luxury.

A second topic we wanted to learn more about was what part age plays in the adjustment to job loss. While those displaced workers that were not able to retire reported their job loss as "generally bad," there were statistically significant differences between older workers, depending on the mill they had worked at, but those differences did not exist between younger workers at the two mills.[4] Table 3.7 shows that at Bucksport, two of the seven younger workers (those 44 and younger) said their job loss had turned out to be a good thing, and 34 of the older workers gave the same response (29 percent and 65 percent, respectively). In the responses of all displaced Sartell workers, 5 of 12 younger workers reported that the job loss was good, but only 33 of 128 older workers gave that response (42 and 26 percent, respectively).

The differences between the older workers from the two mills are statistically significant at the 0.001 level. There are at least five plausible explanations for these differences:

1) Severance pay at Bucksport could have been selective, with those selecting severance being terminated.

2) There was a time factor—some Bucksport respondents had weeks to consider alternatives, while those terminated after

Table 3.7 Bucksport and Sartell Respondents' Answers to Whether Their Job Loss Was Generally Good or Generally Bad for Them

	Workers 44 and younger	Workers 45 and older
Bucksport respondents		
No. workers responding "Generally good" (%)	2 (29)	34 (65)
No. workers responding "Generally bad" (%)	5 (71)	18 (35)
N	7	52
All Sartell respondents		
No. workers responding "Generally good" (%)	5 (42)	33 (26)
No. workers responding "Generally bad" (%)	7 (58)	95 (74)
N	12	128

NOTE: Chi-square = 24.82 with 1 degree of freedom.
SOURCE: Authors' compilation.

the Sartell fire had to make a decision quickly. However, this advantage may not have been as great as we thought: as one respondent from Bucksport said, "I was really stressed out by getting done because of the way it was thrust upon us—we had one day to make a major life decision."

3) While the mean age between the Sartell and Bucksport workers was close, Bucksport workers were, on average, one year older. More importantly, 26 of the Bucksport workers (45 percent) were 62 or older, compared to 18 of the Sartell workers (20 percent).

4) The population, potential for new employment, and unemployment rate of the area where the displaced worker resided could be additional factors influencing a decision to retire. We reasoned that displaced Bucksport workers would be likely to have more frustration or anger than displaced Sartell workers because there would be fewer employment options in a smaller community. Bucksport also had a higher unemployment rate over the previous six months—7.2 in November 2012 compared to 5.6 for Sartell–St. Cloud, according to BLS data.

5) We noted earlier the questionnaire completion rates for the various samples—56 percent for downsized Sartell workers, 44 percent for downsized Bucksport workers, and 66 percent for those discharged in the Sartell closure—but we need to consider methodology in this outcome. If, as we had hoped, we had had nearly 100 percent participation, we could have ignored the low completion rate from Bucksport, but at this stage we cannot rule out response bias. (Readers are encouraged to review Appendix C.)

The third question job researchers are interested in, given the economy of each state, is this: Is there much difference in adjustment/reemployment between those displaced workers who live in Maine and those who live in Minnesota? At the time of the initial downsizing announcement for the Sartell and Bucksport mills (October 2011), the unemployment rate for Minnesota was 6.2 percent, while the Maine unemployment rate was 7.3 percent. The unemployment rates for the mill areas at the downsizing announcement were 5.9 in the Sartell–St. Cloud area and 7.4 for the Bucksport area. In November 2012, comparable area rates were 5.6 and 7.2, reflecting slight improvement in both areas.

Some dislocated Sartell workers reported that the two-month period after the fire was very difficult. One said, "The 2 months of waiting for the decision to close the plant was the worst. There was no information available for anyone. No one knew what was going on." Thus, some of the Sartell respondents who had not been downsized but were in a state of limbo waiting for Verso to decide what it was going to do might have felt relief at finally getting a decision. One man had worked at the mill for 30 years but was too young to retire. He explained why he thought his job loss was bad in three short sentences: "I have no job. I have no income. I have no future."

Some displaced Sartell workers found out from a news conference that Verso had decided to close the mill. They were irritated at the company for not telling them directly. Other terminated Sartell workers believed that the two-month delay in announcing the closure put them at a disadvantage in getting the assistance they needed. And still others expressed frustration that they had had only one day to adjust to their job loss: "On 8/2/2012 Verso told us we were done on 8/3/2012," one said. Displaced Sartell workers described their anger at the company in a variety of ways. One stated, "[I'm] angry at owners who made millions at the cost of our work, and who lost nothing when we lost it all."

One displaced worker—a fourth-generation Sartell mill worker in his family—grew up in Sartell and understood what the mill meant to the community. For him—and the community—the closure was a very sad day. "I liked my job and enjoyed going to work. Now I don't know what I'm going to do for the next 15–20 years. It was a good paying job and they just don't have jobs like that in this area."

Worker Response to the Impacts of Job Loss

Svensen, Neset, and Eriksen (2007) point out that organizational change and downsizing focus mainly on the negative consequences for those that are displaced, as well as for those that are retained. Wright and Barling (1998, p. 339) note that the "executioners" (the individuals who plan or carry out the downsizing) are affected negatively as well, from "role overload, social and organizational isolation, a decline in personal well-being, and decreased family functioning." And Gallup polls show that the threat of job loss is pervasive in the United States.[5] Davis and von Wachter (2011) use these data to show the dramatic jump in 2009 in worker anxieties over hours, wages, and benefits (Table 3.8). Those figures had relaxed only a little by August 2012, indicating that the slow recovery was continuing to trouble workers.

Responding to the loss of one's job could involve much more than an effort to locate other work; it could affect one's physical, mental, and emotional health and significantly reduce one's financial resources. While a portion of displaced paper workers reported that their physical health was worse after job loss (13 percent for Sartell, 18 percent for Bucksport), more noted that their physical health had improved (26 percent for Sartell, 29 percent for Bucksport). Shift workers frequently reported that their health had improved, in part because of their ability to have a regular sleep pattern. Mental health was more of a mixed bag: 51 percent of respondents for Sartell and 26 percent for Bucksport reported worsened mental effects from job loss, but 18 percent for Sartell and 39 percent for Bucksport reported improved mental health.

At the time of data collection, we found that 16 respondents had already moved; 13 of these were from Sartell. Many workers (32 from Sartell and 12 from Bucksport) said they had to budget closely to make

Table 3.8 **Percentage Employed Adults Who Worry They Will Experience Hours, Wages, or Benefits Cut or a Layoff in the Near Future**

	Hours cut	Wages cut	Benefits cut	Layoff
1997	15	17	34	20
2003	15	17	31	19
2004	14	17	28	20
2005	13	14	28	15
2006	16	19	30	17
2007	12	14	29	14
2008	14	16	27	15
2009	27	32	46	31
2010	25	26	39	26
2011	30	33	44	30
2012	26	28	40	28

NOTE: Survey question was asked in August of each year.
SOURCE: Jones (2012).

it through the month, and another 12 Sartell and 5 Bucksport workers reported that their families were struggling with finances. Other respondents said they anticipated they would have to seek some form of public assistance. Still other respondents reported they had missed mortgage or rent payments (8 from Sartell and 3 from Bucksport); had cut back on what they purchased (77 from Sartell and 40 from Bucksport); and had postponed medical or dental care (42 from Minnesota and 19 from Maine).

SUMMARY

The loss of work—through no fault of their own—has the potential to significantly affect displaced workers. If they can find other work quickly, or retire, they may not suffer drastic effects, but if they can't find meaningful employment reasonably soon, all sorts of difficulties may develop. Paper mill workers recently downsized from their Verso employment in Minnesota and Maine reflect the range of those impacts: older workers at the Bucksport and Sartell mills showed significant differences in how severely they were affected.

Although displaced Bucksport respondents had fewer local employment options than those in Sartell, all displaced workers would have a difficult time finding work at the same pay rate and benefit schedule they had while employed at the paper mill. Furthermore, the displaced papermakers were confronted with seeking new work as older workers, and in a slow recovery period. They, like many others in the United States, would find that full-time work was more restricted than in the past, and some would have to accept involuntary part-time employment. Fortunately for the community, several Bucksport Verso workers elected to take early retirement, thus creating an "open position" for younger workers who would have otherwise been involuntarily released.

The displaced workers from both Bucksport and Sartell may have fewer adjustment difficulties than those in other mass layoffs, simply because so many of them were older workers and able to retire. Still, as shown in Table 3.7, older Sartell workers were much more likely than older Bucksport workers (74 percent versus 35 percent) to say their Verso job loss was generally bad for them.

Notes

1. The portion of the WARN Act that notes when circumstances do not trigger WARN is as follows:
   "WARN is not triggered when a covered employer:
   - Closes a temporary facility or completes a temporary project, and the employees were hired with the clear understanding that their employment would end with the closing of the facility or the completion of the project; or
   - Closes a facility or operating unit due to a strike or lockout and the closing is not intended to evade the purposes of the WARN Act.

   "WARN is also not triggered when the following various thresholds for coverage are not met:
   - If a plant closing or mass layoff results in fewer than 50 people losing their jobs at a single site of employment;
   - If 50–499 workers lose their jobs and that number is less than 33 percent of the employer's total active workforce at a single site;
   - If a layoff is for six months or less; or
   - If work hours are not reduced more than 50 percent in each month of any six-month period."

2. While the Verso workers were overwhelmingly long-term seniority personnel, the Holland (2008) report on skills transferability of displaced Fraser paper workers showed the displaced Fraser workers as primarily younger workers. Seventy-five percent of those who completed the Maine Department of Labor survey ($n = 89$) were 21 to 45 years old, with an average length of mill employment of eight years—quite different from the Verso samples.

3. For those downsized at Sartell, 62 percent reported that they never expected to leave Verso through separation, but rather had planned to retire from the mill, while 57 percent of the Bucksport respondents gave the same answer. This was also the response from 72 percent of the displaced Sartell workers terminated after the fire.

4. The "outcome questions" we asked were as follows: "Regarding your job loss at Verso, would you say the job loss was generally good for you or generally bad?" "Then, regarding your family and the Verso downsizing/shutdown, would you say the job loss was generally good for your family or generally bad for your family?" These questions are based on the question created by Little (1976), but used by others, including Adams, Kessel, and Maher (1990); Kessel and Maher (1991); Root and Mayland (1978); Root and Park (2009); and Root, Root, and Sundin (2007). While the percentages of "good" responses or positive comments about job loss vary from 39 to 48 percent in the previously reported studies, the time frame of when the question is asked is crucial. Root and Park (p. 162) note that "job loss researchers generally believe that if you ask the outcome question at the time of job loss when the confusion and unknowns of joblessness are [uncertain], angry and depressed respondents would not have a very positive response. This belief hinges on a view that for those so close to the point of job loss [i.e., after the announcement has been made but before the actual job loss takes effect], anticipating the outcome of displacement would be an exasperating and difficult task, and their worries over finances, personal status, family cohesion, and physical health would be painful. . . . Thus, the outcome question is usually not asked in the initial panel of a longitudinal study, or immediately after the job loss, but at a point after some adjustments have already taken place and where options for the displaced worker are evident."

5. Gallup's annual Work and Education poll has been conducted initially in 1997 and then each year since 2003 among those 18 and older working full- or part-time. The 2012 data in Table 3.8 are from www.gallup.com/poll/156821/benefit-reductions-remain-top-worry-american-workers.aspx.

4

Responding to Job Loss

*Who would have guessed that it would be so hard [to find work],
but it is.*
—Displaced female Sartell worker with 30 years' seniority

Once the downsizing announcement was made, many Verso workers at both the Maine and Minnesota sites expressed great concern. For
some, the announcement upset their career planning and anticipated
retirement outcomes, while for others, it raised concerns about their
finances, loss of fringe benefits, or where to find another good job.
Table 4.1 tabulates responses to Question 59 in the Root-Park questionnaire, showing that Sartell workers, both those downsized and those
terminated in the closure, were more upset than Bucksport workers.
Among job losers from Sartell, the percentages for those terminated at
the closure were larger under every condition than for their mill colleagues who were downsized. The one category in Table 4.1 where the
percentages of all three groups were close was the response, "I was very
depressed," chosen by 19–25 percent of respondents.

EARLIER STUDIES ON JOB LOSS IN THE PAPER INDUSTRY

While the paper industry has had numerous downsizings and closures, there is no comprehensive study documenting the industry's transition over the past 20 to 30 years.[1] And though there have been numerous job loss studies, Minchin's (2006) research comes closest to focusing
on the impacts of job loss for paper mill workers.[2] One chapter in High
and Lewis (2007) does treat job loss impacts for paper mill workers, but
the chapter emphasizes the community adjustment that Sturgeon Falls,
Ontario, had to go through—not the adjustment of the laid-off workers
themselves. We have located a few studies that we deemed tangential to
an assessment of displacement among paper mill workers. One (Univer-

Table 4.1 Workers' Responses to Leaving Their Verso Employment (%)

	Downsized Sartell workers	Downsized Bucksport workers	Sartell workers terminated at closure
I was upset because I had expected to retire from Verso.	45	25	64
I was concerned about my finances, bills, etc.	52	46	67
I was upset over the loss of fringe benefits.	40	25	56
I didn't know where to find another good job.	32	15	50
I was very depressed.	19	25	24
N	96	67	66

NOTE: Multiple responses possible for Table 4.1; each response category is a percentage of the total, N.
SOURCE: This and all other tables and figures in the chapter are constructed from the authors' compilation of survey results.

sity of Maine 2013) consisted of oral history interviews on "the history and culture" of Eastern Fine Paper in Brewer, Maine, a mill that closed in 2003. Although the paper industry in Maine grew from 9 paper mills and 12 pulp mills in 1885 to 109 mills in 1906, the decline hit hard after 1975, and by 1999 only 17 pulp and paper mills remained. The oral history project encompasses "job technique, customary practice, verbal art, and ideological causes"—the traditions of work in a given trade—but does not focus on the impacts of losing one's job. Other sources that were aligned with the broader wood products industry included an assessment of loggers and sawmill workers adapting to periodic layoffs in a declining industry (Stevens 1978), a Maine Department of Labor study on skills transferability of former Fraser Paper employees (Holland 2008), and the Leighton, Roderick, and Folbre (1981) study, which covers the 1977 Penntech Papers shutdown of the Madison, Maine, paper mill with just 90 minutes' notice. Other useful books on job loss for papermakers include Loveland (2005), MacDougall (2009), Osborn (1974), and Ziewitz and Wiaz (2004).

Dislocated workers are described by Kolberg (1983, p. xv) as "those forced from their jobs . . . not because of their lack of competence, but because of sweeping changes in America's technology, production, and marketing." Our definition of job loss follows that of Shaw and Barrett-Power (1997), who characterize it as a constellation of stressor events around the termination of paid work that demands a process of coping and adaptation. The paper industry is and has been involved in significant technological changes, caught up in overproduction when markets have disappeared, and involved in a continuing search for new product development. Austin (2008, p. 26) quotes a pulp and paper executive as saying, "It's not just a question of making paper anymore, it is completely revamping a very old and wise industry into a thriving, new multidimensional one that can successfully live on for another 100 years."

EMPLOYMENT OPTIONS FOR DISPLACED WORKERS

Although Sartell is an expanding suburban city, employment options for displaced mill workers were limited, for several reasons:

- While those displaced were talented and capable, their mill skills were not in great demand in the immediate area.
- The economy was sluggish as recovery from the recession stalled.
- The majority of the Sartell workers were long-seniority older workers, averaging in the mid-50s in age, who, if competing with younger unemployed workers for a new job, may lose out.
- Those displaced were earning $24–$40 per hour (plus benefits), with time-and-a-half for overtime, and considerable opportunity to work overtime. Given the paucity of employment openings locally and the low pay of most available positions, most displaced Sartell workers were confronted with limited options.

Similar if not more restrictive employment options existed in Bucksport, except for one added variable: when the downsizing announcement came, workers knew there would be an offer of early retirement, and that gave them renewed hope they would be able to stay on or be reemployed once early retirees made their wishes known.

Retirement

Seventy-five Bucksport Verso workers accepted the early retirement option. While displaced Sartell workers had not had a retirement option, they might have had easier access to work, or more information about work in the North Dakota oil fields, than Verso's Maine displaced employees.

Some Found Full-Time Work, but at Reduced Pay and Benefits

Aged 55 and a skilled pipefitter, Steve W. felt lucky to get a day job. With 33 years at the Sartell mill, he had some other options, but he took a maintenance position in a nearby smaller town for roughly half his Verso salary. His benefit package is restricted and includes only his health care. His paid vacation period at Verso was six weeks and four days; his present vacation is one week. On the positive side of the ledger, the commute from his home to his present worksite is only three miles. He was offered a paper mill position in Duluth, but that would have meant renting an apartment there and commuting home on weekends. And like several others from Sartell, he could have found work in the North Dakota oil fields, but that too would have meant living apart from his wife in a man camp, able to come home for only five days every five weeks. Another option for Steve was to become an over-the-road trucker, because when he had been unemployed for three months, he took a truck-driving course through DEED. But while trucking was a viable option, it also meant he would be home only once every three or four weeks. Steve opted for quality of life—being at home with his wife and close by his three married children and their families.

Steve maintains there really are no available jobs in the area, certainly not any with the salary and fringe benefit package he had at the mill. He understands that he has a low-wage position, but at least it's not part-time, and he is not separated from his wife or extended family.

Others Had Only Part-Time Work at a Large Pay Reduction

Ken is 59. At the time of the Sartell downsizing, he decided he would retire rather than get bumped from his position in the core room and shuttled to other work that could have been shift work. His 39 ½ years at the paper mill didn't help him obtain full-time work, so he has accepted part-time work as a custodian at his church. He started out at $10 an hour but has received a raise to $12, although he gets no benefits. Ken sets his own schedule, working fewer hours in the summer than the usual 20 hours a week the rest of the year.

Ken's spouse, Karen, was also caught in the layoff. Karen had 30 years' seniority at the mill, having started in the early 1980s after being displaced when the railroad shut down and the rail shops where she worked left the area. Karen came to the mill during an expansion period when several women were added to the workforce. The Sartell mill had 700-plus workers then.

From Blue-Collar to White-Collar, Full-Time

Mark worked on the No. 3 machine and had 20 years' seniority. When he lost his job he wasn't overly concerned, largely because, while working at Verso, he was making an equal income building cabinets. That source petered out when the recession put a halt to home construction. Still, laid off in December 2011, he had three job offers in his first year. He opted to go with an insurance firm, selling life and health insurance and being a financial advisor. He estimates that 30 percent of his displaced coworkers are doing okay but 70 percent are struggling.

Still Unemployed

Don is 60 and unemployed—perhaps partly because, as the last United Steelworkers No. 274 union president, he was still involved in closing down union activities, helping others connect with training and jobs, and cleaning out the union office at the mill. He continues to be optimistic, involved with "his people," and helpful. He knows the impacts of job loss firsthand, but he also knows of them through two sons who were also displaced in the 2011 Verso downsizing.

Don, a maintenance electrician, was never laid off during his 40 years at the mill. He has applied for 60 different jobs, has had 12 interviews, and no offers. Don believes it is because of his age, but he also notes that his union membership may have influenced a potential employer to treat him differently from other prospective employees. Don says he would go back to work at Verso "if it were a possibility."

Tom, another long-seniority Verso Sartell worker, is also unemployed. At age 55, with 30 years of paper mill experience, Tom worked until August 3, 2012. Over the years of his employment at the mill, Tom had been laid off two different times. Tom and his wife have cut back on expenses: driving, "fun stuff," the frequency of eating out, and using medical services when needed. Tom and his family were used to a certain lifestyle and income. "Now it is all new!!!" he writes. Like many others, Tom had expected to retire from Verso. He reports that he was depressed over his job loss and concerned about finances and bills. Responding to the questionnaire, Tom disagrees that his social life is great and agrees with the statement "I feel kind of worthless." If an opportunity arose to go back to work at Verso, he would do so.

Relocating to Another Paper Mill Elsewhere in the United States

Some former Verso workers were able to locate mill work with other employers, but those positions meant relocation. These workers moved to places like Duluth, Minnesota; Clatskanie, Oregon; West Point, Virginia; Nicholasville, Kentucky; Erie, Pennsylvania; Cincinnati, Ohio; and St. Augustine, Florida.

Greg is 53 years of age, an engineer, and had worked at the Sartell mill for more than 25 years. Using professional "headhunters," Greg was successful at getting three job offers in the paper industry. Two of those offers were in the South at more money than the position he accepted, but he reasoned that Oregon would be a better place to live. All three offers were an increase over what he had made at Sartell. Greg noted that getting a new job in a different geographical region was easy—selling his house was where he was going to take a hit financially. Important issues—selling his Minnesota home, buying a property in Oregon, and putting one more child through college—were all confronting Greg and his wife. When he relocated, his wife stayed in Minnesota to sell their home, so he and his wife were 1,700 miles apart.

Greg is positive about the change and would not go back to work at Verso if an opportunity came up. Temporarily physically separated from his wife, Greg disagrees that his social life is great. But he also disagrees with the statement, "I feel kind of worthless" and agrees that "Life goes on after Verso, and it's better!"

John is another mobile paper worker. John, 49, had relocated to Verso Sartell in 2010 after being displaced from an Oregon City, Oregon, mill. As a line manager on Machine No. 3 at Sartell, John had 90 employees reporting to him. Because John anticipated that the mill would not start up after the fire, he began looking for employment. He interviewed during the summer, receiving job offers in Rome, Georgia, and West Point, Virginia. In early September, he accepted the Virginia position with RockTenn and began his paper machine superintendent position October 1. John appears positive about his employer and his future in that company—in part because RockTenn makes several grades of paper, including cardboard boxes, that are in demand, which makes his long-term future more secure than it was at Verso. For John, who has a college degree, the unemployment experience was short-term: he was looking for work for only four weeks. John reported that his Verso job loss was generally good for him, as well as for his family.

STUDIES ON CHANGES IN HEALTH

Studies both here and abroad note that displaced workers suffer changes in health, both physical and mental: typically, 20–30 percent of unemployed respondents indicate that their health has deteriorated since job loss, and only 10 percent report health improvements (Payne, Warr, and Hartley 1984; Warr and Jackson 1983). However, Root and Park (2009) found that 54 percent of older displaced armament workers reported no change in their physical health, while 22 percent attributed some health problems to job loss and 24 percent replied their health had improved since becoming jobless. But when it came to their mental or emotional health, the displaced armament workers responded quite differently: only 35 percent reported no change in their mental health, 39 percent reported mental or emotional health problems, and 25 percent reported improved emotional health.

In England, Fryer and Warr (1984) found that for displaced men nearing retirement (60 and above), their scores on that country's General Health Questionnaire did not vary over time since their job loss. On the other hand, men who were somewhat younger (under 59) often had high scores for distress and depression.

Warr, Jackson, and Banks (1988) suggest that there are two types of stabilization that occur among displaced workers after a few months of unemployment. One type is "constructive adaptation," where those remaining unemployed take positive steps to develop interests or participate in activities outside the search for work. These activities could include hobbies or volunteer work, for example. Displaced workers who remain continually unemployed but active, remaining positive, are sometimes referred to as "good copers." A second and more prevalent form of adaptation is "resigned adaptation," where people withdraw from searching for work and from social contact, and they avoid situations that expose them to new experiences. Warr, Jackson, and Banks describe this as avoidance behavior: "By wanting less, long-term unemployed people achieve less, and they become less" (p. 55).

Many workers appear worried over the economy—Jones (2009) maintains that's true for 40 percent of Americans. However, Jones also notes that there are opportunities in starting over. He cites the example of a 30-year-old New Yorker displaced from her editing work at a publishing firm who started to do freelance editing and found it to be financially rewarding. "If it continues to be this steady, I will be better off financially than I was as a full-time employee," she says. "In one way it was a bad thing to lose my job, but it's created room for all these other things that so far have proven very fruitful and fulfilling" (p. 5).

THE TIMING OF THE SEARCH FOR REPLACEMENT WORK

Two factors are important in the speed with which displaced workers search for replacement employment: 1) financial responsibilities and 2) the worker's perception of the job market (Leana and Feldman 1995). While financial responsibilities varied, displaced paper workers commonly reported that some families were "hurting." That "hurt" stemmed from having to meet steep monthly mortgage payments and other budget items with finances now dependent on unemployment compensation or severance payments. Some workers had paid off their mortgage years earlier, so their financial distress was not as great; others were in serious difficulty. Some workers had limited reserves, in part because they had lived "paycheck to paycheck." Eating out several days each week had consumed much of their Verso income.

Cutting Back on Expenses

Once displaced, many respondents initiated efforts to reduce their costs by cutting back on activities that would cost them money. All three groups were consistent on the specific ways they cut back on expenses. The most common specific way of reducing expenses was to cut back on eating out. Other means of saving money included minimizing driving, going to the movies less often, and not using needed medical services. Some of those displaced, especially at Bucksport, also cashed in some pension or stock options. And some borrowed money from relatives, took out loans, or pawned items, but those were the least common approaches (Table 4.2).

Table 4.2 Respondent Cutbacks to Reduce Expenses (%)

Strategies to adjust financially	Downsized Sartell workers	Downsized Bucksport workers	Sartell workers terminated at closure
Cut back on expenses generally	78	61	86
Borrowed money from relatives	7	7	2
Cut back on eating out	57	40	62
Pawned items	8	9	0
Have taken out a loan	8	6	2
Have not used medical services as needed	40	21	21
Let some needed home repairs go	28	27	21
Cashed in some pension/ stocks	15	27	20
Cut back on driving	51	33	50
Cut back on going to movies	38	27	30
N	93	67	66

NOTE: Multiple responses possible; each category a percentage of the total, N.

Displaced workers and their families also tried to find ways to increase their income. A total of 22 respondents obtained a second job. Family members also helped; Table 4.3 shows the increase in work taken on by the spouse or significant other. Although half or more of spouses were already working, employed Sartell spouses in particular were more likely to increase their work hours.

Is Upgrading One's Skills Necessary to Get a Job?

When respondents were asked if they thought it was necessary to upgrade their skills in order to get a job, the percentage agreeing was inversely related to age (Table 4.4). Among the Sartell workers terminated at the closure, at least two-thirds of each respondent age category

Table 4.3 Change in Employment by Respondent's Spouse or Significant Other after Respondent's Own Job Loss (%)

	Downsized Sartell workers	Downsized Bucksport workers	Sartell workers terminated at closure
Spouse/sig. other was not working but took a job.	8	2	2
Spouse/sig. other was already working but began to work more.	13	4	10
Spouse/sig. other was already working but changed jobs to get more hours or higher pay.	2	4	6
Spouse/sig. other was already working and took a second job.	2	0	2
Spouse/sig. other was not working and did not start to work.	22	33	17
Spouse/sig. other was already working and continued to work at the same job.	52	56	63
N	77	48	52

NOTE: Columns may not sum to 100 because of rounding.

thought a skill upgrade was necessary. The percentage of Bucksport respondents agreeing was considerably less than for either Sartell group.

Mill respondents were also asked if, since their job loss, they had attended a training or educational program to obtain new skills or help them get a job (Table 4.4). Interestingly, among those downsized, the number of respondents who were participating in an educational or training program was far fewer than the number reporting that it was necessary to upgrade their skills in order to get a job—often half or less. However, among those terminated from Sartell because of the closure, the percentages who had been involved in training or an educational program were highest for those in the youngest group and lowest for those in the 63-plus age range.

Clearly, these terminated Sartell workers were more consistent in their views and behavior about needing new skills and actually obtaining skills, as their numbers in the corresponding charts match quite closely. Given that the Bucksport workers were less upset over their displacement than the Sartell workers, it is understandable that they would be less likely to attend a training or education program.

Our questionnaire also inquired about the type of training or education workers needed or desired to obtain the work they wanted to do, as well as what the respondent would need in order to be able to enter a training program. Additional training desires focused on three responses: 1) skill training, 2) expanding computer skills, and 3) obtaining a college degree or taking college courses. Downsized Bucksport and Sartell respondents had the largest percentages of respondents who wanted skill training, while the Sartell respondents terminated at the mill closure were most interested in computer training (Table 4.4). Bucksport respondents appeared to have the least interest in additional training or education—only 16 percent expressed such a desire, in contrast to 40 percent of downsized Sartell workers and 45 percent of terminated Sartell workers.

For those displaced workers who wanted training, Table 4.4 shows the prevalence of worker-identified need for tuition assistance or, alternatively, tuition assistance plus a stipend for books and equipment in order to participate in a training program. This need was particularly important for Sartell workers. Compared to both categories of Sartell workers, displaced Bucksport workers were most likely to reply that they did not need any assistance to participate in a training program.

Table 4.4 Respondents Who Attended a Training or Education Program to Obtain New Skills to Help Get a Job, and Other Survey Responses on Training

	Downsized Sartell workers	Downsized Bucksport workers	Sartell workers terminated at closure
Respondents agreeing skills upgrade necessary to get a job (%)			
63 and older	6	7	5
56–62	42	37	40
22–55	52	56	56
N	62	27	43
Respondents who have attended training or educational programs to obtain new skills (%)			
63 and older	3	18	8
56–62	53	45	33
22–55	45	36	59
N	89	62	63
Kind of training desired (%)			
Skill training	50	54	30
Computer training	24	9	37
College courses/degree	26	36	33
N	38	11	30
Respondent-identified needs to be able to enter training program[a]			
Tuition	50	37	66
Tuition + books/equip. stipend	50	35	59
Free child care	2	4	0
Transportation	6	0	4
Spouse to get a better job	14	6	5
N	78	46	56

NOTE: Columns may not sum to 100 because of rounding.
[a] Multiple responses possible; each category a percentage of the total. N.

FAMILY IMPACTS OF JOB LOSS

While displaced worker-family units were adjusting to job loss by "tightening their belts," one could expect that personal relationships might also require adjustment. Two questions were asked about changes in relationships between workers and spouses or significant others and other family members since job loss. Respondents could answer in three ways: 1) the relationship was closer, 2) there was no change in the relationship, or 3) the relationship had difficulties or individuals had become more distant from each other. Most respondents (57–80 percent) reported no change (Figures 4.1 and 4.2). Sartell workers, both displaced and terminated, were more likely to report difficulties with their spouses or partners, while Bucksport workers were more likely to report increased distance in family relationships, but these differences

Figure 4.1 Change in Relationship with Spouse after Job Loss (%)

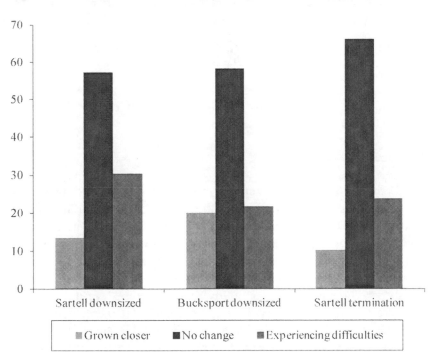

Figure 4.2 Change in Relationships with Family Members after Job Loss (%)

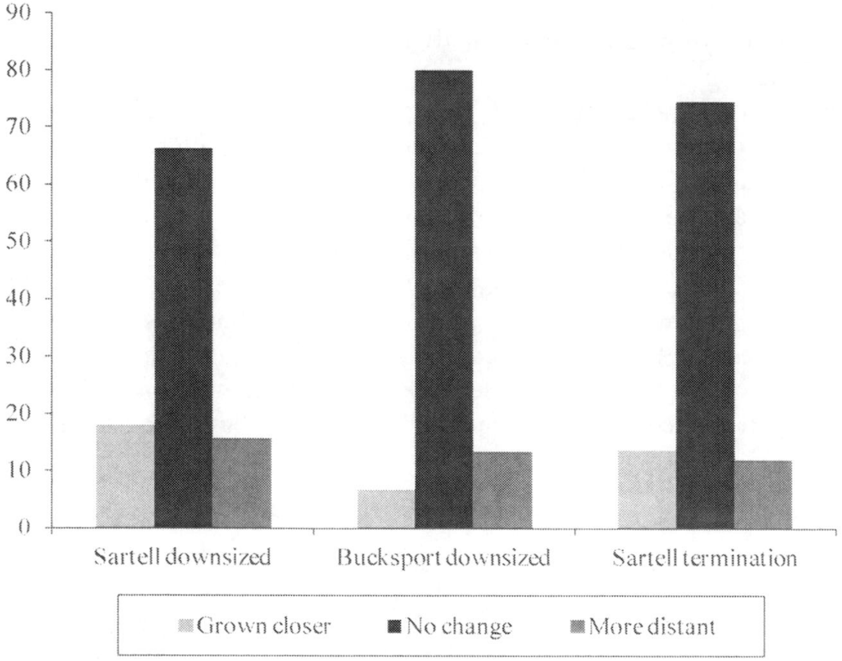

were not statistically significant. Both categories of Sartell workers reported family relationships as being closer.

Finances

Being a displaced worker is a broad categorical descriptor, and there are many variables affecting the degree of personal and family functioning, which creates a number of subcategories. One could be unemployed or retired, employed or too ill to work, and one's relationship to the work world could determine how satisfactory one's personal and family relationships were. While we did not ask former Verso respondents for their monthly family income, we did ask how they were doing financially. Forty respondents (19 percent) reported that they were doing well (Table 4.5). This could be because they had found new work (in the case of 19 individuals) or were retired (21) and

Table 4.5 Financial Situation for Dislocated Paper Workers after Job Loss (% of total respondents)

	Downsized Sartell workers	Downsized Bucksport workers	Sartell workers terminated at closure
Finances are not a problem.	12	33	16
Present income is less than at Verso.	31	34	42
We have to budget closely each month.	34	21	30
Finances are a major problem/receiving assistance or will soon apply for assistance.	24	11	12
N	89	61	64

NOTE: Chi-square = 16.32 with 6 degrees of freedom. Significant probability < 0.01. d = −0.12. Columns may not sum to 100 because of rounding.

had a pension or other income. Seventy-five of the displaced respondents reported they had less income but indicated that finances were not a major problem for their families and that they did not have to budget closely in order to survive each month. However, 85 respondents did say they had to budget closely in order to make it each month, and 36 said finances were a major problem or that they were either receiving some kind of assistance or would need to apply for assistance soon.

Bucksport workers had the highest percentage of respondents reporting finances were not a problem, while downsized Sartell workers had the largest percentage reporting finances were a major problem. Table differences are statistically significant with an acceptable measure of association (d = −0.12).

Changes in Physical or Mental Health as a Result of Job Loss

Workers were asked whether the Verso job loss had affected their physical health and were instructed to check one of five options, ranging from "Yes, having serious health problems" to "Having considerable improvement in health since leaving the mill." Most respondents, regardless of location or timing of job loss, reported no change in their physical health (data not shown). For each mill contingent downsized or terminated, at least 20 percent reported an improvement in their health. Of these, five or six respondents downsized from Sartell and Bucksport indicated they had had *considerable* improvement in their health. However, 22 percent of Bucksport respondents reported slight or serious health problems, compared to 14 percent for each of the two Sartell categories.

A follow-up question focused on the impact of job loss on their overall mental and emotional health (Table 4.6). Sartell respondents, particularly those who lost their jobs in the shutdown, reported that their Verso job loss harmed them to a greater degree than did Bucksport respondents. Bucksport respondents were much more likely to say their mental and emotional health had improved.

At least 25 percent of those in each job loss category reported no real mental health impact. However, rather large percentages of Sartell respondents said the job loss affected their mental and emotional health. The Bucksport respondents were more likely (41 percent) to report improvement. While the differences are statistically significant, the measure of association (Somers' d) is not strong.

Job loss may have significant negative effects on psychological well-being, including lowered self-esteem, increased anxiety, depression, and indicators of psychological distress. While coping resources vary among individuals, such resources would include individual skills, levels of support, and energy levels (such as possessing a positive outlook). Thus, citing others, Leana and Feldman (1995, p. 1383) write that "the greater the person's reservoir of coping resources, the more

Table 4.6 Has Job Loss Affected Your Overall Mental/Emotional Health? (%)

Assessment of mental and emotional health	Downsized Sartell workers	Downsized Bucksport workers	Sartell workers terminated at closure
Harmed by job loss	49	28	59
No real effect	29	31	24
Improved by job loss	22	41	17
N	92	64	66

NOTE: Chi-square =18.57 with 4 degrees of freedom. Significant probability < 0.001. d = −0.04. Columns may not sum to 100 because of rounding.

likely he or she is to have the ability and the inclination to cope effectively with stressful or uncertain situations." Those confronted with job
loss could focus on solving the problem—be involved in retraining,
relocate for better employment options, or be proactive in job-search
efforts—all efforts that would be the most likely to gain reemployment.
Alternatively, what Leana and Feldman refer to as symptom-focused
coping activities are not directly related to solving their employment
problem, but are efforts to alleviate the stress of being a job loser and
would include seeking social support or financial assistance.

Was Job Loss Good or Bad?

One question asked of displaced workers from a range of occupations over several years has been whether their job loss was good or bad
for them.[3] Since Little (1976) initially asked the question to a sample of
100 laid-off technical professional males along Route 128 on the East
Coast, different researchers in six studies have found that between 39
and 48 percent of displaced workers reported that their job loss was
"good." Those studies were done between 1976 and 2008 and included
displaced workers from several occupations, such as meatpacking, clerical, unionized production workers, public school teachers, and defense
workers (Table 4.7).

While one might imagine that most workers would not want to
lose their jobs—particularly on the heels of a recession—there was
considerable variation in the responses of paper mill workers in this
study, depending on which mill they were downsized from, as well as
the timing of their job loss from the Sartell mill. Table 4.8 shows that
Bucksport workers were more likely to view job loss as "good," with
60 percent of those displaced from Bucksport expressing that view. In
stark contrast, 79 percent of those Sartell workers terminated said the
impact of their job loss was "bad." In Table 4.8, we also see that the
percentages of workers who viewed the job loss as good or bad for them
are nearly identical, for all three cohorts, to the percentages of workers
who viewed it as good or bad for their families. A more detailed way
of looking at what job loss meant for our sample is to assess how the
respondents saw their job loss for themselves, cross-tabulated with how
they saw it for their families (Table 4.9).

Table 4.7 A Sample of U.S. Research Employing an Outcome Question

Researcher(s)	Year	Sample	Statement or question asked	% reporting "Good" or agreeing	Timing of outcome question	Completion rate
Little	1976	Laid-off technical-professional males, "for the most part engineers."	"I am beginning to think that losing my technical-professional position might not have been such a bad break after all."	48	Respondents were unemployed from 1 to 33 or more weeks and had higher incomes than others registered at the Route 128 Professional Service Center in Waltham, MA.	Convenience sample of 100 from 8,600 registrants.
Root & Mayland	1978	Displaced meatpacking workers, primarily a male sample.	"Was the closing generally good for your family or generally bad for your family?"	40	The outcome question was asked in the third interview two years after the Mason City Armour meatpacking plant shut down. The sample was a 10% random draw of those displaced.	81% in the third displaced worker interview.
Adams, Kessel, & Maher	1990	Clerical and unionized production workers involved in a plant shutdown.	"How did the layoff affect you and your family?"	42	Question initially asked one year after termination and again in the second-year survey, two years after job loss. The figure provided is from the second survey; the responses from the first survey were similar and so are not reported.	70% in first year; 74% in the second interview.
Kessel & Maher	1991	Downsized hourly production, clerical, and professional-managerial employees.	"How did the layoff affect you and your family?"	40	The sample comprised the majority of respondents terminated from the Burlington, VT. G.E. facility between January 1988 and October 1990. Respondents were asked the question in	82%

Source	Year	Description	Question	N	Details	%
					early 1991, which for some was only four months after job loss and for others more than three years.	
Root, Root & Sundin	2007	Laid-off public school teachers, overwhelmingly female (74%).	"Has the downsizing been good or bad for you?"	39	The sample comprised a 20% random draw of teachers downsized from 2000 to 2001 through the 2003–2004 school years. Data were collected in May 2005, with respondents having been terminated from 1 to 4 years earlier.	37%
Root & Park	2009	Displaced defense workers involved in the fifth downsizing over 15 years to create "flexibility" and increase outsourcing.	"Would you say the downsizing was generally good for you or generally bad?"	42	Longitudinal study of 227 defense workers displaced in 1998–1999. Data were collected in the last wave of mailed questionnaires in April 2002, 3–4 years after job loss.	84%
Root & Park	2016	Paper mill workers were downsized from (a) Minnesota and (b) Maine mills, and (c) after a fire in the Minnesota plant, the mill was shut down.	"Would you say the downsizing was generally good for you or generally bad?"	(a) 33 (b) 60 (c) 21	For those downsized from the Maine and Minnesota mills, the question was asked in a mailed questionnaire sent out in mid-July 2012, nine months after job loss for Maine workers and seven months after for most of the Minnesota mill workers. Those terminated in the Minnesota shutdown were asked the question in a mailed questionnaire three months after job loss.	(a) 55% (b) 44% (c) 66%

Table 4.8 Respondents' Views about Whether Their Downsizing Was Generally Good or Generally Bad (%)

	Downsized Sartell workers	Downsized Bucksport workers	Sartell workers terminated at closure
Panel A[a]			
Job loss was "good" for me.	33	60	21
Job loss was "bad" for me.	67	40	79
N	89	60	59
Panel B[b]			
Job loss was "good" for my family.	31	60	20
Job loss was "bad" for my family.	68	40	80
N	89	57	61

NOTE: Significant probability < 0.001. d $= 0.05$ is not significant.
[a] Chi-square $= 20.46$ with 2 degrees of freedom.
[b] Chi-square $= 21.75$ with 2 degrees of freedom.

Table 4.9 Comparison of Respondents' Views on Whether Their Downsizing Was Good for Them and/or Their Families (%)

Downsized Sartell workers ($n = 89$)		
Question: Was the job loss good or bad for you and/or your family?	Job loss was good for my family.	Job loss was bad for my family.
Job loss was good for me.	27	6
Job loss was bad for me.	4	63

Downsized Bucksport workers ($n = 57$)		
Question: Was the job loss good or bad for you and/or your family?	Job loss was good for my family.	Job loss was bad for my family.
Job loss was good for me.	56	2
Job loss was bad for me.	4	38

Sartell workers terminated at closure ($n = 59$)		
Question: Was the job loss good or bad for you and/or your family?	Job loss was good for my family.	Job loss was bad for my family.
Job loss was good for me.	19	3
Job loss was bad for me.	2	76

Some 32 of the 57 displaced Bucksport respondents (56 percent) reported that their job loss was good for them and good for their family. Thus, Bucksport respondents generally had positive views about it. Among the job losers downsized from Sartell, 63 percent perceived that their job loss was bad for them and also bad for their families, while 76 percent of the terminated Sartell respondents said their job loss was bad for them and for their families. The positive response to job loss from the Bucksport respondents was much higher than that of job losers in earlier studies (Adams, Kessel, and Maher 1990; Kessel and Maher 1991; Little 1976; Root and Mayland 1978; Root and Park 2009; Root, Root, and Sundin 2007).

The wide variation of response from the displaced Bucksport workers (56 percent positive) as opposed to the terminated Sartell workers (76 percent negative) is puzzling. There were similarities in those displaced: all workers at the two plants were employed by the same company, all were paper mill workers, all became job losers within a seven-month period, and all were "left behind" on the heels of a recession. What might account for the wide discrepancy?

While Bucksport workers were aware of difficulties in the paper industry, they might have thought the industry difficulties would bypass them, if for no other reason than that Verso had recently committed $40 million in modernization and expansion at their mill. In essence, while their mill was safe, they were out of a job. No comparable corporate investment had been recently made, or proposed, at Sartell. Furthermore, those downsized from Bucksport were aware of the early retirement option available for long-term Bucksport workers and anticipated (or even had been told) that they would be rehired within a few weeks.

Sartell workers who were terminated in the mill closure had survived the downsizing, then, two months later, were confronted at the time of the fire with the prospect of losing their mill employment. Many of those survivors went from elation to depression—they were not only denied the opportunity to continue to work, they were also following other Sartell paper workers displaced earlier who had the advantage of procuring "first options" in any available local employment.

Initially we thought it might be a matter of age difference—i.e., the Bucksport workers might be younger and therefore more positive about the options from being unemployed and looking for work. As shown in Table 4.10, however, age range, mean, and median are comparable, and,

Table 4.10 Age of Displaced Mill Workers and Years Worked at Mill

	Downsized Sartell workers	Downsized Bucksport workers	Sartell workers terminated in the closure
Age			
Range	26–66	23–70	34–66
Mean	54.0	56.0	54.0
Median	57.0	60.0	54.5
Years worked			
Range	2–45	1–47	2–40
Mean	24.0	23.4	29.2
Median	26.0	29.0	30.0

counter to what we expected, the mean and median age of Bucksport workers were in fact greater than those of Sartell workers. Table 4.10 also compares the span of years employed and the mean and median employment period for each cohort of workers. Most workers in both mills were long-term employees. Although the table does not show this, the displaced Bucksport employees were also much more likely to be short-timers, because 13 of those downsized in Maine were employed for one year or less, while all of the Sartell workers were into at least their second year. The longest-seniority employees who were displaced were two workers from Bucksport, one with 46 years of service, the other with 47. These two individuals balance out the means.

We also made a cross-tabulation to determine if gender played a part in assessing whether job loss was bad or good (Table 4.11). Responding to this question were the 13 women downsized from Sartell, plus six women who were downsized from Bucksport and six who were displaced from Sartell when the mill was closed. Of the 13 downsized

Table 4.11 Ratio by Gender Reporting That Job Loss Was Good

Gender	Downsized Sartell workers	Downsized Bucksport workers	Sartell workers terminated in the closure
Female ratio (%)	6 of 13 (46)	3 of 6 (50)	1 of 6 (17)
Male ratio (%)	24 of 76 (32)	31 of 51 (61)	12 of 54 (22)

Sartell women, six reported that their job loss was "good," and so did three of the six Bucksport women, but only one of six Sartell women terminated at the closure gave a "good" response. Bucksport workers—both women and men—were more likely to perceive their job loss as being good for them than the displaced Sartell workers.

One of the Sartell workers terminated responded to the question of whether there were "good paying jobs available in the Sartell area that you would like to have" by writing, "Never make what I made at the mill." He also wrote that the job loss was generally bad, because "it was a big change. I did not worry about other jobs, I was going to retire from the Mill!"

Verso workers were aware of the excess product the company had on hand. At the time of the Sartell explosion and fire, that mill had rolls of paper in inventory, largely owing to slow sales. As noted earlier, a major issue in the pulp and paper industry is the ability of U.S. paper producers to increase production at the same time that export opportunities have dwindled and competition with low-cost Asian imports has risen.

Temporary Workers in Bucksport

One difference between the Maine and Minnesota mills was that the Bucksport mill utilized temporary workers: 41 of its workers were temps. Of these 41, only eight returned our questionnaire. Temporary workers were provided the same questionnaire as all others, $10, and a stamped, addressed envelope for returning the completed questionnaire. Our temporary worker respondents ranged in age from 23 to 56; the mean age was 42, and four of the Bucksport temps were in their 50s. The temps were downsized from May 2011 to early January 2012—six of the eight in our sample were released in mid-October 2011.

Five of the eight temps believed the job loss was bad for them and for their families; only one believed it was good for him and for his family. Another thought it was bad for him but good for the family. One wrote that the job loss had both good and bad components for himself.

While three temps had worked for Verso for less than a year, three others had been there for one year, one had been there for two years and another for three. Two had come to work at Bucksport after the Eastern Fine Paper mill closed in 2005, one after having worked there for 17 years.

THE CONTINUING IMPACT OF THE GREAT RECESSION

Because of a somewhat sluggish recovery, displaced workers could anticipate a longer lag period before they were able to find new employment (Lippman 2013). While women have regained the number of jobs they lost in the recession, in 2013 men were still more than two million jobs short of the number they had held. "The gender gap is expected to persist until the job market is much healthier," write Rugaber and Wiseman (2013, p. A:1). "To understand why, consider the kinds of jobs that are, and aren't, being added. Lower-wage industries, like retail, education, restaurants, and hotels, have been hiring the fastest. Women are predominant in those areas. Men, by contrast, dominate sectors like construction and manufacturing, which have yet to recover millions of jobs lost in the recession."

Greenstone and Looney (2011, pp. 2–3) note that two years after the Great Recession ended, one of every 11 American workers was still unemployed. And for many of those who found work, their reemployment comes at lower wages—48 percent lower than their average pre–job loss earnings. One reason for the large earnings losses is that their skills in previous employment are less valuable in the present economy. According to Poletaev and Robinson (2008), the largest earnings losses are incurred by displaced workers who take new jobs utilizing different skills. Thus, Nedelkoska and Neffke (2011) suggest that workers seeking employment look for opportunities where they can use existing skills and limit the need to learn new skill sets.

Although workers with a college degree may respond better to earnings shocks, job loss reduces the rate of home ownership and private health insurance coverage—an indication that "job loss appears to reduce workers' lifetime outcomes along multiple dimensions" (von Wachter and Handwerker 2009, p. 1).

Quick Adjustments, and Some Not So Quick

When confronted with job loss, a few Verso workers (six from Sartell, one from Bucksport) were fortunate to have another job lined up before they left the mill. For Max, having had a part-time job while working for Verso worked to his advantage: he was able to work full-time at his side job until he located another full-time position. "Things are going fine," he said. "I work at a full-time job I don't mind and a part-time job I enjoy. I make far less than I did at Verso, but we knew the job would come to an end sometime, so we prepared for it financially. I am happier than I ever was working in the paper industry."

Raymond is another downsized Sartell worker highly satisfied with the outcome of his job loss. Raymond wrote, "Everything is going great, and the best thing to happen to me was getting laid off." He elaborates: "Verso was a miserable place to work. My new job is enjoyable; managers listen." Would he return to work at Verso if such an opportunity came up? "No way in hell!"

Sam was a displaced Sartell worker who secured a new position through an Internet posting prior to his downsizing. He was without work for four weeks, but part of that time was spent getting his family moved to another state. His home sold in two weeks. While his household income is half of what it was in Sartell, Sam maintains that it is better to be in a new position than be unemployed in Sartell. This does not mean it has been easy to relocate. The move has been difficult for the children, and leaving parents and extended kin behind has been hard. However, taking everything into account, Sam reports that he is very satisfied with his new work, and given an opportunity to go back to work for Verso, he would reject the offer.

Some downsized Bucksport workers were also able to find work quickly—but, like those downsized from Sartell, there were also others who had 30 weeks of unemployment or remain unemployed. Ron was one of the Bucksport respondents who benefited from the early retirement plan Verso initiated at the Maine mill. Downsized after working for Verso for three years, Ron looked for work for a week, then was rehired full-time by Verso. Still, Ron said the downsizing was generally bad, and he thought the company should have given more notice to those who were downsized.

Jimmy had worked for Verso-Bucksport for a year as a temporary worker. He was without work for three weeks before he became self-employed. In large part, his self-employment came about because "there are no good paying jobs in our area." He would return to the mill if that was an option because he really liked working there; he was "proud to walk past that gate every morning." But a return to Verso would be conditional on the job being full-time and "no temp stuff."

Others at Bucksport were still without work many weeks after job loss. Amos was downsized in late October 2011 after 37 years at the mill and had not had work since then. Although in his early 60s, he was planning to relocate out of state and had tried to sell his house. While he recognizes he needs to find work, he wasn't interested in looking for work locally because he wanted to move closer to family in another state. Once he moved, he expected he would find work. If given the option to return to Verso, he would decline, because, as he wrote, "I am glad to be out of the job that hates older workers; with no raises and more work—a very bad environment."

In a comparable position to Amos, Stan and Mike had been without work since the closure of the Sartell mill, and each had been at the mill for well over 20 years, were in their late 50s, and had expected to retire from the mill. Stan considered his job loss bad for him and for his family. He and his wife worry about losing their home. Stan wrote, "I don't look forward to getting up in the morning." Mike is divorced and recently moved. He has been searching for work for the past three months. He worries about not having health insurance, seeing that as a major concern.

Leaving Verso

All respondents were asked to think back to when they left the company and what their feelings were then (Question 59). Sartell respondents—both downsized and displaced at shutdown—were more likely than Bucksport respondents to report being upset and concerned. For example, 52 percent of the downsized Sartell respondents, 46 percent of downsized Bucksport respondents, and 67 percent of the Sartell workers displaced at the closure reported being concerned about their finances. Some 63 percent of those displaced from Sartell at the closure reported being upset because they had expected to retire from Verso; the same was reported by 45 percent of those downsized from Sartell but by only 25 percent of those downsized at Bucksport. Eighteen percent of the Bucksport respondents (12 individuals) reported they weren't particularly concerned about their job loss, as did 11 percent of the downsized Sartell workers (11 respondents) and 15 percent of Sartell workers (10 respondents) caught in the shutdown.

Regarding what the company or union could have done to better prepare them for job loss, only 6 percent of Bucksport respondents but 14 percent of those downsized from Sartell said the company or union should have offered classes on money management. Considerably more workers favored offering classes to upgrade skills: 32 and 12 percent of those downsized from Sartell and Bucksport, respectively, and 20 percent of those terminated from Sartell at the closure.

SUMMARY

Job loss is a stressor event requiring a range of adjustments—seeking work, consideration of relocation for some, and for others, accepting part-time employment. For most Americans, losing a job one expected to have until retirement could well constitute a crisis situation. And losing a long-term position that paid well and included good health care for workers and their families when the workers were in their mid-50s could only inflame the stress and anxiety. Additional pressure would likely be felt when job loss adjustment was impeded by a slow economic recovery. The outcomes from such stress could affect one's health, relationships with others, and concerns about the future. Such was the situation for displaced Verso paper mill workers.

Changes in the paper industry, exacerbated by a slow economic recovery, meant that finding comparable local employment would be difficult. This constituted the situation in Bucksport for sure, whereas the St. Cloud metropolitan area offered better options for work opportunities outside the Verso mill. In addition, many of the displaced workers carried two liabilities: 1) they were older, and 2) paper-worker skills were not in demand in the immediate area. Because demand for coated paper had diminished and foreign competition had increased, none of the displaced Verso production workers were offered a transfer to another Verso mill.[4] Employment options at mills belonging to other companies were also limited and were difficult to undertake given the need to relocate. Relocation for work in the North Dakota oil fields was not desirable because that would require separation from, or relocation for, one's family. Whatever jobs might be available were likely to be lower-paid and, often, part-time. Given their concerns about finances and the loss of benefits, displaced workers sought to reduce their expenses in any way imaginable, and spouses often took on additional work.

Most former Sartell workers viewed their job loss as being bad for them *and* bad for their family. Most former Bucksport workers saw their job loss more positively, largely because the company had announced an early retirement option just before the announcement to eliminate 125 positions, which meant younger workers could fill the slots opened by older workers who took early retirement.

Notes

1. Given that more than 175 paper mills became inoperative between 1998 and 2013 (Rieland 2011), it is clear that sociologists, labor economists, and others who study economic displacement have been selective in their focus on U.S. industries, resulting in a serious void in job loss research in the paper industry.
2. Minchin's (2006) study has some drawbacks, primarily having to do with his focusing on a sample of 15 from a workforce of more than 800.
3. Comparisons of what is sometimes described as an outcome question (i.e., "Has the downsizing been good or bad for you?" or some comparable variation) are difficult—in part because the question is not always stated exactly the same, but also because *when* the question was asked could well make a difference. For example, in the Root and Park (2009) longitudinal study of displaced defense workers, the question was asked three to four years after their job loss. In this study, the question was asked seven to nine months after the downsizing in Maine and Minnesota and three months after termination when the mill was shut down.
4. Two transfers from Sartell to Bucksport were made—the mill superintendent and one manager.

5

Assistance Provided to
Help Dislocated Workers

If a community, the families, and the individuals going through a major workplace adjustment are to make a healthy transition, they need the companies and unions to plan the programming and supports together. Families need to use their strengths and develop skills, including the ability to communicate and solve problems together. Individuals need to be able to ask for support, and to create a vision of a new future. The road through this transition has many potholes, blind corners, and crossroads, and sometimes the map seems faded, but a healthy transition means reaching that new place in your life, with the anger, fear, and discouragement worked through.
—Peggy Quinn (1999, p. 41)

According to the Center for Paper Business and Industry Studies (CPBIS 2014a), there were 163,000 employees in U.S. pulp and paper mills in January 1998. By May 2003 that number had dropped sharply to 111,000; it then dropped more slowly, to 83,000 in 2010. Pulp and paper mill employment in February 2014 in the United States was 76,000 workers, about 47 percent of the 1996 level (Figure 5.1).

Of course, displaced paper workers are only some of the U.S. workers that have become job losers. In December 2013, the U.S. unemployment rate (seasonally adjusted) was 6.7 percent, while the corresponding rate for Maine was 6.2 and for Minnesota was 4.6. One year earlier, the unemployment rate had been 7.2 percent in Maine and 5.4 in Minnesota. Maine's unemployment rate of 6.2 percent translates to 45,100 individuals; Minnesota's 4.6 percent rate to 139,987.

Even though the good news is that the Maine and Minnesota unemployment rates are lower than the national unemployment rate, the bad news is that thousands of recently employed workers are now without work or have found only part-time employment since displacement. Shaw and Barrett-Power (1997) maintain that displacement without

Figure 5.1 Paper Industry Employment, 1998–2014

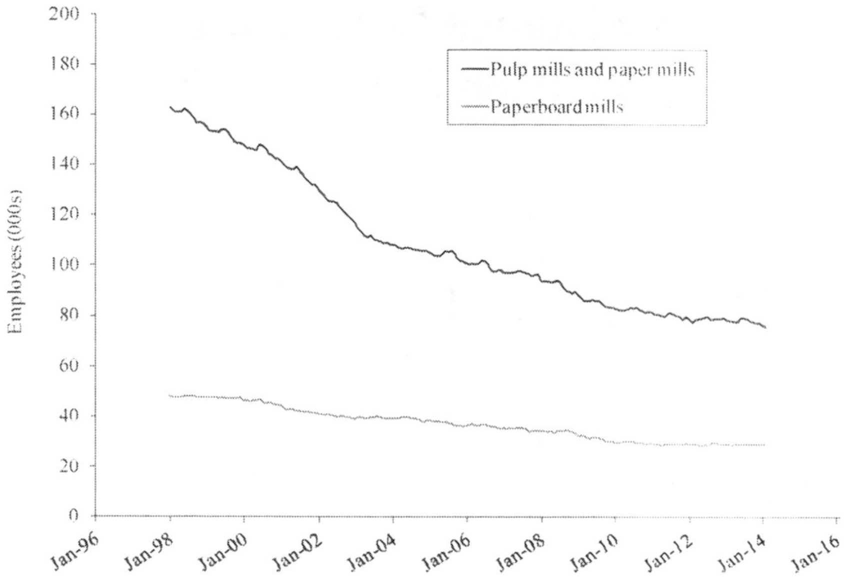

SOURCE: CPBIS (2014a).

outplacement assistance is more severe for job losers than when assistance is provided. They point to several individual, work group, or organizational aids that could help:

- A work group developing a plan for addressing potential layoffs
- Implementing employee assistance programs, including retraining incentives, job search help, or outplacement counseling
- Encouraging organizational decision makers and group members to actively deal with the job loss problem
- Minimizing negative and unintended outcomes, particularly by reducing instances where positive outcomes for individuals are followed by negative actions

WORKER ADJUSTMENT AND RETRAINING NOTIFICATION

One of the major aids to U.S. employees confronting job loss is the Worker Adjustment and Retraining Notification (WARN) Act, which was introduced in the U.S. Senate in June 1988 and within a month had been passed by both houses of Congress. It was left unsigned by President Reagan and became law on August 4, 1988 (Wikipedia 2015c). WARN gives workers and their families time to adjust to and plan for anticipated employment loss, either 60 days' notice prior to displacement or "pay in lieu of notice" for the 60-day period. WARN also requires that notice of closure or mass layoff be given to employees' representatives, the local chief elected official, and the state dislocated worker unit. Perhaps as importantly to workers and their families, the WARN notice given to governmental agencies provides officials with a brief period to prepare for retraining programs or other supportive services that might be provided in the community.[1]

WARN represented a tremendous advance in helping dislocated workers. Until then, a downsizing or closure could be announced and occur on the same day. While the WARN Act protects workers, their families, and their communities by requiring most employers with 100 or more employees to provide notification of plant closings and mass layoffs (USDOL 2015b), some loopholes exist. For example, WARN is not triggered when various thresholds are not met, including 1) when a plant closing or mass layoff results in fewer than 50 people losing their jobs at a single site and 2) when 50–499 workers lose their jobs but the number displaced is less than 33 percent of the employer's total active workforce at a single site (Wikipedia 2015c).

While downsized Sartell workers were given 60 days' notice, those in Bucksport were, for the most part, let go in October (and the balance displaced in November and December) without a WARN notice because 33 percent of the workforce was not affected. Essentially, Bucksport workers terminated in October had about one-and-a-half weeks between the time they learned of the impending downsizing and the actual termination. To reach the desired reduction in the number of workers at Bucksport of 125, the company and the unions agreed to offer early retirement for those volunteering to accept it; thereafter, they would issue involuntary layoffs to get to 125. In Maine, a worker can take a voluntary layoff and still collect unemployment compensation as long as there is an announced number of layoffs. In the Bucksport downsizing, some 75 older workers within six months to a year of retirement took the voluntary layoff, which allowed 75 younger workers the opportunity to remain on the job. Even though some Bucksport workers complained that they had to make major decisions too quickly after the announced downsizing, two supportive elements are reflected in the Bucksport approach: 1) the company and union worked together to create and approve the early retirement program, and 2) the retirement offer was sufficiently attractive to entice 75 workers to accept.

At Bucksport, there were 41 workers classified as temporary workers; they were paid $12.50 per hour, did not have benefits, and did not have union representation even though they paid union dues. Of these temps, 13 were hired permanently by Verso after the recalls. Of the remaining temporary workers, 18 are working elsewhere (4 at higher-paying jobs and 14 at lower-paying jobs), and 10 are either not working or have moved out of state.

Maine does not require a report when state services are provided at a downsizing or closure. However, of those displaced at Bucksport, 65 workers signed up for the TRADE program; 46 attended résumé writing and interviewing skills workshops, 48 attended job search workshops, and 9 were involved in training programs.

In Minnesota, displaced Sartell workers who had secured employment used the term "scammers" to describe those who were "working the system"—particularly in taking training only for the income provided, not for the skills that would provide them with new work. Scammers turned down employment opportunities; however, the training did provide some income, and it did provide for continuing interaction with other displaced Verso workers. Training gave these displaced workers a place to go, status, and allowed them to stay on the fringe of the labor force. In short, participation in training provided them with legitimacy, and from their perspective, no one would have to know that they did not expect to accept a job following training. However, the Stearns-Benton Employment and Training Council (SBETC) staff feared that prospective employers would, after being turned down by scammers, react negatively and disregard all displaced Verso personnel.

Maine's mass layoff law says, "Whenever an employer lays off 100 or more employees at a covered establishment, the employer within

7 days of such a layoff shall report to the director the expected duration of the layoff and whether it is of indefinite or definite duration" (warnactlaw.com 2012). Minnesota, along with Maryland and Michigan, has a statute that asks employers to voluntarily provide advance notice to workers in the event of a mass layoff, but these three states do not require compliance (Wikipedia 2015c).

Assistance to Verso Mill Workers Terminated in the Shutdown

In Minnesota, the Verso-Sartell mill had already downsized 151 employees when the May 2012 explosion and fire led to the mill's August shutdown and another 434 workers' losing their jobs. The SBETC renewed its efforts to assist those terminated. An SBETC overview (Zavala 2013, p. 1) reported that "the Verso jobseeker profile reflected males, average age 44, who were union members in obsolete jobs, 50% of whom had been with Verso 30+ years, 80% with 25+ years or more. The wage for the majority was $24–$40/hour with benefits." The SBETC provided dislocated worker assistance to former Sartell mill workers, while displaced Bucksport workers were provided assistance through one of 12 full-service Maine Career Centers.

Working Part-Time for Economic Reasons

In 2002, there were 58,300 Minnesotans who worked part-time for economic reasons, but by January 2011 that figure had nearly tripled, as 165,100 remained stuck in part-time work (Forster 2011). Comparative measures of labor underutilization for Maine, Minnesota, and the United States in 2003, 2009, 2011, and the second quarter of 2014 from the Bureau of Labor Statistics (BLS) are shown in Table 5.1. Kletzer's (2000) earlier research supports the assertion that as the Chinese paper industry has grown considerably and Chinese imports have become more competitive, domestic industry displacement has increased.

The U-6 category in Table 5.1 includes total unemployed, plus all marginally attached workers, plus total employed part-time for economic reasons, as a percentage of the civilian labor force. In this category (and most others), the U.S. percentage is higher than that of both Maine and Minnesota, while Maine has a percentage equal to or higher than Minnesota's.

Table 5.1 Alternative Measures of Labor Underutilization for Maine, Minnesota, and the United States, 2003, 2009, 2011, and 2014[a]

	U-1	U-2	U-3	U-4	U-5	U-6
			2003			
Maine	1.7	3.0	5.1	5.2	5.9	9.3
Minnesota	1.6	3.0	5.0	5.1	5.9	8.9
U.S.	2.3	3.3	6.0	6.3	7.0	10.1
			2009			
Maine	4.0	4.9	8.1	8.5	9.5	14.7
Minnesota	3.5	5.0	7.8	8.1	8.9	14.2
U.S.	4.7	5.9	9.3	9.7	10.5	16.2
			2011			
Maine	4.1	4.6	8.0	8.5	9.5	15.1
Minnesota	3.3	3.6	6.5	6.8	7.6	12.8
U.S.	5.3	5.3	8.9	9.5	10.4	15.9
			2014			
Maine	2.6	3.3	6.1	6.4	7.2	12.8
Minnesota	1.9	2.5	4.6	4.9	5.6	10.0
U.S.	3.5	3.5	6.8	7.2	8.1	12.9

NOTE: The state measures are based on the same definitions as those published for the United States (BLS 2011) and include the following:

- U-1: persons unemployed 15 weeks or longer, as a % of the civilian labor force
- U-2: job losers and persons who completed temporary jobs, as a % of the civilian labor force
- U-3: total unemployed, as a % of the civilian labor force
- U-4: total unemployed plus discouraged workers, as a % of the civilian labor force plus discouraged workers
- U-5: total unemployed plus discouraged workers, plus all other marginally attached workers, as a % of the civilian labor force plus all marginally attached workers
- U-6: total unemployed plus all marginally attached workers, plus total employed part-time for economic reasons, as a % of the civilian labor force plus all marginally attached workers

[a] 2014 figures are for second quarter.
SOURCE: BLS (2003, 2009, 2011, 2014).

Workforce Development Approaches in Maine and Minnesota

According to the Maine State Workforce Investment Board, Maine has set a goal of developing a globally competitive workforce—i.e., building a cadre of appropriately trained and educated workers through industry partnerships (Mills 2013). The Minnesota approach appears to use job fairs, such as the Department of Employment and Economic Development's (DEED) Twin Cities hiring and recruiting event "The Get Jobs Job Fair." Workforce development is created through pre–career fair workshops in résumé writing, interviewing, networking, job search, self-motivation strategies, and overcoming employment obstacles such as the "Don't call us, we'll call you" employer response.

Within Maine's 16 counties, pulp and paper mills numbered among the top 25 private employers in nine counties and among the top 3 employers in four counties. To rank in the top three, an employer had to have at least 500 employees. The Verso Bucksport mill ranked third in employment in Hancock County, behind a biotech research and development firm and the hospital (Maine.gov 2015b).

THE WORKFORCE INVESTMENT ACT OF 1998

The Workforce Investment Act of 1998 (WIA) replaced the Job Training Partnership Act (JTPA), tying together federal programs in employment, training, adult education, and vocational rehabilitation into a "one-stop" system. According to Wikipedia (2015d, p. 1), the goal of WIA was to "induce business to participate in the local delivery of Workforce Development Services." The vehicle for business involvement was participation in Workforce Investment Boards, composed of area business and community representatives. Displaced workers benefited from WIA because as "customers," they had a choice in deciding which training program best fit their needs. WIA also promoted a quick return to work through core services provided to laid-off workers, including labor market information, assessment of skill levels, and job search and placement assistance.

Implementing WIA in Maine

WIA created a "one-stop" system of workforce investment and education for adults, youth, and dislocated workers. In Maine, there are four regions of Local Workforce Investment Boards, composed of business, labor, public, and nonprofit organizations that collaborate with the Maine Department of Labor in establishing 12 Career Centers and 18 satellite offices to provide services to job seekers and employers.

Those seeking employment can obtain a range of services, including

- an assessment of skill levels, aptitudes, abilities, and support service needs;
- workshops on networking, job search techniques, and resume writing;
- information on education and training service providers;
- help filing claims for unemployment insurance;
- career counseling and job search and placement assistance; and
- up-to-date labor market information about job vacancies and required skills for in-demand jobs (Mainecareercenter.com 2013).

Maine has two special programs for laid-off workers, the first of which is Trade Assistance Programs. These programs include Trade Adjustment Assistance (TAA), Alternative Trade Adjustment Assistance (ATAA), and Trade Readjustment Allowances (TRA). They help trade-affected workers who have lost jobs because production has left the United States or imports have increased. The U.S. Department of Labor determines eligibility for these programs. Certified workers may receive job search assistance, training, relocation allowances, and additional weeks of unemployment compensation. ATAA provides those eligible over the age of 50 with a wage subsidy if their new employment has lower wages than their previous job (Maine.gov 2015a).

A second Maine program is the Dislocated Worker Benefit Program, which provides up to 26 extra weeks of unemployment benefits to those in approved training programs; these persons are not required to look for work as long as they are attending school (Maine.gov 2015a).

The Maine Department of Labor has Internet postings of useful information on trade assistance programs, unemployment compensation for laid-off military, and dislocated worker benefits.

Sartell Programs to Help with the Transition

The SBETC established the following assistance programs:

- Those displaced after the fire, their spouses, and their families could join an employee assistance program, in which a counseling professional helped the group understand and work through grief and generate forward movement.

- A client assistance program provides terminated workers with financial counseling and personal needs counseling (mental health, family issues). Because of displaced workers' high earnings, severance, and retirement accounts, health and investment service providers targeted them with marketing campaigns.

- Informational sessions on health care options were provided.

- Because the displaced workers had worked together in a closed community for so long, the city of Sartell provided a drop-in center where they could congregate—initially city hall; later the Veterans of Foreign Wars (VFW) building in Sauk Rapids.

Sartell Programs to Prepare Displaced Workers to Find New Work

- Adult Basic Education (ABE) provided on-site "Introduction to Computer" classes to assist the displaced workers in their job search. The computer information and skills carried over to UI claim applications and employment and training options.

- Area employers provided tours and made presentations in sessions titled "Career Trek Workforce U," which helped job seekers connect and look forward. Employers involved in the program were able to talk with displaced workers and found them motivated to go to work. This helped dispel rumors that because of their high earnings, the displaced paper workers would only look at jobs with comparable wages.

Sartell Programs to Prepare Displaced Workers for School

- SBETC created cohorts of displaced workers who could begin training as a group in "off-semester start" classes.

- SBETC and St. Cloud Technical and Community College (SCTCC) developed support groups and tutorial processes for students.

- SBETC and SCTCC developed sessions to help nontraditional adult-learner students acclimate to school. SCTCC provided sessions on "Intro to Technology," on TRIO Student Support Services, and on learning how to study, how to maneuver in the college computer system, and how to submit homework.

- SBETC contracted with the Minnesota Resource Center (MRC) to design and implement refresher classes on math and writing, how to use the Internet, and practical computer applications. These classes built on the ABE classes provided earlier.[2]

Unemployment insurance benefits are not standardized in the United States for either the weekly benefit amount or the number of weeks for which benefits are available. For example, Georgia allows benefits for only 18 weeks and Florida and North Carolina for 19 weeks, while most states and the District of Columbia cover 26 weeks. Only two states, Massachusetts and Montana, allow benefits for more than 26 weeks (USDOL 2015a). Weekly benefit allocations vary from a low of $221 in Louisiana to a high of $679 in Massachusetts (FileUnemployment.org 2015). Maine ranks fifteenth among all states with a weekly benefit of $378, while Minnesota, at $629 weekly, ranks third.

Businesses Pledge to Consider the Long-Term Unemployed

Schafer (2014) notes that some of the unemployed have said that it is necessary to lie to get a job—and have done so themselves. While that advice is difficult for career advisers to accept or understand, for some among the more than 2.5 million Americans out of work for at least one year, lying has been used successfully. Many long-term out-of-work Americans feel they can't win. It is against this backdrop that President Obama has recruited some of the nation's largest companies to revamp hiring practices and initiate procedures to employ those who have been out of work for long periods of time. Baker (2014) writes that the president has persuaded some 300 businesses to agree to new hiring policies, including more than 20 of the nation's largest companies. In an effort to assist the nearly four million Americans who have been unemployed 27 weeks or more, the companies have pledged four things: 1) to ensure that advertising doesn't discriminate against the unemployed, 2) to review recruiting procedures, 3) to encourage all qualified candidates to apply, and 4) to share information about hiring the long-term unemployed within their companies.

The Minnesota Dislocated Worker Program

In the 2012 annual report for the Minnesota Dislocated Worker (DW) Program, the program's director, Anthony Alongi, writes that the program, through its Workforce Development Fund, allows the state the flexibility to integrate TAA services for trade-affected workers or participate in federal pilot projects (Minnesota DEED 2012). Services provided by the state's DW program include career planning and counseling, job search and placement services, job training, and financial support services that cover transportation costs, family care costs, health care costs, or other emergency aids to help displaced workers reach their employment goals.

According to this annual report (p. 5), "Minnesota is unusual in having its own, state-funded DW program. Most states only have a federally funded DW program, as established by the Workforce Investment Act (WIA) of 1998. Minnesota's two DW programs work side by side and are virtually indistinguishable in the eyes of the customer. Our state DW program allows services to many more job seekers than what the federally funded DW program can provide alone." The report says 19,741 people were helped in 2012—13,568 in the state DW program, another 7,868 in the WIA DW program, and 2,256 in other programs.[3] Total expenses were nearly $32 million.

Whenever appropriate, the Minnesota DW program utilizes TAA if jobs have been lost because of foreign trade; it also relies on National Emergency Grants (NEGs), which temporarily expand service capacity when there is an economic event that causes significant job loss. All TAA-eligible customers are coenrolled in the Minnesota DW program. Table 5.2 compares TAA data for Maine and Minnesota.

Not everyone thought sufficient assistance was provided, as shown in the following unsolicited letter, which one of this book's authors received in May 2014:

Ken:

It has been a long 2 years since the paper mill in Sartell shut down. What I have found out in these 2 years is that there really is nobody out there that will help people like me or others in my situation [displaced workers]. My mortgage company, the State of Minnesota, the surrounding counties, city of Sartell, or even Verso Paper. Everything that was written in the paper, or shown on tv, or on the radio, was really all bullshit, because nobody did anything to really help us. They did no more than they had to. The severance checks from Verso were taxed at around 48%, where in a case like this they could have taxed it a lot less and the State could have given us some tax breaks. They could have been a little more lenient on the unemployment payouts; as this was no fault of any worker at this mill.

I am in the process of filing for bankruptcy, but finding out that this is not an easy process either. I am trying to save my house as I built it myself. I will probably have to get a 2nd job to save my house and pay for the bankruptcy fees.

I have found out that if I go look for help, you will get calls and emails from a lot of people that want to scam you. I have had this happen to me twice. One was for my house payment; they told me they could save me $400–$500 a month, but it was a scam as I called Washington, D.C. and they confirmed this. My mortgage company said they could put me into a HAMP program, but 2 ½ months later they said after 6 months I would owe them a balloon payment to make up what I was saving on my monthly payment. So who do you really trust anymore? Nobody. I have really lost my trust in the American population.

But on the bright side I finally landed a good job on March 5, 2014 at Dezuriks [sic], across the river from Verso Paper. Everything is going good there, and I was able to join the union a short time ago. In around 3 years I will be making about the same as I did at Verso, wage-wise. I believe the benefits are better at Dezuriks. I do know that the working conditions are better! I know that the next 3 years are going to be real tough on me; just to get my finances straightened out.

I would be interested in the book that you are planning to have out this fall or winter. Let me know about it. Thanks for everything.

Max

Table 5.2 Trade Adjustment Assistance: 2010 State Profiles for Maine and Minnesota

	Maine	Minnesota
Number of TAA petitions certified	26	52
Estimated workers covered by new certifications	1,546	4,057
Federal funding allocated to state to provide benefits and services	$7,099,605	$12,275,723
Top TAA certifications	Approx. 150 WestPoint Home Inc. workers	400 U.S. Steel Corp. workers
	150 Formed Fiber Technologies workers	Approx. 300 Coloplast Mfg. workers
	130 Bumble Bee Foods workers	200 Farley's and Sathers Candy Co. workers
	Approx. 100 Fraser Papers workers	
Number of workers covered by 2009 expanded TAA program (statutory expansions have since expired)	914	4,325

SOURCE: Authors' formulation from state profiles.

National Emergency Grants

National Emergency Grants provide temporary funding to state and local workforce investment boards in response to large, unexpected economic events that cause significant job loss. The Oklahoma Employment Security Commission (2008) says such events typically involve company layoffs of 50 or more workers.

Minnesota has benefited from NEGs, having received four in 2011, one in 2012, and four in 2013. Elsewhere, the Center for Paper Business and Industry Studies reports that the U.S. Department of Labor provided a $1.8 million NEG to assist in training and case management services for those displaced from International Paper's Courtland, Alabama, mill (McCarthy 2014).

SUMMARY

The pulp and paper industry has continued to cut employment, often in large numbers, because of mill closures or reductions in the number of operating paper machines. The WARN Act has been an important asset to job losers, as it requires most large employers to provide either 60 days' notice prior to displacement or 60 days' pay. WARN also notifies state Dislocated Worker programs of large downsizings and sets in motion the creation of assistance options available to those confronted with job loss.

Although labor underutilization has declined since the recession, current figures do not indicate a full recovery. WIA attempts to involve both business and community leaders in programmatic planning by knitting together numerous programs related to employment, training, adult education, and vocational rehabilitation. The U.S. Department of Labor awards discretionary National Emergency Grants in response to significant dislocation events. Minnesota also has a state-supported WIA program and thus has additional monies with which to assist displaced workers.

Notes

1. Eder (2008) notes that some companies lay off large numbers of workers but fail to provide the required notice. In 2007, then-U.S. senators Sherrod Brown, Hillary Clinton, and Barack Obama introduced legislation to overhaul the law after the *Toledo Blade*'s 2007 series on WARN.
2. Information provided by Kathy Zavala in an e-mail message, dated July 3, 2014. MRC operates out of 34 sites in the Twin Cities metro area plus St. Cloud, seeking to help people achieve greater personal, social, and economic success. MRC assists laid-off workers and other segments of the population who are facing struggles.
3. The numbers of the separate programs sum to more than the total because some people enrolled in more than one program.

6
When Women Are Job Losers

"Brenda moved from Packing to the all-male Mixing department, but after meeting with what she describes as severe resistance from coworkers, she went back. 'They didn't even give me a chance,' she says. When Sue became the first woman in Processing, she says her partner forced her to work unreasonably quickly. 'He just wanted to see if I would break,' Sue told me."
—Judith A. Levine (2009, p. 270), relating how female food processing employees characterize the sex segregation in male-dominant work sites

WOMEN ON THE WORK FLOOR

Like most heavy manufacturing industries, the pulp and paper industry predominantly employs men.

In the Bucksport and Sartell Verso mills, only 12 percent of our sample were women (27 of 224 workers), and most of those (21) were employed at Sartell in Minnesota. Some of the questions we raised about women working the production line at a paper mill included the following: Why were women employed in such small numbers and mostly at one location? What were the experiences of these women, and how were they dealing with downsizing and dislocation? What insights could be gained from their responses to our survey and interviews?

The fact that most of the women were employed at one site is in itself instructive. The employment of 21 women at Sartell was the result of efforts at diversifying the workforce some 25–30 years ago. When the company was under pressure to create a more diverse workforce, the plant manager chose to recruit women rather than other people belonging to protected classes. At that time, the African American and Native American populations in Sartell were almost nonexistent, while women were, of course, around 50 percent of the local population. Since that time, the Sartell population has expanded and diversified because of its proximity to St. Cloud, a community an hour northwest of the Twin

Cities. However, the downward trajectory of the paper industry has not led to increased hiring of either gender; overall, the Sartell workforce shrank from 700 at the time management first hired female production workers to about 450 just before the 2012 downsizing.

Breaking into Male-Dominated Work

For women to obtain work in a traditional male environment was not, and is not, easy. Women made up just under 25 percent of manufacturing workers in 1959, according to data from the Bureau of Labor Statistics. Their share crested at more than 32 percent starting in 1989 but since then has steadily tailed off, falling to 27.1 percent in April 2013. Note that women's share of manufacturing employment reached its height in the late 1980s, at a time when the Sartell mill (along with other manufacturers) was actively diversifying its workforce.

The women who had been hired at the Sartell mill fought hard to get accepted into what was, and still is to a large extent, a male environment. The Sartell women had worked through the initial difficulties and had become accepted after what was invariably a rough introduction in overcoming male reluctance to have women on the work floor.[1] In the Sartell interviews, women made it clear that there was harassment at the beginning of their employment, but that it was in the distant past and not a current issue. In addition to harassment at the work site, Ortiz and Roscigno (2009, p. 338) note that firms or workers may engage in other patterns of discriminatory practices once women are hired in segregated workplaces, such as "wage inequality, or other types of inequality related to their lower status positions." This differential treatment can include lack of promotion.[2]

The hiring pattern in Minnesota contrasted with that of the Maine plant, where in an equally homogeneous community few women found their way to the shop floor. The Bucksport mill had been under no pressure to diversify, and the women we met there were in administrative and human resource management positions, not production. This Maine pattern of employment for women is by no means unusual. Women in manufacturing and construction find that administrative and clerical positions are available, where their presence is more accepted and the work is less physically demanding. Clerical and administrative positions have traditionally been "women's work."

Why would women seek out jobs in challenging circumstances where they are not initially welcome? What might encourage women to pursue employment in traditionally male jobs? Simply, men's jobs pay more. In times of economic hardship, the need to maintain family income is critical. Economic need—linked to the number of mouths one is responsible for feeding—causes women to seek these jobs. Reskin's (1993) study of sex segregation in the workplace highlights these economic factors.[3] The probability of women working in nontraditional occupations increases with the number of children they have, according to Beller (1982).[4] Rosenfeld (1983) finds that being married does not affect the "sex-typicality" of women's job moves. Single women were slower than women with young children to leave "female work" for traditionally male jobs (Rosenfeld and Spenner 1992). And even when children are grown, the economic burden may not decrease: one woman in our sample mentioned helping grown children through college. Then, too, there is the financial burden of aging parents. In the past, a woman's income was traditionally thought of as a way to deal with these additional expenses.

Challenges Go beyond Male Bias for Women

Male hostility may not be the only challenge for women looking for work in heavy manufacturing. The preference for putting women into administrative slots rather than on the work floor, as we found in Maine, may also be a result of the fact that women are more at risk for injury in physically demanding work. Oyebode et al. (2009) sought to determine if female workers in a heavy manufacturing environment have a higher risk of injury than males when performing the same job. Evaluating sex differences in type and severity of injury, they used human resources and incident surveillance data for the hourly population at six U.S. aluminum smelters. They find that female workers working in aluminum smelters have a greater risk for sustaining all forms of injury after adjusting for age, tenure, and standardized job category. This excess risk for female workers persists when injuries are dichotomized into acute injuries and musculoskeletal disorder–related injuries.

The Oyebode et al. (2009) study provides evidence of disparity in occupational injury, with female workers at higher risk than their male counterparts in a heavy manufacturing environment. It is not hard to extrapolate from the smelting industry to the manufacture of pulp and paper. Pulp, paper, and paperboard mills in the United States produce 9 million tons of pulp annually and 26 billion newspapers, books, and magazines. According to OSHA, pulp and paper manufacturing can also be hazardous because of massive weights and pulpwood loads that may fall, roll, or slide. Workers may be struck or crushed by loads or suffer lacerations from the misuse of equipment, particularly when machines are used without proper safeguards.[5]

Some Women Accept the Challenge

However, some women were willing to take on the risks involved in production work in male-dominated paper mills. Kara, 58 years old, worked at the Sartell plant. She describes working in 120-degree heat with caustic foam present. (In this heat, men often wrap towels around their heads to absorb the sweat.) Kara agreed that work on the shop floor was hard but said that it was a good job and that she and other women enjoyed it. Female respondents at the Sartell mill expressed pride in their work. However, after spending time at the Bucksport mill, it is easy to understand why few women wanted to work in a physically demanding and sometimes dangerous situation.

Technology is a two-edged sword and is changing the workplace for both the better and the worse. Although in some instances paper mill work has become less dangerous through the introduction of technology, technology in Maine is used extensively to monitor the production of paper and energy at the site. However, technology has not seemed to reduce much of the danger inherent in the production process: We were aware of at least two major explosions at paper mills during the period we were collecting data. When we visited Maine, the union was collecting money for another Maine mill that had just experienced a temporary shutdown when a compressor exploded. Recall that it was also an exploding compressor that led to the death of a worker at Sartell and the closure of the mill when one side of the building was completely blown out. Hard physical labor remained in many areas where workers shoveled wood-chip waste into the furnace to produce energy and wrestled with huge rolls of paper to maneuver them through the plant.

The Role of Technology

In some aspects, technology has changed the nature of work in manufacturing by opening up new jobs that may be more acceptable to women. Some older men at the Maine plant expressed frustration at having to learn new skills to manage the system. Could women be hired to do this work? This is unlikely, since technology has also reduced the need for workers. Women generally have worked in manufacturing for a far shorter time than men; this lack of seniority has acted to reduce their employment as downsizing occurred, since the operative principle in most union shops is "Last hired/first fired."

National manufacturing employment figures show that overall, the manufacturing sector added 530,000 jobs from February 2010 through March 2013, with men gaining 558,000 jobs while women lost 28,000 positions (BLS 2013). The wood products industry lost ground in the total number of women hired, while the number of men hired shows a small percentage gain. Fabricated metal products hired over 120,000 men and fewer than 10,000 women. Blue-collar women in declining industries are consequently more vulnerable to layoff. In addition, as Smith (1991) points out, women tend to suffer permanent job loss, particularly in rural areas. In Canada women lost a disproportionate share of manufacturing jobs over the five years from 2002 through 2006: employment of women declined by 9 percent, whereas that of men declined by 7 percent (JEC 2013). Thus, women, who make up nearly one-third of employees in the manufacturing sector, have largely been excluded from the current job expansion (*Reliable Plant* 2007).

DOWNSIZING AND STRESS

As described above, women have been making some inroads into nontraditional occupations, although the shrinkage of the manufacturing industry has threatened these job gains. The women in our sample felt the loss of a good-paying job—particularly single women with children. Involuntary loss of a job you depend on to support the family is a huge stressor. However, continuing to work at the plant had its drawbacks, too: future uncertainty took its toll on those that remained. When we asked workers to comment on the work environment, the majority responded with answers naming tension and stress.

Uncertainty and lack of communication made the situation worse. The stress caused one woman, a 60-year-old machine operator, to quit as the work atmosphere and general conditions of work deteriorated. She put it this way: "Working at the mill for 27 years was a good providing job for me, especially as a single mother with 3 children. I would have liked 2 more years until retirement but . . . it almost seemed like I would have some serious health problems if I did [continue]."

Staying at the mill was hard, but so was undergoing the stress caused by economic hardship. Research indicates that the experience of the woman quoted above is not atypical (Rayman 1987). Some research finds that stress caused by financial worries is similar in women and men, but according to Grayson (1985) and Parks (2009), the stress lasts longer for women. Rayman, in summarizing the literature on the health impacts of job loss for men, finds that men are susceptible to increased drinking and to respiratory and stomach ailments, while women are more likely to experience depression, eating disorders (with weight gain or loss), and erosion of self-esteem.

Retire or Find a New Job?

Numerous factors influence older women's job choices. Do older women leave the job for retirement, or to seek another occupation? The downsizing at the Bucksport mill gave women the option of taking a severance package, but since their job tenure was less than that of the men, their financial benefit was less. Staying on in the Bucksport mill presented its own problems as the workforce was reduced and management changed: Not only was there stress and tension around the question of whether the factory would survive—a tag sheet on the conference room wall read "Survival Strategies"—the downsizing also led to changes in working conditions. The remaining workers had to take on more responsibility. Rotating shifts were introduced, which wreak havoc with child care and elder care needs, especially when a worker has no spouse. Both in our research and in other studies (Padavic 1991), when women were asked to go back on the night shift, they found their stress increased, and they often quit. Older women may not have had the issue of child care, but they faced other issues related to work environment. The deterioration of working conditions led to mental and physical strain. One of the most common responses when we asked about the quality of life after leaving the mill was, "Now I get to sleep at night." Not that retirement is all roses—paying for health care and stress over finances stood out as the major concerns for the female workers that took part in our research.

While women in our sample were generally older, Rayman (1987, p. 372) notes that women report facing age discrimination during their job hunt at a younger age than men—"as early as in their late thirties, women experienced sex and age discrimination."

Dealing with Physical and Mental Health Care Costs

Hard work at the mill left many of the workers in their fifties and sixties, both men and women, with accumulating health problems. The average age of the workers was 54 years. Not only were women dealing with their own health issues, but many married women were also dealing with ailing spouses and elderly parents. The worry and stress of poor health and lack of insurance pervaded the responses of both women and men. Loss of a job meant losing health care and being unable to pay over $1,000 per month for COBRA or extended health care benefits offered to the unemployed. One 57-year-old woman expressed the enforced leisure this way: "Having 24 hours a day to live and decide how to live— thinking about being 57 years old, no job, no good prospects or what to do about it. Paying COBRA cost and what about after COBRA?" Since we conducted these interviews, the Affordable Care Act has been passed. Whether or not this act has ameliorated the situation for these mill workers who have now become long-term unemployed remains to be seen. Most of these workers were not yet able to qualify for Medicare. In his article on the closure of a factory and its impact on health, Grayson (1985) notes that the level of stress felt by wives is not that different from that of their husbands and remains more or less constant over a longer period of time. Women in this older group are keepers of the household budget. Making do with what they had was a major challenge. Most were coping by drastically reducing the family budget and doing more with less. Questions forced their way to the surface: What could be given up? What could they still afford? Wrestling with these issues, by themselves, was a major source of stress.

For Married Women, the Stress Is Compounded

To add to their own stress, some of the women found themselves having to deal with the emotional toll of a dispirited or sick spouse. One 42-year-old Sartell worker whose marital life was suffering wrote this: "I'm feeling like [I'm] not contributing to something that mattered—very sad—I am not able to provide financially to my college child as I did before. I am not happy and satisfied with life like it was [before], so its hard for me to be social. There is a hardship now between my husband and self because I don't have a paycheck and benefits."

A woman's social life can also be threatened by the physical or mental health issues of a spouse. A 65-year-old woman from Sartell noted, "My husband has multiple sensitivities, so it makes us hermits—we stay home to keep the peace on the home front." Women have frequently relied on a network of female friends to help them through hard times, and it is easy in this comment to sense the isolation from friends and family who could provide crucial social support for the woman who keeps the peace by staying home.

Older married couples face the stress of terminal illness (perhaps caused by the work at the mill), exacerbated by uninsured health-care costs. For widows, the situation is dire. One 60-year-old widow whose husband worked at the Sartell mill wrote, "Jim passed away Feb 28th from lung cancer. I think it was asbestos that he worked with on a regular basis. He was a pipe fitter the whole time he worked at the mill."

Women Are the Traditional Caregivers

Adding to the burden of many women is the care of elderly parents. The phenomenon of this "sandwich generation" has been well documented by the Pew Research Center in its Social and Demographic Trends project (Parker and Patten 2013). By age 55, the bodies of workers involved in physical labor are showing signs of wear. This is especially true in construction and in the mills. Particularly the male workers we interviewed, many with a work life of more than 20 or 30 years at the mill, had led hard lives, and it showed in their faces and in their gaits. Although some women had not worked as long as many men, they had also led physically demanding lives. Just when they had to confront health issues in their own lives, their parents were reaching their eighties and becoming increasingly frail.

Responsibility for elder care, spousal care, and child care has traditionally fallen on women. Support networks and assisted living may be less available in small towns for assisting families with elderly parents. They face issues both with availability and, in hard times, with the cost of care, which is typically very high. The nursing home industry itself is feeling financial pressure, and for-profit nursing facilities often stretch employees to the limit. One displaced female mill worker, Kay, described the job she found in a local care facility for the elderly as being too strenuous, and she quit. It is conceivable that this type of care is neither desirable nor affordable in the eyes of the local community. The lack of availability of care, combined with the high cost of elder care, makes it inevitable that family members take care of elders if they can. All in all, the effects of job loss compounded with health issues affect not only the displaced women themselves but also their college-age children and aging parents, just at a time when they themselves are more vulnerable physically, emotionally, and financially.

Rayman (1987) notes that when unemployed women are asked about the traits of their ideal new job, their response of "good pay" is exactly the response of unemployed men. "But the other two principal responses from the women," she writes, "are rarely, if ever, cited by men: supportive coworkers and a flexible schedule" (p. 375).

Finding Work in a Rural Community

For displaced workers to find reemployment when jobs are scarce is hard on both men and women.

Oftentimes, available work is lower paid, which may be why it is available. Krueger, Cramer, and Cho (2014) show that the older long-term unemployed find it increasingly hard to find work the longer they remain without a job. There is also the reality that even when they obtain work, a replacement job may pay less. Women often take what they can get, but the circumstances can be humiliating. For example, at age 57, Kay believed she had obtained the job in the nursing home because the manager "felt sorry for her." Not only was the pay less, but the schedule was demanding and the work physically hard, and she couldn't continue. Her age and the obvious wear and tear on her body made it easy to understand her plight. She was desperate and had taken to selling vitamins on the Internet in an attempt to earn some money.

This type of desperation is easily taken advantage of—not only by peddlers of dubious selling-from-home schemes but also by all sorts of "financial advisers" who descended on the laid-off workers, attracted by a notion that workers would receive a severance package, were anxious about their financial future, and had little knowledge or sophistication when it came to financial management of investments. The Minnesota Dislocated Worker Program did provide counseling and workshops on financial management, but several of the displaced women were not attuned to programs like this and were skeptical of government-funded programs. Although the women were keepers of the family budget, their financial literacy—especially among older women—was a major deficiency (Lusardi 2012). Female respondents typically viewed large financial decisions as the perogative of the men.

Finding Work in a Stratified Workplace

There remain gender-stratified workplaces, and finding suitable work is hard on a generation of women who grew up in a more traditional time, when women could work but did not expect to be thrust into the position of becoming breadwinners. At Kay's age, women don't see a long work life in front of them that would justify the expense and the physical and intellectual challenge of a year or more of training for what younger women embrace as a career or life's work. Our female respondents may be unwilling to break out of gender roles they grew up with; in general, participating in job training or postsecondary education is threatening for someone of their age and status. Many of them are fearful of going into an academic environment after decades of absence. Thus, many women, like many men that Root and Park (2009) interviewed in their study of dislocated defense workers, were glad to get out of high school and into a job at a mill or factory, where there was often a family tradition of going into this work.

Workers in Sartell and Bucksport talked about grandparents and parents working at the mill. Academia had never been a comfortable place for them, and they recalled their high school English teachers with less than favorable memories. They settled into a place where work paid for a reasonable middle-class life that provided the necessities. Women filled a role that often included part-time employment, with family responsibilities having precedence. One women mentioned that the loss of her job at least meant she could take "better care of her family." Going back to the classroom was—for either gender—not something that the majority of our respondents relished. Only 8 percent of the Maine sample and 14 percent of the Sartell group opted to take part in the retraining programs offered by the state-sponsored Dislocated Worker Program.

Sliding into Retirement

Displaced women in our study were faced with the same dilemma as men; their options were to find a new job to tide them over (perhaps even part-time), risk retraining, or slide into retirement. Somehow getting by until they qualified for retirement (not looking for work) was preferred by 40 percent of the men in the Bucksport sample. In Sartell, by contrast, 34 percent were unemployed and looking for work.

Retirement has its own difficulties. Adjusting to retirement was hard for the men, but it meant additional problems for women. For displaced women, suddenly having a man underfoot around the house every day inevitably leads to changes in relationships. Women lose independence and the paycheck that work provides. (We earlier mentioned the husband who resented his wife's loss of income.) They must adjust not only to their own lack of work but also to the disruptions in their husbands' traditional role, which may cause unhappiness (documented in Chapter 7, on the effect of unemployment for married couples). Marriages do not always survive hardship and separations. Some men moved to accept new jobs in distant mills, some accepted jobs as long-distance truck drivers. One man, 52 years old, wrote, "My wife left me for greener pastures." One way or another, the turmoil caused by job loss affects all aspects of family life. However, some displaced workers found a silver lining in their situation.

Release from Work Is Not All Bad

Some women (and men) found that dislocation from a worksite that is frequently being downsized was not something they missed. Rotating and uncertain shift schedules particularly were a source of distress. After all, work at a mill is hard, punishing work in difficult conditions. Some women felt that they had even benefited and their mental health had improved since displacement. One 64-year-old female shift worker wrote, "I was one of the lucky ones close to retirement—now I eat regular and sleep." Twenty-three percent of women and men found that their mental health had indeed improved since job loss. As work continues to evolve in the United States, women find increased financial pressure to work. But what jobs are available, and what training and other supports do they need in order to succeed?

OLDER WOMEN AND THE FUTURE OF WORK

How do women see their future? The number of women in our sample is small, and it is impossible to extrapolate from the experiences of these women to women in heavy manufacturing generally. However, several questions do arise: Do women, as much as men, see their identity framed by the work they do? As families change and more women work, do young women identify as "wife and mother" as much as women in past generations have? The women still employed at the Maine mill had made sacrifices to keep their jobs. At least two had relocated from Minnesota—one to join a spouse who had relocated to Maine. Both were in management positions. As more women work, is work becoming a larger part of women's identities? Notwithstanding these considerations, in line with Maslow's hierarchy of needs, more immediate concerns dominated these women's lives. Worries about finances and health were clearly uppermost in the women's minds.

The Joint Economic Committee of the U.S. Congress is seeking to address the issue of the shortage of women in manufacturing. It has a set of recommendations that include getting more girls in school interested in STEM programs. Through vocational and community college programs, the committee wants to prepare women with the skills and knowledge that employers in manufacturing want. The committee also wants employers to develop mentoring programs for women in all areas of manufacturing (JEC 2013). This approach takes the long view and certainly does not address the needs of older women in a threatened industry such as pulp and paper. For older women, their needs are immediate—primarily health care and day-to-day living. Women in our sample were vulnerable to the financial investment hucksters and Internet selling schemes mentioned earlier. What makes sense in this situation? Counseling and support from governmental and nongovernmental agencies were available. To what extent did these help? Were women more willing than men to take advantage of them? Were services for mental health and depression available, and to what extent did women take advantage of them? There is a strong faith-based community in the St. Cloud area. One woman mentioned that her church had invited Dave Ramsey, a faith-oriented financial adviser, to help her congregation.

Tracking the Unemployment Figures for Older Women

Warr (1987) maintains that women form the bulk of the "hidden unemployed"—i.e., those who want employment but are not counted in the official unemployment figures. For women, the relationship between employment status and psychological well-being is often less clear than for men, because many other variables, such as the quality of occupational and nonoccupational involvement, marital status, and childbearing status, all mediate this relationship. Indeed, Warr argues that the employment/unemployment distinction is less appropriate for women than for men. Women without partners who are also mothers are likely to experience the conflicting roles of breadwinner and nurturer and may display an ambivalent attitude toward employment. According to Frey (1986), most single parents also report the issue of child care as a major barrier to workforce reentry. Thus, the findings on the psychological effects of employment and unemployment based on the usual samples of school leavers and male redundant workers may not fit well with our sample of female single parents.

Finding Solutions That Work

Harry and Tiggemann (1992) find that certain interventions for displaced workers can improve the mental health of women. Participation in a three-week job reentry preparation program in Canada decreased depression compared to the control group, and increased self-esteem. The psychological effects of the course on reentry to the workforce were clearly beneficial for the participants. As predicted, the participants displayed greater confidence and firmer expectations of paid employment upon completion of the course, as well as a significant increase in psychological well-being on all four measures: 1) displaying less depressive affect, 2) higher self-esteem (shared by the control group), 3) less negative mood, and 4) less minor psychiatric disorder. The Harry and Tiggeman study did not include whether these women were indeed successful in becoming employed.

Recommendations

How can we increase women's participation in an occupation that traditionally has been thought of as dirty, dangerous, and dead-end? Certainly there are changes in several areas that could make work in the mills better—not inconsequentially, for both women and men.

Changes in the perception of manufacturing as dirty and dangerous have to be backed up by making the work floors less so. Industry groups need to address this negative image as they recruit and hire in the future. In the past, the danger and physical challenge of the work only increased the belief, certainly held amongst the workers we met, that this was "men's work." Explosions in paper mills still happen, as was apparent in our visits to the Bucksport mill. The industry needs to ensure worker safety, and OSHA regulations should be enforced, with the welfare of a female workforce as a primary goal. The success of the women in Minnesota in breaking into a male-dominated industry shows that women can and will take on this work when given the opportunity. In the future, more work needs to be done by high school counselors, and in federally and state-funded job counseling and training programs, to make women aware that there is a future, if not in paper mills then in manufacturing generally. Technology is making jobs less physically demanding, less dangerous, and more technically challenging. Jobs require less brawn and more brain, and women can supply both.

Changes in industrial technology mean that women can operate heavy machinery as well as men. Women pilot commercial and military aircraft and can certainly operate cranes and the huge production-line machinery common now in many mills and factories. The men who survived the layoffs in the mills did so because they had advanced technical skills that enabled them to operate state-of-the-art machines. Human resource managers have a role to play in encouraging women to take on a career trajectory to prepare for these niche jobs. The key to survival seems to be continuous and high-level retraining as an integrated part of the job, not as a voluntary add-on during the worker's own time. Voluntary retraining, even when paid, was not popular with the great majority of our laid-off workers—women or men.

Should women seek jobs in what appears to be a declining industry? The heavy industries that survive must adapt. These changes, prompted by technology, give women a window to higher-paying, family-supporting jobs. Those women who are willing should be given the opportunity, even if somewhat grudgingly, as in Minnesota. There is a long history of women fighting discrimination in the workforce. Legal avenues have opened up such male-dominated professions as firefighting and the military to women. The Department of Labor, state workforce and dislocated worker programs, employers and the unions all have a role in opening up these last bastions to women by enforcing current discrimination law.

SUMMARY

Parks (2009) points out that although the media image of the unemployed factory worker is usually male, the impact of job loss is often worse for women, because many women are single parents. Being a single parent is the strongest predictor of women seeking employment in nontraditional jobs.

We gained information on the women in our study through interviews, mailed questionnaires, and site visits. Our samples, while small, provide quantitative, qualitative, and anecdotal data. A more systematic qualitative approach should be taken to comprehend the lived experiences of displaced women. Their concerns over finances, health care, and the stresses and strains of job loss were real, palpable, and near universal. Too young to retire and too old to be hired should not be the life story of these displaced women.

Notes

1. Minchin (2006) describes the same pattern of male reluctance to accept women as equals or allow women to work on the paper machine at the International Paper Company mill in Mobile, Alabama.
2. Roth's (2002) research supports the Ortiz and Roscigno (2009) statement.
3. Reskin (1993) is perhaps the most comprehensive and frequently cited review of sex segregation. However, that study does predate the Great Recession and perhaps does not reflect the changing views of the current generation of women. A study on women in manufacturing done by the Joint Economic Committee Democratic Staff (2013) is both more comprehensive and more current, but it does not provide the depth and research analysis that Reskin does.
4. Cited in Reskin (1993, p. 255).
5. United Steelworkers union newsletter, 2013.

7
When Couples Lose Their Jobs

"We can laugh and joke, just to keep our strength up, because all of us are feeling it inside. My wife is out of work too, because of all of this change—free trade stuff. She used to work downtown at a clothing place and they closed up. They moved all their equipment. But what they do is get another factory, make all the things there and ship it. That's cheaper. They lay off all the folks. Both of us are out of work."
—A laid-off worker quoted in Sobel and Meurer (1994, p. 86)

Job loss for one adult family member can be problematic, particularly if new work isn't quickly available, but the potential for stress when both adult members of a family unit are displaced has the potential of creating additional havoc, personal stress, and marital strain. While the Sobel and Meurer quotation above is not from a displaced paper worker, nor were the couple employed at the same work site, the anxiety of the speaker is evident.[1]

While there were six married couples that were working at the Sartell mill prior to the downsizing, there were no employed couples among the Bucksport workers. Four of these Sartell couples were in production, and two were in management. In late October 2013, we mailed all six couples a letter inviting them to be interviewed and offered them compensation for their time (see Appendix D). Four couples agreed to an interview, for which they were paid. Those interviewed included three production couples and one couple in management.

Of the four couples interviewed, three individuals were downsized, and the rest lost their jobs when their mill was shut down. Like the majority of the mill workers, these individuals were older and had worked at the mill for many years. All of the interviewed couples had started working at the mill under St. Regis ownership. St. Regis purchased the mill in 1946 and merged with Champion International in 1984; the mill was later sold to International Paper, and the coated paper segment was spun off to Verso in 2006. Thus, all displaced couples had worked through three ownership changes at the Sartell mill.

As job loss researchers, our interest in creating this chapter was stimulated when we read the returned questionnaires and noted that for each of the four couples we interviewed, a spouse had commented on the job loss of both partners, as in the "Both of us are out of work" quote from Sobel and Meurer (1994). While their comments were brief, displaced Sartell mill couples told us that their family was doubly affected by the downsizing or closure at Verso Sartell. As one said, "The biggest downfall was when my husband also lost his job at Verso."

INTERVIEWS WITH THE DISPLACED COUPLES

All interviews were conducted in the homes of the displaced couples. While three of the eight individuals interviewed had been divorced, the others were married for the first time. All four couples had been together for several years and had either created blended families by bringing children into their marriage or had children during the marriage who were now adults. They were now grandparents and, for those with extended family living close, were involved in child-care duties with grandchildren. At the same time, some of these displaced couples were part of "the sandwich generation"—those trying to help adult children and simultaneously assist older parents.

None of the couples interviewed lived in Sartell—they all had an acreage out of town or lived on a farm or a lake. All homes were ample, substantially built, well-furnished, and up-to-date. All respondent homes were within a reasonable commute of several miles to Sartell and the paper mill. Conflicting work schedules necessitated that each individual drive to Verso independently of his or her partner.

The interviews with the couples usually required about one-and-a-half hours to complete. The structured interview had 11 segments, including 1) background, 2) courtship/marriage, 3) work schedule/environment, 4) response to downsizing/closure announcement, 5) other family members, 6) job loss pressures, 7) strains as a result of lack of income, 8) adjustments, 9) patterns used to resolve issues/problems, 10) remaining difficulties, and 11) "advice for others in the same situation, where both adults are experiencing job loss at the same time."

The average length of work history among the interviewed couples was 33 years, with a range of 29–37 years. They were older, with an average age of 58 and a range of 55–61. None of the eight individuals we interviewed were yet receiving Social Security. Total family annual incomes were each $100,000 or more while they were both employed at Verso. Some of the annual wages came from overtime, at one-and-a-half times the hourly wage. For those individuals who worked in maintenance, overtime was an obligation if a particular project wasn't completed during their shift. Not all Verso workers wanted to work over-time—including one or two of these married couples—but researchers did hear stories of a few others who wanted as much overtime as possible, and those individuals had a reputation for "living at the mill."

The married couples that were interviewed possessed a range of skills, including different maintenance skills (electrician, welder, mill-wright) as well as instrument technician, department manager, training specialist, and day utility worker.

The Significance of Social Support in Times of Crisis

While many families have support structures that enable them to adjust to difficult times, including networks of friends, neighbors, extended family, and social groups, as well as a history within the family of providing assistance to one another, there are times when other resources are called for. While families may receive an outpouring of support during a loved one's death and funeral, losing a job is usually a more solitary experience. The dislocated individual and family are left to their own devices. The Holmes and Rahe Stress Scale ranks dismissal from work as the eighth most stressful out of 43 life events,[2] and it may be that the stress of job loss is so great largely because a social mechanism to assist in job-loss situations hasn't been created.

For those who are job losers in a major downsizing or closure, Quinn (1999, p. 39) provides a community model for maximizing the adjustment to job loss. Quinn describes the support structure for a single-industry Canadian mining community where companies and the unions "worked closely with community organizations in Elliot Lake and developed their own adjustment services so that there were supports available" during downsizings. Financial planners, job-search experts, healthy lifestyle advisers, and personal counselors helped employees normalize the feelings and effects of the downsizing and identify their strengths and challenges.

Wilkinson and Robinson (1999) also favor local adjustment committees as being most helpful in providing assistance to displaced workers in the job search tasks, serving as an important source of information, and simply being available for support. Shultz and Weber (1964,1966) and Stern (1969) have documented the value of local adjustment committees, particularly from a period when several meatpacking plants were closing and the companies were heavily involved in assisting their employees who were terminated in the shutdown.

Factors Influencing Displaced Worker Adjustment

Neitzert, Mawhiney, and Porter (1999) list some of the causal factors influencing displaced worker adjustment, including duration of unemployment, occupational switching, migration, and bouts of unemployment between spells of employment. Finding a new job and having a stable income constitute a successful adjustment to displacement.

Neitzert, Mawhiney, and Porter (1999, p. 62) found that out of 4,500 workers, only 38 women were employed by the two mining companies in Elliot Lake at the time of the layoff announcements. These 38 women were primarily in clerical positions (55 percent), production (13 percent), health (10 percent), administration (8 percent), and service (5 percent). The authors note that "few women have been employed as mining production workers," which is likely true for other production fields as well, such as the paper industry. For instance, 25 women were terminated from the Sartell mill at the time of the downsizing, which displaced 180 workers, and at the closure, 31 of the 229 displaced were women. Thus, for both the downsizing and the closure, women made up about 14 percent of the affected workforce.[3]

For women and their families in the downsizing and closures of Elliot Lake's last two mines, job loss carried significant impacts: "Household income per adult equivalent dropped to the lowest in the period, equity indicators deteriorated seriously among displaced families, health levels declined, divorce rates increased, and empowerment as measured by participation in community organizations declined" (Neitzert, Mawhiney, and Porter 1999, p. 64). Displaced worker families in Elliot Lake lost wealth (as measured by value of the home), converted other assets, or increased indebtedness during that difficult time.

Neitzert, Mawhiney, and Porter (1999) find that displaced families in Elliot Lake were immediately affected by reduced income and unemployment, and then "soon after" by diminishing relationship quality and higher divorce rates. The process suggests that good communication, mutual support, and a continuing effort to maintain the functioning of the family as a cohesive unit are important steps in maintaining family equilibrium and cohesion in times of job loss.

Part of an appropriate response to job loss is the alignment of current expenditures with present income. Neitzert, Mawhiney, and Porter (1999) maintain that the displaced family unit must create and implement a new provisioning strategy. Finding new employment is but one solution; early migration—or relocation—to another community for work, or having a partner who had not been in the labor force step into new employment, are other options. Some displaced worker-family units may be able to continue their search for new employment for an extended period of time, and in some family units that had dissolved under the strain, the remaining partner might locate a new income-earning partner.

While Neitzert, Mawhiney, and Porter (1999) acknowledge that locating new employment, or having the realistic option for retirement, are important in determining a successful adjustment to job loss, they stress that family characteristics may be equally important—especially for female workers: "In particular," they write, "marital status and age and presence of children are significant factors in determining the ability of families to cope with layoffs" (p. 70). Boushey (2011) affirms that since the 1970s there has been a significant increase in dual-earner married couples, particularly for mothers. Marital status, age, and presence of children are not only likely to influence the choice of adjustment strategy, they also affect the allocation of adjustment costs.

PREVIOUS STUDIES OF DUAL-FAMILY EARNERS

In research on Australian families, Miller (1997, p. 5) maintains that the burden of unemployment on family units is intense: "Almost 25 percent of total unemployment among couple families in 1994," he says, "was to families where both husband and wife were unemployed."

Displaced dual-earner families are expected to have more acute hard-ship and are particularly significant in Australia, where in the 20 years between 1974 and 1994, the figure had increased threefold. Corre-spondingly, unemployment is more concentrated in family units—in part because of women in the labor force, a greater likelihood of short-term unemployment, and increased movement of professionals from one occupation to another.

Boushey (2011) reports that married couples with both spouses in the labor force reached a high of 67 percent in the late 1990s, only to have that increase wiped away with two recessions—the first in the early 2000s and the second in 2007–2009. Figure 7.1 provides a histori-cal perspective of dual-earner family units.

Shaw (1986, pp. 368–369) makes the point that unemployment results in financial hardship in only a minority of cases, in part because of an increase in dual-earner families, increases in support from unem-ployment insurance, and finally, because of the growth of public wel-fare systems. While it is true that multiple earners cushion the family when one family member becomes unemployed, there is also the pos-sibility that other family members (who have not been employed) join the labor force to assist the family.

Belz (2014a, p. A12) describes one case: "Bob McLean, now 65, was 60 when he lost his job in January 2009. It wasn't a huge surprise—he was among the oldest in his department, he said. He took a year of severance, went to the state's dislocated worker program, rewrote his resume, took classes in computer-assisted design programs and started looking for jobs." Now McLean drives a school bus and earns one-third of what he earned prior to his job loss. In February 2009, Bob's wife, Liz McLean, also lost her job. Since dislocation, she has worked stints in information technology for other companies, but she now works for a company that sells books to colleges and notes, "Every job since I got laid off at that other place has been lower in pay." At age 60, Liz reports, "We don't go out, we don't travel; we're figuring out if I can even retire."

Married women who enter the labor force are examples of the "added worker effect," which reduces the vulnerability of the family when one person is unemployed. Thus, Shaw (1986, pp. 370–371) reports that those "most vulnerable to the financial consequences of unemploy-ment are likely to include both female and male heads of single-parent

Figure 7.1   Percentage of Married Couples with Both Spouses in the Labor Force

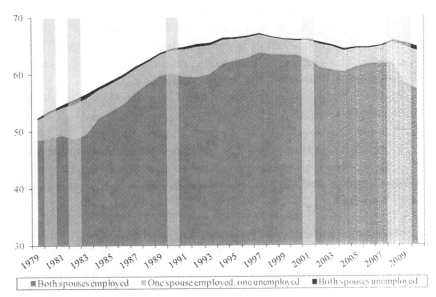

NOTE: The vertical bars represent periods of recession.
SOURCE: Boushey (2011).

families, male and female unattached individuals, and male and female family heads that are 'traditional' or principal breadwinners." Multiple income earners in a family cushion the impact of unemployment. The presence of dependent children is an important variable influencing the outcome of job loss—possibly preventing another adult from working, but also necessitating additional family costs.

Jin, Shah, and Svoboda (1997, p. 291) note that "most aggregate-level time-series analyses demonstrated increased rates of adverse health outcomes following unemployment." There is strong support for a relationship between unemployment and physical or mental illness or use of health care services. Strom (2003, p. 399) also documents the deterioration in psychological well-being, physical health, and the family economic situation once a breadwinner is displaced.

Unemployment insurance, financial hardship, and unemployment duration are all factors that help determine whether the job loss is a stressor event. Financial assets, family size and composition, and quality of family relations are elements that determine whether families grow more cohesive or crumble under the stress. Social support, effective coping strategies, and attributing unemployment to other factors are likely to reduce a family's vulnerability to stress (Strom 2003). Other considerations are socioeconomic status, the gender of the person displaced, age, family size, and family composition.

Figure 7.2 shows the impact of the Great Recession on couples with one spouse being unemployed for six months or more. Boushey (2011) notes that in 2010, on average, five people were looking for work for every job vacancy. The recession affected unemployment for older workers—particularly husbands—to a greater degree than for younger couples, and older workers likewise had a harder time finding reemployment.

The Need for Research on Displaced Married Couples

Mawhiney and Lewis (1999) recognize the impact of job loss for two adult partners as a needed area for research. Wilkinson and Robinson (1999, p. 87) summarize their experience: "Our respondents have dealt with the problems arising from the layoffs with forbearance and fortitude. Even so, experiencing a layoff is highly stressful. It causes important problems for the individuals concerned, for other members of their households, and for the community they reside in. Providing more effective help is not charity; it is good social management."

The stress of job loss from the principal wage earner's unemployment has long been a focus of research (Thomas, McCabe, and Berry 1980; Turkington 1986). Rook, Dooley, and Catalano (1991b) summarize how undesirable events such as job loss occurring to those close to the job loser might affect their health as well: distress may occur because of empathizing with the job loser, demands for support may be created on others, and the crisis experienced by someone may reduce the social support available to those close to him or her. These demands may drain the resources of family and friends.

Family researchers assert that the quality of the marital relationship is key to influencing marital stress processes (Rook, Dooley, and Catalano 1991a). When both adults in a given family experience simultaneous job loss, the financial strain is likely to be deeply felt, but the

Figure 7.2 Married Couples with One Spouse Unemployed (% long-term unemployed, by gender)

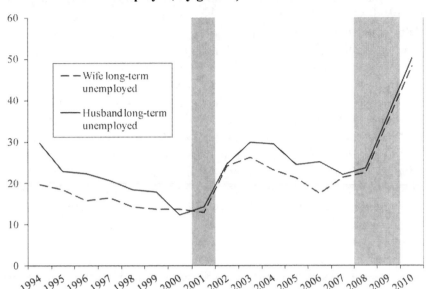

NOTE: Gray bands denote recessions.
SOURCE: Boushey (2011).

advantage is that this double pressure may facilitate increased communication, heighten the intensity of efforts to resolve the problem, and prompt both partners to commit to bringing about some positive resolution to their situation. The major difference between a single parent confronting job loss and a married couple who both lose their jobs at the same time is the strength of the dyad: shared common goals, longevity of the relationship, and the social support that is provided in a marriage are all pluses that push the commitment forward.

MARRIED COUPLE RESPONDENTS IN OUR SURVEY

Of the four married couples who consented to an interview after having been either downsized or terminated when the Sartell mill shut down, some were single when they started working at the paper mill; others were married but became divorced and married their current partner. With two good incomes in the family, they did not have significant debt. Their children were independent adults. All four couples were long-term employees of the Sartell mill, and all recalled mill ownership under St. Regis and staying on through multiple ownership changes.

Each couple commented that work conditions and safety became increasingly more problematic under each new owner. Some remarked that the most recent owners wouldn't replace parts; instead, the machines had to be repaired. The mill workers were aging, and there were few new employees. Respondents thought the pay and benefits were good, and they acknowledged that six weeks of vacation was "just plain nice." However, after the 2011 downsizing, there weren't enough personnel to cover positions during vacation periods, and some of those who had been downsized were called in to serve as temporary replacement personnel.

Table 7.1 focuses on problem-solving procedures for displaced couples. The four married couples from Sartell who had both lost their jobs all reported cutting back on expenses, driving, eating out, and attending movies, but they did not mention postponing medical or dental treatment or pawning items. And none mentioned considering a smaller residence. Two of the four women in the couple subset had enrolled in educational/training programs, while some other couple members were picking up part-time work as best they could.

Not all of the couples had the same situation at the time of the downsizing and closure. Two couples had weathered the downsizing and were terminated in the closure, while another couple had one partner who took retirement at the time of the downsizing, but the spouse became dislocated at the shutdown. Both partners in the fourth couple took retirement at the time of the downsizing. Our married couples started at the mill under different conditions as well. Although some came to the plant as married individuals, none had the same partner they now have.

Courtship in Our Sample

These four couples had been married from 14 to 31 years, with varying courtship experiences. One couple, describing their courtship,

Table 7.1 Variables in How Couples Cope with Reduced Income

Problem-focused coping		
Cutting back on expenses, personal belongings	Increasing funds	Improving one's status
Decided not to buy something that respondent or household members had planned to buy.	Borrowed money from relatives.	Sought training to improve job status.
Postponed nonemergency medical or dental treatment.	Borrowed money from a financial institution.	Sought an additional job to increase income.
Cut back on customary purchases considered nonessential.	Refinanced a mortgage.	
Cut back on purchases considered necessary to respondent's health or well-being.	Using credit cards or installment purchase plans more than usual.	
Sold or pawned household or personal items.	Drew from savings more heavily than usual.	
Sought another residence to lower rent, mortgage, or real estate taxes.		

SOURCE: Rook, Dooley, and Catalano (1991a).

said they were not aware of any company policy regarding dating and marriage, but even so they kept their dating quiet. They knew that one couldn't date a direct supervisor, but they didn't know the company policy regarding dating/marriage among coworkers. Since they didn't work in the same department, they thought they would be OK if they just kept their relationship quiet. Their "keep it quiet" practice was upended when they were holding hands while waiting to board a plane for a weekend trip and met a mill manager coming off the plane. Another couple needed to get both union and company (St. Regis) approval prior to their marriage.

Working at the Mill

One couple expressed the view that since both of them worked at the same place, they were able to share insights into work conditions and an understanding of mill work in a way that couples who did not share a common work site were unable to. In part, their shared insights related to the deteriorating conditions at the mill as new owners took over or as the company was trying to become more efficient and in the process increased demands on workers. Another example of couples' familiarity with each other's work environment was a shared awareness of the presence of hazardous chemicals. Some workers viewed their job as dangerous—not only because of chemicals but also because of the high heat; temperatures inside the mill could reach 120 degrees.[4]

The married couples we spoke with did not fraternize with their partners at work—none of them did the same work as their partner, so they were not nearby their partner once at the worksite, and they were sometimes on different shifts from their partners. None of the couples had lunch or took breaks with their partners.

Finances—or Lack Thereof

A financial pinch is one of the first things one anticipates when job loss occurs. The couples we interviewed reported they were now using their severance package or savings, but what we heard most often was, "We just don't spend," or "We watch what we spend." Sometimes luck appeared to work in their favor: one couple had a large building on their property that was demolished in a storm. The building had a large monthly payment, but since their insurance covered the building and it was not replaced, the payout eased their financial situation considerably.

Most couples commented on the high cost of health insurance, which had been a low-cost benefit when they worked at the mill. Health insurance was now typically $1,000 or more per month. Another advantage had been the six weeks of paid vacation annually (although the couple could not take the entire six-week period together).

Once displaced, some couples needed to spend some of their severance "to make it through the week," while other couples had managed to save at least six months' salary as a fallback cushion. Using some of that cushion, cutting back on expenses, and finding limited part-time work helped them balance expenses. Two of the four women were attending school, which allowed them to be reimbursed for school expenses. Additionally, those attending school were receiving unemployment compensation, so retraining through school could be viewed as a part-time job.

When our married couples started at the mill, they were among 700-plus workers employed there. After the 2011 downsizing, they were among the last 275 employees, and it had been a long time since new workers in any number had joined the mill workforce. Two of the individuals interviewed reported that when Verso became the mill owner, "they [Verso management] said they would keep us open five years, then shut us down—and that's what they did."

Married-couple respondents had a long and shared view of mill work under four different owners. Virtually all couples expressed the view, or agreed with others, that problems at the mill increased with each successive owner. These problems included having an insufficient number of employees, little interest in part replacement, and an emphasis on a "make it work" approach and other general cost-cutting measures. One spouse described the couple's last weeks at Verso Sartell as "a constant state of correction."

The resultant stress was evident in their responses. At least one individual in each of three couples had decided to retire at the time of the downsizing, or had been looking at retiring early, partly because "this was a stressful job, and I couldn't last until I was 65." For most interviewed couples, the goal was to "get out early" (i.e., retire).

One of the Sartell couples we interviewed was also featured in a *St. Cloud Times* article, which focused on their activities since their job loss. Bob and Ginger Johnson worked in maintenance, Bob as a welder, and Ginger as an electrician. Bob's interests in horses led him to start a business after retirement (The Common Horseman) that provides carriage rides for weddings, anniversaries, birthdays, or other occasions. Bob was quoted as saying, "Now that I'm retired, I think about two things. Number one, why didn't I do this sooner? Number two, I'm keeping so busy, where would I find the time to work now anyway?"

Ginger Johnson became one of the first women to work at the Sartell mill as an electrician. She didn't start at that job, but rather, like most new workers, she began by pitching logs in the pulp mill. Working her way up, it took her 13 years to get to the electrician's position, which she had from 1990 to May 2012. Ginger viewed displacement "as a golden opportunity when I found out what was possible through the Workforce Center." She is enrolled in a community health program at St. Cloud State University, where she is the oldest student in her classes. Ginger earned an associate's degree by taking night classes several years ago. Once she completes her bachelor's degree, she hopes to work for the Veterans Health Administration in St. Cloud.

Even though couples faced necessary cutbacks on expenditures once there was no mill job, there were benefits to not having to go to work daily, such as being able to spend more time with grandchildren, assist in caring for a grandchild, or be of greater assistance to parents or in-laws. If still employed full-time, these couples simply wouldn't have had time for such things. While some couples commented on how they were now able to do almost everything together, others noted that occasional distance was important in maintaining their relationship.

Table 7.2 shows the strategies that the individuals in our married-couple subset used to respond to job loss compared to all separated Sartell workers. All of the activities of the couple-sample individuals in Table 7.2 focused on saving cash, earning replacement dollars, or creating an improved financial posture. Both groups had a similar distribution of activities used to maintain one's financial standing. Fewer than 10 terminated workers either borrowed money from relatives, pawned items, or took out a loan, and none of the individuals in our married couple subset used any of these approaches to maintain their financial position.

Although all four couples said they had cut back on expenses of all kinds, most indicated that lack of income was not yet an issue—in part because they had a good budget plan or because their home was paid for and they were watching what they spent their money on. One couple noted that while they were working they had an understanding that either partner could make a commitment, or spend, $500 or less without discussing this with their mate, but now that they were not working, that level of individual-initiated expenditure had dropped considerably.

Advice for Other Couples in the Same Situation

When asked what advice they would give another couple who had lost employment, the couples stressed "getting finances in order." However, some added that "getting things in order" should be done earlier, because doing so at the time of job loss was too late. They also emphasized maintaining an upbeat attitude regardless of one's circumstances. This attitude was generally apparent in the couples we interviewed.

Table 7.2 Activities Utilized to Maintain Financial Posture among Married Couples Compared to Other Separated Sartell Respondents

	Couple-sample individuals	Others
Obtained extra paid work.	2	16
Cut back on expenses generally.	6	126
Borrowed money from relatives.	0	8
Cut back on eating out.	5	91
Pawned items.	0	8
Took out a loan.	0	9
Not used medical services as much as needed.	3	49
Let some needed home repairs go.	2	39
Cashed in some pension/stock.	2	25
Cut back on driving to save money.	5	77
Cut back on attending movies.	4	53

SOURCE: Authors' compilation of survey data.

One couple expressed their advice in three phrases: 1) "There is life after Verso," 2) "Keep an ace in the hole," and 3) "It's not all doom and gloom." These statements reflect 1) their involvement in home activities and in helping relatives with tasks or helping other family members keep appointments as being part of living a good life; 2) having a backup plan with alternatives, including something owned that is valuable and could be, if required, converted to cash; and 3) the attitude that there are continuing positive and negative experiences, as there are positive and negative people, so enjoy the positives and handle the negative components, just as you would enjoy being around positive individuals and avoid those who whine or are always negative.

Another couple, dissatisfied with having worked for a corporation, would encourage others confronted with job loss to explore being their own boss. Yet another couple focused on social networking and program participation (retraining), as well as being involved in workshops initiated by the union or by the Minnesota Department of Employment and Economic Development. Networking for useful information and asking questions were also viewed as helpful to making a good adjustment.

In response to whether the downsizing was "generally good for you or generally bad" and to whether it was "generally good for your family or generally bad for your family," three of four individuals in down-sized couples reported a "bad" response for the individual and also for the family. In contrast, among the individuals in couples who both lost employment in the shutdown, three of four reported a "good" response for the individual and also for the family. The data for all Sartell respondents is quite different from the data for married respondents, since 60 percent of those who were downsized expected the results to be "bad" for an individual, while 82 percent displaced at the shutdown reported a "bad" response for individuals and families.

In the questionnaire, these individuals were asked what problems they expected to encounter in the next two to three years. While one individual in the couple subset noted finances, four noted health insurance. Among all other Sartell respondents, 45 noted finances, while 34 mentioned health insurance. Thus, individuals in the married-couple subset were more concerned with health insurance issues, while among all job losers from Sartell, finances was the issue that loomed largest.

At the end of the questionnaire that was mailed to all the downsized Sartell workers and 100 of those terminated at the shutdown, we asked two questions that related to satisfaction, one being, "Taking everything into account, how satisfied are you with what you are presently doing compared to working at Verso?" They could answer either "very satisfied," "satisfied," "dissatisfied," or "very dissatisfied." Among our married-couple subset, four individuals chose "very satisfied," and the remaining respondents each selected a different remaining category; thus, five of the eight respondents were at least satisfied, and half were very satisfied. A second question asked, "If it were a possibility, and an opportunity to go back to work at Verso came up, would you return to work there?" Among the four married couples, two people circled "Yes," three circled "No," and two wrote in, "Don't know."

THE ABCX MODEL

Applying the McCubbin and Patterson (1981) model provides insight in understanding the adjustment to economic displacement. The four variables are as follows: A = the displacement (job loss), B = the family's crisis-meeting resources, C = the family's definition of the event, and X = the crisis produced by A, B, and C in interaction. Considering all components in this model, the four married Sartell couples that lost jobs (A) had the following crisis-meeting resources (B):

- Years of having been a two-paycheck family
- Homes without debt
- No dependent children (family composition)
- Some income (even part-time work)
- Quality of family relations (cohesion)
- Previous experience with problems/difficulties
- Social support from partner
- Good communication
- Effective coping strategies with other events in their married life

Various definitions of the event (C) included these:

- It's not what we wanted, but now that it's here, we will adjust.
- It slows down retirement, it doesn't stop it.
- There's not much we can do about it.
- The economy (and the demand for paper) is in difficulty.

Job loss impact of the crisis (X) included the following:

- Looking for work
- Getting caught up with work around the house
- Getting retrained (going to school)
- Accepting work at a lower wage

SUMMARY

Among six married couples where both partners lost their jobs in either the downsizing or the shutdown of the Sartell paper mill, the four couples we interviewed appeared to be making a good adjustment to their situation. These couples were long-time employees and had purchased substantial homesite properties in the area, which they did not want to leave. Moreover, most of these couples had been interested in leaving their mill position early and had been saving to be ready for the planned retirement. Even though the timing of their departure wasn't of their choosing, the couples seemed comfortable with "making do" with the decisions made by Verso. Some respondents were close to receiving Social Security, several had severance packages, two were attending school and receiving unemployment compensation while doing so, and some had part-time jobs or had created self-employment opportunities. Piecing their present situation together financially, most respondents in the married-couple subset appeared satisfied with how they were adjusting to their Verso-Sartell job loss.

Notes

1. The authors acknowledge that the impact of job loss for a single parent may be as stressful—or even more so—as the impact of job loss for a married couple, simply because the burden of locating employment falls to a single individual. Still, assessment of dual-earner job loss is a topic that deserves focus, and we broach it in this study. The authors recognize that while there are many couples that might lose their jobs at roughly the same time, it is not likely that many of them had the same employer.
2.   The Holmes and Rahe Stress Scale is a measure of the link between life events and illness. Job loss, ranked eighth of 43 life events, is less stressful than marriage (ranked seventh) but more stressful than retirement (ranked ninth).
3. At Bucksport, nine women were downsized, two of whom retired. The five from the permanent roster were recalled, while two temporary workers were not recalled.
4. Getman (1998, p. 5) similarly notes the dangers of working in a paper mill: "The inside of the mill is hot, the machines are dangerous, and the noise is deafening. The bleaching and pulp making operations use dangerous chemicals that can cause serious health problems if they come into contact with the skin or are inhaled." Getman also describes a major leak of chlorine dioxide at the International Paper mill in Jay, Maine, in February 1988 that required the evacuation of the community (p. 138). Had the weather been warmer, the gas could have proved lethal to anyone within a 25-square-mile area. Loveland (2005, p. 13) relates the death of five men from hydrogen sulfide gas while they were cleaning out a sewer at Champion International Paper in Canton, North Carolina.

8
Islands in the Storm

The Plight of Two Communities

From St-Quentin to as far down as Bathurst, without the mill, people don't really realize the outcome that's going to happen. Not only to people at the mill, but a lot of people around the area. It's the last nail in the casket for a lot of us people—a big, big downfall.
—Comment from a 50-year-old paper mill worker with 29 years at the Dalhousie mill, in White (2008, p. 1)

This chapter focuses on a comparison of two communities in two geographically different states and poses the question of whether the impact of job loss is more problematic in one compared to the other. While the situation in Minnesota became much different once the explosion and fire occurred and the Sartell mill was shuttered, here we are comparing the situation at the downsizing—which occurred in both Minnesota and Maine at about the same time. In a downsizing, does location make a difference?

Table 8.1 provides a comparison of basic community character-istics between these two communities. Each community had unique strengths. For Sartell, the proximity to St. Cloud and a broad range of employment opportunities in the St. Cloud area was probably the great-est benefit, even though salaries and fringe benefits might not be as good as what they had been at the paper mill. Probably the primary ben-efit helping the displaced Bucksport workers was the fact that 75 older Verso workers took early retirement and thus "saved" 75 involuntarily displaced workers who would be competing for available employment in the community. Because of the limited employment opportunities in Bucksport, those displaced Maine workers would likely be aware of a need to relocate. Although there are more paper mills in Maine than in Minnesota, relocation or a longer commute might be a necessity for those displaced from Bucksport.

Table 8.1 Descriptive Characteristics of Sartell and Bucksport

	Sartell, MN	Bucksport, ME
Incorporated	1907	1792
2010 population	15,876	4.924
2014 unemployment rate (%)		
January	7.2	8.7
February	6.9	9.4
March	7.3	8.6
April	5.3	7.0
May	4.5	7.8
June	4.8	6.4
Geographical area	10.05 sq. miles	56.53 sq. miles
Closest city of 50,000	St. Cloud, MN	Portland, ME
Mill employment (prior to downsizing)	485	700+
Age of paper mill in 2010	107 years	82 years
Annual mill production capacity	310,250 tons	482,800 tons with 4 paper machines
Most recent mill modernization	1982	2014
Unions represented	United Steelworkers	United Steelworkers, Int. Brotherhood of Electrical Workers, Int. Assoc. of Machinists and Aerospace Workers, Office and Prof. Employees Int. Union
Number displaced	175	151
Date downsizing announced	Oct. 11, 2011	Oct. 11, 2011
Date when most employees were downsized	Dec. 31, 2011	Oct. 23, 2011

SOURCE: Authors' compilation.

DO STATE DIFFERENCES AFFECT DISPLACED WORKERS?

Mass layoff statistics report large job cutbacks (Table 8.2). The number of mass layoffs in 2009 reached almost 200 events in Maine, and there were 377 mass layoffs in Minnesota; state unemployment rates for that year were 8.4 and 8.0 percent, respectively.

Joe Johnson (2013, p. 4) reports that Mainers are "working harder yet falling further behind" because in the four-plus years since the Great

Table 8.2 Mass Layoff Events, 2004–2012, Maine and Minnesota

	Maine		Minnesota	
	Events	Separations	Events	Separations
2004	83	9,987	213	24,607
2005	123	13,473	237	26,689
2006	102	9,864	205	25,729
2007	130	12,073	199	19,231
2008	138	10,138	245	23,370
2009	192	15,141	377	34,255
2010	149	11,764	221	20,543
2011	123	9,517	259	28,202
2012	133	10,056	—	—

NOTE: "—" = data not available. (As of 2012, Minnesota no longer tracks layoff events.)
SOURCE: Bureau of Labor Statistics (2015b).

Recession nearly 50,000 residents had searched for work, over 9,000 had stopped looking for work, and 42,000-plus had part-time work but desired full-time work. The unemployment rate in Maine in October 2011 was 6.9 percent and for the following month was 7.2 percent. It reached 8.5 percent in February 2012. Two years earlier, in February 2010, the Maine unemployment rate had been 9.7 percent, with nearly 67,000 Mainers unemployed (TheLedger.com 2015a).

In the months following the downsizing announcement at the Bucksport and Sartell mills, the unemployment rate in Maine was usually higher than that for Minnesota. The peak in Minnesota occurred from April through June of 2009 at 8.3 percent, a time when Maine unemployment varied from 8.7 to 8.0 percent. The February 2010 unemployment rate in Minnesota was 7.7 percent (TheLedger.com 2015b).

Cooper (2014) notes that long-term unemployment is at record levels in every state. Utilizing an interactive map to illustrate the share of each state's unemployed who have been jobless for 27 weeks or more, he cites Maine as having a 30.4 percent long-term share of unemployed, while Minnesota had 26.8 percent.

Population Characteristics

Located in Benton and Stearns counties, which have a combined population of nearly 190,000, Sartell had 16,183 residents in 2012. Not all Sartell mill workers lived in Sartell; a number lived in St. Cloud, while others lived in Rice, Sauk Rapids, St. Joseph, or other nearby towns. Sartell is part of the St. Cloud Metropolitan Statistical Area and is St. Cloud's most populous suburb. A rerouting of U.S. Route 10 in the 1960s resulted in the razing of much of the downtown, and a new bridge over the Mississippi River in the 1980s destroyed more downtown buildings. This lack of a downtown pushed Sartell residents into closer links with St. Cloud. From 1960 to the present, Sartell's population has grown from under 800 to over 15,000 residents (Table 8.3). While in operation, the Verso Paper Mill was Sartell's largest employer. Median age in Sartell was 33 years in 2010.

Bucksport, Maine, is located in Hancock County, whose population was 54,558 in 2012. The county's labor force was 30,200 in 2011, but it has dropped to 29,800 since then. From 2000 to 2008, the county's unemployment rate ranged between 4 and 6 percent, but it jumped to 8.7 percent in 2009 and reached 9.0 percent in 2010. It dropped back to 8.1 percent, or 2,400 people, in 2013. Maine had a civilian labor force of 709,800 in January 2014. Of these, employed residents totaled 665,600, and unemployed numbered 44,100, for an unemployment rate of 6.2 percent. Bucksport itself had just under 5,000 people in 2010.

Table 8.3 Sartell and Bucksport Population Change, 1910–2010

	Sartell		Bucksport	
Census	Population	% change	Population	% change
1910	240		2,216	
1920	510	112.5	1,906	−0.14
1930	521	2.2	2,135	0.12
1940	532	2.1	2,927	0.37
1950	662	24.4	3,120	0.06
1960	791	19.5	3,466	0.11
1970	1,323	67.3	3,756	0.08
1980	3,427	159.0	4,345	0.16
1990	5,393	57.4	4,825	0.11
2000	9,641	78.8	4,908	0.02
2010	15,876	64.7	4,924	0.003

SOURCE: U.S. Census Bureau (2015).

State Labor Force Characteristics

State labor force characteristics at the time of the 2011 downsizing compared with the fourth quarter of 2014 show that the labor force increased in Maine during the three-year period but decreased in Minnesota (Table 8.4). As well, in Maine employment is up, unemployment is down, and there are fewer job losers and fewer discouraged workers, but just the opposite is true for Minnesota.

Metropolitan labor markets are characterized by having at least one urbanized area of 50,000 or more population, plus adjacent territory that is socially and economically integrated by commuting links. While Bucksport is located in the Ellsworth labor market area (LMA) along with 36 other communities, including Bar Harbor, Cranberry Isles, Deer Isle, and as far north as Steuben (Center for Workforce Research and Information 2015a), Sartell is in the St. Cloud metropolitan statistical area (MSA).

The St. Cloud MSA is projected to grow to a population of over 250,000 by 2035, an increase of 38.5 percent. The St. Cloud MSA labor force in 2010 was 160,000, up 17 percent over the 2000 labor force of 136,000. In December 2013, the unemployment rate for the St. Cloud

Table 8.4 Labor Force Characteristics of Maine and Minnesota Residents at Time of 2011 Downsizing and in 2014[a]

	Maine 2011	Maine 2014	Minnesota 2011	Minnesota 2014
Labor force	700,700	710,000	2,957,800	2,940,800
Employed	646,100	662,000	2,813,000	2,771,100
Unemployed	54,600	48,000	144,800	169,800
U-6[b] (%)	14.9	13.7	10.6	11.9
Unemployed 15+ weeks	27,800	21,600	61,700	79,000
Job losers	31,800	26,300	80,600	88,700
Discouraged workers	2,500	1,700	8,300	9,700
Invol. part-time employed	39,400	41,600	140,400	145,500
Part-time as % of total	6.0	6.0	5.0	5.2

[a] Numbers are from the fourth quarter of each year.
[b] % for U-6 is comprehensive unemployment rate, which includes involuntary part-time workers as well as unemployed workers who have stopped looking for work and left the labor force.
SOURCE: Bureau of Labor Statistics.

MSA was 4.8 percent, while the state unemployment rate was 4.6 percent (Greater St. Cloud Development Corporation 2014).

Verso's reduction of 175 people at the Sartell mill is the largest layoff involving a St. Cloud–area business since Electrolux terminated 204 employees in 2004. Sartell itself hasn't experienced a larger layoff since 2001, when DeZurik/Copes-Vulcan eliminated over 1,000 positions.

More than 40,000 Maine residents (6.5 percent of all employed Mainers) are working part-time because they cannot find a full-time position. Maine ranks sixth-highest in the nation for the number of involuntary part-time workers, and the number of involuntary part-time workers is coming down very slowly (Johnson 2014).

COMPARISON OF SARTELL AND BUCKSPORT WORKERS

Those downsized from their Verso employment at Sartell were given 60 days' notice, while those in Bucksport were given neither the 60-day notice nor 60 days' pay in lieu of notice because the number terminated did not total one-third of the Bucksport workforce. Up until 1989, when the WARN Act was implemented, it was possible for a company to announce and execute a downsizing or closure on the same day. While that didn't occur at Bucksport, most of the paper mill workers there were released within a two-week period from the day the downsizing was announced. Those not terminated then were released a month or two later. For the majority (69 percent) of those downsized at Sartell, their last day at work was December 31, 2011, whereas for those who were displaced after the fire, the last day for most was May 28, 2012, and all workers were dismissed by August 2, 2012.

While the communities of Bucksport and Sartell each possessed some relative advantages over the other community, the question remains: were the workers different, and did these worker differences influence their ability to find reemployment? Tables 8.5 through 8.9 provide a comparison of select characteristics of the downsized Sartell and Bucksport workers. Table 8.5 shows that the Sartell sample is more likely to be married, less likely to have attended or finished college, and less likely to be 62 or older than the Bucksport sample. Table 8.6 shows that the Sartell sample is more likely to think a skill upgrade is necessary and to be involved in retraining or education.

Table 8.5 Marital and Educational Status and Age Distribution of Sartell and Bucksport Displaced Workers (%)

	Sartell sample	Bucksport sample
Marital status		
Married	86	73
Living with significant other	3	8
Divorced or separated	6	12
Single, never married	4	8
N	96	67
Education level		
Less than high school	0	2
High school	52	40
Some college	41	43
College degree	7	12
Graduate or prof. training	0	3
N	96	67
Age range		
23–34	4	8
35–44	7	10
45–61	73	33
62+	15	50
N	94	52

NOTE: Categories may not sum to 100 because of rounding.
SOURCE: Authors' compilation of survey responses.

Although downsized Bucksport workers were more likely to have claimed unemployment compensation than Sartell respondents (48 percent vs. 38 percent), those differences are not statistically significant. The shortest recipients of UC were Bucksport respondents who claimed only one week, while the longest claim was a Bucksport worker who received 104 weeks of benefits.

There were 37 Sartell respondents who reported they were retired, one of whom had collapsed at work while suffering a heart attack and sustained a head injury (in 2009) and was now disabled. He had to leave the workforce 10 years earlier than he had planned. Thirty-four Bucksport respondents and 14 displaced Sartell respondents said they were retired.

Table 8.6 Downsized Sartell and Bucksport Workers on Whether It Is Necessary for Them to Upgrade Their Skills to Get a Job, Retraining Efforts, and Job Search Results (%)

	Sartell sample	Bucksport sample
Skill upgrade necessary?		
Yes	76	50
No	24	50
N	82	54
Involved in retraining or educational opportunity?		
Yes	43	18
No	57	82
N	89	62
Weeks took to find a new job		
0	21	9
1–4	28	45
5–9	14	9
10–14	10	14
15–19	7	—
20–24	14	4
25+	7	18
N	29	22

NOTE: Categories may not sum to 100 because of rounding.
SOURCE: Authors' compilation of survey responses.

Table 8.7 provides the one-way mileage workers traveled to get to their Verso mill jobs. Most Sartell workers had to travel 10 miles or less to get to work, while the largest percentage of Bucksport workers traveled 11–25 miles.

Impact of Job Loss on Spouse or Significant Other

One of the survey questions asked whether, as a result of the respondent losing his or her Verso job, that person's spouse or significant other had changed jobs or altered his or her employment status. Table 8.8 shows the distribution of responses for those displaced from Sartell and Bucksport. While the differences are not statistically significant, there are indications that Sartell spouses were more active in finding additional employment options.

Table 8.7 Responses to the Questions "Are There Good-Paying Jobs Available in Your Area That You Would Like to Have?," Distance Traveled to Work (one way) at Verso, and Reason That You Moved

	Sartell	Bucksport
Are there good-paying jobs in your area that you would like to have? (%)		
Yes	42	24
No	58	76
N	82	53
Distance of commute in miles? (%)		
1–10	63	38
11–25	21	46
26+	16	16
N	92	63
Why did you move? (*n*)[a]		
To be closer to family members	3	2
To be closer to my new work	1	4
To reduce my housing costs	7	4
Medical reasons forced relocation	1	0
We moved to a warmer climate	1	1
We were in foreclosure	1	0
House/apartment was too large	2	0

[a] Respondents were encouraged to check all categories that applied.
SOURCE: Authors' compilation of survey responses.

Most displaced workers at both Sartell and Bucksport reported that their relationship with their spouse or significant other had not changed since their job loss (58 percent vs. 59 percent), although 13 percent of Sartell respondents and 20 percent of displaced Bucksport workers reported that they had grown closer to their spouse or significant other, while 29 percent of the Sartell workers and 21 percent of those from Bucksport reported "some difficulties." Family cohesion appeared to remain strong, as 67 percent of Sartell workers and 80 percent of Bucksport workers reported that the worker-family relationship had not changed since job loss. Eighteen and 7 percent, respectively, said those relationships had grown closer; 16 and 14 percent said they had grown more distant.

**Table 8.8 Spouse Employment Response to Displaced Worker Job Loss
at the Verso Mills in Sartell and Bucksport (%)**

Spouse's employment status	Sartell	Bucksport
Spouse not working and didn't start to work after downsizing.	21	33
Spouse wasn't working but took a job after downsizing.	8	2
Spouse was working and continued to work at the same job after the downsizing.	50	56
Spouse was working but began to work more hours at his/her job after the downsizing.	12	4
Spouse was working but changed jobs to get more hours/ better pay after the downsizing.	2	4
Spouse was working & took second job after downsizing.	2	0
Spouse quit job and relocated with me.	4	0
N	80	48

NOTE: Categories may not sum to 100 because of rounding.
SOURCE: Authors' compilation of survey responses.

Several Displaced Workers Sell Their Homes

Ten Sartell displaced worker families had sold their homes since the downsizing, compared to only one from Bucksport. Moreover, 29 Sartell families had discussed possibly selling their homes, compared to 17 from Bucksport, and 10 Sartell families had actually tried unsuccessfully to sell their homes, compared to four of the displaced Bucksport families. Nine Sartell and three Bucksport respondent families had already moved. Table 8.7 provides responses as to why displaced mill workers moved. Twenty-five Sartell respondents (28 percent) and 22 Bucksport respondents (36 percent) replied "Yes" to the question, "If the economy were different, would you be interested in moving?"

PROBLEMS AND CONCERNS FACING THOSE DOWNSIZED

Table 8.9 lists concerns of downsized workers from Sartell and Bucksport. Concerns not listed here, which drew fewer responses, included moving, depression, age issues, and how to occupy one's time. Table 8.9 suggests that displaced workers from Sartell were more con-

Table 8.9 Number of Respondents Identifying Problems and Concerns Facing Those Downsized from Sartell and Bucksport

Concerns	Sartell sample	Bucksport sample
Trouble receiving buyout or trouble with human resources department	3	4
Finding work	15	2
Health insurance	27	14
House issues: selling, losing through foreclosure, moving	4	4
Finances	41	11

SOURCE: Authors' compilation of survey responses.

cerned with finances, health insurance, and finding work than those from Bucksport, but the differences are not statistically significant.

Many of the same concerns identified in Table 8.9 (finances, health insurance, and finding work) were identified again when respondents specified the problems that could arise for them in the next two to three years, although Bucksport respondents ranked them differently. Additional concerns included keeping one's home, elderly parents, disability, and relocation.

Issues Dealing with Finances and Locally Desirable Work Options

Table 8.7 shows that regardless of which mill the workers were displaced from, the majority perceived that there were not good-paying local jobs that they would like to have. Here, the percentage difference between the two locations is statistically significant and indicates greater employment options for displaced Sartell workers. In Table 8.10, the categories progress downward from least need to most. Responses indicate Sartell respondents were experiencing more financial pressure than Bucksport respondents.

Utilizing a Workforce Center

Seventy-two percent of Sartell respondents reported they had visited a workforce center to look for work, whereas only 46 percent of Bucksport workers had. Since 75 of the Bucksport workers took early

Table 8.10 Responses to Present Financial Issues for Downsized Sartell and Bucksport Workers (%)

Financial issues	Sartell sample	Bucksport sample
No problem, we have retirement income or new work.	12	33
Not a major problem, but present income is less than Verso earnings.	31	34
We need to budget closely each month.	33	21
Finances are a major problem; family is struggling.	16	10
We will soon have to apply for some kind of assistance.	7	1
We are receiving fuel assistance or food stamps.	1	0
N	90	61

NOTE: Categories may not sum to 100 percent because of rounding.
SOURCE: Authors' compilation of survey responses.

retirement, their age and minimal interest in securing other work may have accounted for their bypassing the job search. In addition, fewer Bucksport respondents reported that good-paying jobs they would like to have were available locally (Table 8.7), which may be why fewer visited a workforce center. Other reasons for not visiting the workforce center could include the larger number of Bucksport workers who reported they had retired (21 for Bucksport to 13 for Sartell) or a greater distance for Bucksport workers to travel to a workforce center. Of course, there are good reasons for displaced workers not to go to the workforce center, and some of those listed by individuals who had not visited the center were 1) having been called back to Verso Bucksport, 2) already having a job, and 3) using alternative job search options, such as headhunters, LinkedIn, CareerBuilder, or Monster.

The Physical and Mental Health Impacts of Job Loss

Downsized workers were asked whether the loss of their Verso job had affected their physical or mental health. About half of respondents reported no change in their physical health, and more respondents reported a positive effect on their physical health than a negative

Table 8.11 Downsized Sartell and Bucksport Worker Responses on the Impact of Job Loss on Their Physical and Mental Health (%)

| | Sartell sample | | Bucksport sample | |
Impact on health	Physical	Mental	Physical	Mental
Affected health negatively	14	49	22	28
No change	55	29	47	31
Affected health positively	31	22	32	41
N	94	92	60	64

NOTE: Chi-square = 8.6 with 2 degrees of freedom, significant at the 0.01 level. Somers' d = 0.22. Categories may not sum to 100 because of rounding.
SOURCE: Authors' compilation of survey responses.

one (Table 8.11). In contrast, 49 percent of Sartell respondents reported that their mental health was negatively affected, while 41 percent of the Bucksport respondents reported just the opposite—that their mental health was affected positively. Differences between the respondents from the two paper mills were statistically significant when comparing mental health outcomes, and Somers' d, a measure of association, was sufficiently strong at 0.22.

Minimum Wage in Minnesota and Maine

Maine's minimum wage is $7.50 an hour, raised to that level in October 2009. Tipped employees may be paid as little as 50 percent of the minimum but are allowed to keep all tips. Maine exempts several categories of workers from this minimum wage, including agricultural and farm workers, taxi drivers, fishermen, home assembly workers, and employees at seasonal recreation camps (Minimum-Wage.org 2015).

In August 2014, the minimum wage in Minnesota was moved to $8.00 for large employers (enterprises with annual receipts of $500,000 or more) and $6.50 for small employers. The recent increase raised the Minnesota minimum wage from $6.15. Political discussions in 2014 suggested that the minimum would move to $9 an hour in 2015 and to $9.50 an hour in 2016 for large employers. When the Minnesota minimum wage was $6.15, only Georgia and Wyoming, both at $5.15 per hour, had a lower minimum wage (Stassen-Berger 2014, p. A:7).

Burgard, Brand, and House (2009, p. 784) note that perceived job insecurity may be more problematic for a worker's health than job loss, in part because of continuing ambiguity, the inability to respond (unless the worker loses his or her job), and the lack of a support structure. Burgard, Brand, and House explore two possibilities: 1) whether organizations could intervene to help reduce the insecurity, and 2) whether broader government policies to reduce the negative effects of job loss would be helpful.

Carnevale, Smith, and Strohl (2015) see the future for Maine's workforce as positive, particularly for those with postsecondary education. New jobs requiring postsecondary education and training are expected to grow in Maine by 15,000, while jobs for high school graduates and dropouts will grow by only 2,200. During the period from 2008 to 2018, there will likely be 196,000 job vacancies from new jobs and retirements, with nearly 60 percent of those positions going to applicants with postsecondary credentials. In 2018, Maine is expected to rank twenty-ninth among states in terms of the proportion of its jobs requiring a bachelor's degree and forty-ninth in jobs for high school dropouts.

The future for Minnesota's workforce is also positive, but with an increased demand that those seeking work will have completed their postsecondary education. New jobs requiring postsecondary education and training are expected to grow by 152,000, while jobs for high school graduates and dropouts will grow by 28,000. From 2008 to 2018, there will likely be 902,000 job vacancies from new jobs and retirements, with nearly 70 percent of those positions going to those with postsecondary credentials. Minnesota ranks fifth in terms of the proportion of its 2018 jobs requiring a bachelor's degree and is forty-eighth in jobs for high school dropouts (Carnevale, Smith, and Strohl 2015).

Table 8.12 provides a further comparison between Maine and Minnesota on several labor force variables. In addition to these, both states had a higher percentage of home ownership among residents than did the United States: in Minnesota, 72 percent of adult residents were homeowners in 2012; the figure for Maine was 74.1 percent, and the figure for the nation was 65.6 percent. Maine ranked fifth nationally and Minnesota tenth in home ownership.

**Table 8.12 Minnesota and Maine Rankings for Labor Force,
Unemployment, Personal Income, and Education**

	Labor force partic. rate	Rank	2013 Unempl. rate	Rank	2013 per capita income ($)	Rank	% pop. w/ high school educ. or higher	Rank
Minnesota	70.1	3	5.1	9	47,856	12	92.5	2
Maine	65.4	17	6.7	23	41,014	30	91.6	8
United States	63.2		7.4		44,543		86.4	

SOURCE: Center for Workforce Research and Information (2015b).

SUMMARY

This chapter focuses on two communities in different regions of the United States, each with a paper mill downsizing that was announced by a common owner. Characteristics of the communities differed substantially—one was an Eastern Seaboard community settled in the late 1700s, while the other was a Great Plains community created by the availability of work at a mill started in the early 1900s. With a population of slightly more than 4,900, the Bucksport, Maine, community is less than a third the population of Sartell, Minnesota. Sartell, a large suburb of St. Cloud, provides shopping, housing, and employment options, while displaced Bucksport employees have fewer local employment options and a greater distance to travel to a larger city.

In Bucksport, displaced mill workers needed more time to find employment, and more Bucksport respondents reported taking early retirement. More Sartell respondents were involved in retraining or in an educational opportunity, but the majority in each community were *not* involved in retraining. In Sartell, there were indicators that spouses of displaced mill workers were more active in locating additional employment options than were Bucksport spouses, in part because Minnesota respondents viewed financial needs as being more pressing than did Maine respondents.

Marital status, attained education, and the number of weeks the downsized workers were unemployed and looking for work were but some of the aspects where those displaced in each community were similar. In each sample, the majority of workers were aged 45 or older; 15 percent of Sartell respondents and 50 percent of Bucksport respondents were 62 or older.

At one time, the Sartell mill had 700 employees, but just before the downsizing Verso employed fewer than 500 workers there. The Bucksport mill had more than 700 employees before the downsizing and ranked as the town's third-largest employer. Mass layoff events in Maine dropped from a high of 192 in 2009 to 123 (with 9,517 worker separations) in 2011. In Minnesota, the 377 mass layoff events in 2009 dropped to 259 in 2011, with 28,202 displaced workers.

9

A Canadian Comparison

In numbers of towns across the United States displaced workers are standing in job lines, welfare lines, and unemployment insurance lines. Because many of them received no warning of their plants' closing down, they and the towns they live in are unprepared for the loss of employment. The emotional and economic shock these workers and towns suffer is great. Up north in Canada, the lot of the displaced worker is much better. Because by law a company has to give advance notice when it closes a plant, Canada's Manpower Consultative Service has time to put a remedial plan in motion. In an advisory capacity, the service helps the company, union, and workers devise and operate a joint effort to place workers in other jobs before the gates close. When necessary, the service helps workers move to where jobs are, retrains them, offers them job search assistance, and supplies major benefits such as health insurance during the transition period.
—William L. Batt Jr. (1983, p. 6)[1]

Comparing U.S. and Canadian labor force characteristics is not unusual—numerous U.S. and Canadian social scientists have looked at various issues, including job vacancies (Zagorsky 1993), unemployment rates (Baker, Corak, and Heisz 1998; Burtless 1998; Card and Riddell 1993; Helliwell 1998), labor market behavior (Department of Finance Canada 2014; Jones and Riddell 1998), unemployment insurance (Moorthy 1990; Prasad and Thomas 1998), unemployment persistence (Amano and Macklem 1998), jobless durations of displaced workers (Gray and Grenier 1998), skill demand (Kuhn and Robb 1998), STEM workforce (Lee and Mossaad 2010), wage inequality (Storer and Van Audenrode 1998), and structural policy (Sheikh 1998).

The focus on comparative studies was largely during a period when there was a new and large "unemployment gap" between the two countries. From the 1950s until the 1980s, measures of the labor market policies for Canada and the United States were similar and appeared to respond to conditions in a similar way, even though the labor force differences were considerable. However, from 1982 on, the unemployment differences were no longer running in tandem, and economists, sociologists, and psychologists in both countries attempted to explain the change. Zagorsky (1996, p. 13) notes that after the rise in the Canadian unemployment rate, it remained about three percentage points above the unemployment rate in the United States. Figure 9.1 depicts unemployment rate differences between Canada and the United States in the years after the Great Recession and shows that Canadian unemployment has remained lower.

A current assessment of Canadian labor market conditions is available from the Department of Finance Canada (2014), which reports that the Canadian economy has gained over one million new jobs since recovery from the recession began in July 2009, and that it has expanded at a faster pace than any other G-7 economy (Figure 9.2).[2] Canadian job creation has focused on high-wage, high-skilled, full-time private-sector employment during the recovery and has resulted in the

Figure 9.1 Comparison of Canadian and U.S. Unemployment Rates, 2006–2014 (%)

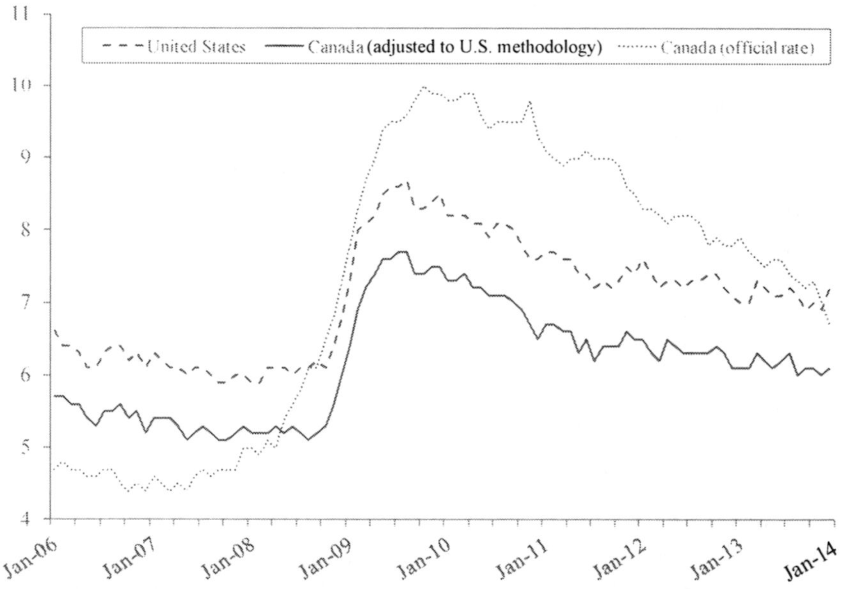

SOURCE: Department of Finance Canada (2014).

Figure 9.2 Improvement in Employment since 2006 for G-7 Countries (%)

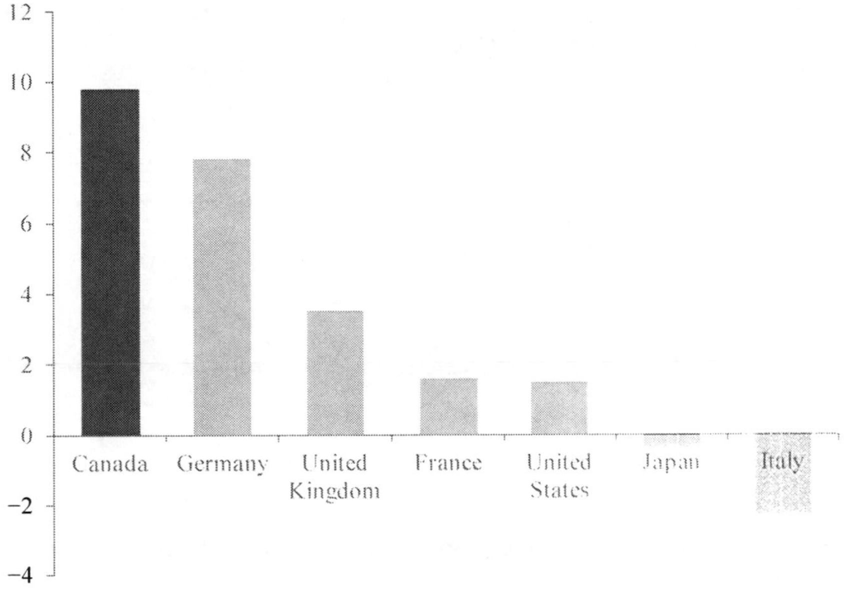

SOURCE: Department of Finance Canada (2014).

lowest long-term unemployment rate among G-7 countries.[3] However, Figure 9.3 illustrates how employment improvement in the recovery has varied greatly in Canadian provinces and territories.

There are important labor force differences between Canada and the United States. These include the following:

- From the early 1980s until early 2008, the Canadian unemployment rate has exceeded the U.S. rate.

- In Canada, the average length of unemployment is longer.

- Displacement through a plant or mill closure is more common in the United States than in Canada (Gray and Grenier 1998).

- The Canadian labor market has maintained a higher labor force participation rate than the United States, which indicates that there are fewer discouraged workers in Canada (Department of Finance Canada 2014).

Figure 9.3 Improvement in Employment since 2006 in Canadian Provinces and Territories (%)

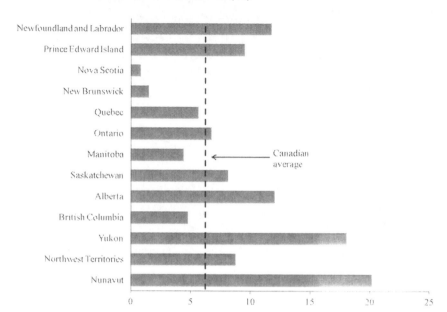

SOURCE: Department of Finance Canada (2014).

- The Canadian economy has recouped all the jobs lost during the Great Recession, and the number of employed Canadians is similar to or surpasses prerecession levels in most age groups.

The question, then, is whether Canada remains a model of assistance (as described by Batt in the epigraph that opens this chapter) to those who have become displaced workers.

UNDERSTANDING THE DIFFERENCES BETWEEN THE CANADIAN AND U.S. SYSTEMS

Differences in labor force policies between Canada and the United States exist on several levels. For example, jobless Canadians in high unemployment areas are able to apply for a "regional extended benefit" provision. Gray and Grenier (1998) note that in Canada there are also numerous regional development programs that are earmarked for high unemployment areas, a programmatic effort that is less widespread in the United States. Other differences include the following:

- Displaced older (55-plus) Canadian workers fare worse than their American counterparts.

- Being a union member is a greater handicap for American workers than for Canadians.

- Canadian workers are in more depressed labor markets than American workers.

- There is a "greater inclination in Canada for governments to assist workers and firms in distress" (Gray and Grenier 1998, p. S165).

Baker, Corak, and Heisz (1998) note that Canada has a higher incidence of unemployment than the United States. Employer-initiated separations are more typical in Canada, where unemployment also lasts longer than in the United States. However, Amano and Macklem (1998) ascribe the Canada-U.S. unemployment gap largely to a more generous Canadian unemployment insurance (UI) program, particularly UI extensions within regions. Other plausible contributing factors could include the strength of unions in Canada, along with minimum wage differences and the rigidity of wages.

To further explain the differences in the unemployment rate between the two countries, researchers have examined labor force policies. For example, Zagorsky (1996) emphasizes the importance of definitions that could explain some of the measurable variations in unemployment, pointing out that while the United States distinguishes between active and passive job seekers ("passive" methods include reading the want ads or taking a class), Canada makes no such distinction, treating all employment search methods as equally valid. (In 1993, 55 percent of the Canadian unemployed "looked at ads.") Zagorsky thus concludes that definitional differences account for nearly 20 percent of the current gap. He also assesses job vacancies—the option for the unemployed to fill a slot and become employed. At the time of his assessment, comparable job vacancy data for Canada and the United States were not readily available and required proxy data. However, using analogous synthetic vacancy rates, Zagorsky concluded that labor supply functions were similar in the two countries, although labor demand was not. The *Jobs Report* (Department of Finance Canada 2014) provides a needed update, indicating Canadian labor demand now appears strong for high-skilled employment that requires postsecondary education. Zagorsky suggests further research will be required to ascertain why labor vacancies follow different patterns in the United States and Canada.

Officials must consider globalization, technological change, and population aging as they affect Canadian workers. To support the development of a skilled mobile workforce, Canada has aligned training funds with private-sector labor needs, promoted postsecondary education and skills development, and provided labor market support for underrepresented groups, including older workers. Furthermore, Canada has made improvements in matching workers with available jobs, has increased timely labor market information to facilitate job search efforts, and has created daily job postings to alert unemployed residents about available jobs (Department of Finance Canada 2014).

The Canadian Unemployment Insurance System

Among the major features of Canada's social safety net is its unemployment insurance system—a $15 to $20 billion annual expenditure that came after the expansion and after program changes from the 1970s were relaxed. The program reflects a continuing view that UI contributes significantly to labor market impacts. In 1976, new Canadian UI regulations disentitled residents between the ages of 65 and 70, influencing many elderly to withdraw from the labor force (Green and Riddell 1993). Further changes in 1996 restructured the Employment Insurance (EI) program to reduce the percentage of unemployed eligible to collect EI benefits, which increased self-employment, part-time work, and other forms of contingent employment. Silver, Shields, and Wilson (2005) note that self-employment, as well as part-time and contingent work, either was disallowed for EI benefits or made qualification more difficult. They maintain that the restructuring of the Canadian labor market in the 1990s helped bring about an erosion of the welfare state, along with a deemphasis on full-time sustaining employment. For example, they contend, by 2001, 47 percent of all jobs in Canada lasted for only a year or less.

Canada's UI system was created through the Unemployment Act of 1940 to provide insurance against the risk of having income be lost to unemployment. With some exceptions—workers in agriculture, forestry, and fishing, for example—coverage was limited to those with labor market experience who were willing and able to work. According to Green and Riddell (1993, p. S102), "when the program began to pay benefits (1942), 42 percent of the labor force was covered by UI."

In 1971–1972, changes in the Canadian UI program became more comprehensive and generous—reducing the minimum qualifying period, increasing the maximum duration of benefits, and introducing extended benefits in specific regions. As a result of these amendments, UI benefits grew from $700 million in 1970 to almost $2 billion in 1972 and almost $12 billion in 1983. Government fiscal restraint and the 1974–1975 recession altered the program to reverse the liberalization of 1971–1972 (Green and Riddell 1993). Besides the reduction in UI coverage from age 70 to 65 in 1976, other changes included a reduction in benefit rate as well as an increase in the disqualification period for those who voluntarily quit their jobs. Further changes in 1978–1979 made UI benefits for those with "marginal labor force attachment" (i.e., part-time workers, new entrants) more restrictive. Other system changes made in 1989–1990 shifted resources away from income maintenance into job market training and reemployment programs—i.e., to more active labor market policies. Even with the change to more restrictive UI policies, Green and Riddell note that according to 1990 OECD figures, Canadian UI expenditures were higher than those in the United States, Japan, Italy, Australia, France, Germany, Sweden, and the United Kingdom.

In 1996, the name of the Canadian unemployment insurance system was changed to Employment Insurance (EI). The EI system has workers pay a premium of 1.78 percent of earnings, while employers pay 1.4 times the amount of employee contributions. Since 1990, there has been no government contribution to the EI fund. EI benefit amounts and duration vary with previous salary, how long an individual has worked, and the unemployment rate in that area. EI pays for maternity and parental leave, compassionate care leave, illness coverage, and retraining programs (Wikipedia 2015b).

As the period of unemployment lengthens for displaced workers, options for finding work decrease, and the need for prompt assistance increases. Silver, Shields, and Wilson (2005) find that even two years after job loss, significant numbers of job losers were not fully integrated into the labor force. Those who were unsuccessful in finding a full-time job that lasted more than one year were unemployed, had left the labor market, or only had part-time or unstable full-time work.

Since 2009, the Canadian unemployment rate has been lower than that of the United States (Corak 2012). A study of subjective employment insecurity finds Canadian residents are less likely to worry about losing a job than U.S. residents (Anderson and Pontusson 2007).

PAPER MANUFACTURING IN CANADA

On the face of it, the Canadian paper mill environment is not too much different from that in the United States. Similarities include

- decreased demand for paper products (newsprint, coated papers);

- increased concern for environmental regulations;

- the shutdown of several paper mills in recent years;[4]

- the expansion of ownership in paper mills abroad, as well as for-eign acquisition of Canadian and U.S. paper mills; and

- the turnover in corporate ownership.

The two countries are similar in the number of newsprint paper producers (47 in Canada, out of 289 paper mills, and 46 in the United States, out of 450 mills), according to Manta, a Web business directory. Sweeney and Holmes (2013, p. 223) point to "endless rounds of restruc-turing" in the Canadian pulp and paper industry beginning in the early 1980s, when expenditures increased while employment decreased. For example, the pulp and paper workforce in British Columbia declined by almost 6,000 workers in 2001, the year the Canada-U.S. Softwood Lumber Agreement expired.

Pulp and paper workers are unionized in Canada through member-ship in either the Pulp, Paper, and Woodworkers of Canada (PPWC) or the Communications, Energy, and Paperworkers Union of Canada (CEP). After the mill closed in Port Alice, British Columbia, CEP remained active in the community, funding essential services and providing groceries to displaced workers and their families and moral support to union members (Sweeney and Holmes 2013).

Silver, Shields, and Wilson (2005) suggest that the 1990s eroded the postwar Western welfare state and restructured the labor market toward unemployment, part-time and contingent employment, and declining full-time work. Canada had a slow post-1992 recovery from the recession of the early 1990s—not until 1998 did it recover the number of full-time jobs that had existed in 1989. During the 1990s, the Canadian labor force exceeded demand, which created job insecurity and made it difficult for displaced workers to find employment. Restructuring appeared as a permanent component of the Canadian economy. For example, in 1993, of the 11,258,000 full-time jobs in Canada, almost three million ended. Primarily this was through layoffs, but 45 percent ended because of structural displacement. Using Statistics Canada's Survey of Labour and Income Dynamics (SLID), Silver, Shields, and Wilson point out that among those displaced in 1993, only 41 percent were employed in stable, full-time work after two years. Seven percent had part-time work, 10 percent were self-employed, 12 percent had full-time jobs lasting less than one year, and 30 percent were not employed. "The stark conclusion," they write (p. 797), "is that if you are a restructured worker and have not been successful in securing full-time employment after one year, your prospects for doing so over the next year are rather bleak."

Structural unemployment is an embedded feature of the Canadian labor market. Silver, Shields, and Wilson (2005) note that when a paper mill downsizing or closure occurs—whether in Nova Scotia, British Columbia, or elsewhere—one option for those displaced is to leave their family to find work in western Canada's oil and gas industry. There they adopt a two-weeks-on, two-weeks-off pattern, living in "man camps" while on the job and at home while off.

We look at provincial or state policies and programs versus national ones to compare how they improve or at least maintain the lot of paper workers. According to Batt (1983), the Canadian government was involved in assisting companies and unions to relieve serious unemployment in the area and lessen unemployment insurance costs by providing alternative employment to displaced workers. How do state or provincial versus national policies and programs compare? In an effort to make a comparison, we examine the shutdown of the Bowater Mersey Paper Company Limited, which was closed in June 2012.

Background of the Bowater Mersey Paper Company Limited

Bowater Mersey began operation in Brooklyn, Nova Scotia, as the Mersey Paper Company in 1929. Located on the estuary of the Mersey River, the operation consisted of a pulp and paper mill, as well as a power plant created when the company dammed the river 20 miles upstream. Financier Izaak Walton Killam began his pulp and paper and hydroelectric empire in Canada and Latin America with Mersey Paper, then created the Mersey Shipping Company in 1930 to carry raw materials to the Brooklyn mill and finished product from it.

Killam died in 1955, and the mill was sold the next year to Bowater and renamed the Bowater Mersey Paper Company in 1959. In 1963, the Washington Post Company purchased 49 percent of the common stock; Bowater retained the remaining 51 percent. The name changed to AbitibiBowater with the merger between Montreal-based Abitibi-Consolidated and U.S.-based Bowater in 2007, and in 2011 it became Resolute Forest Products (*Globe and Mail* 2012a). The 2007 merger made AbitibiBowater the third-largest pulp and paper producer in North America and the eighth largest in the world. Resolute claims to be the world's largest newsprint producer by capacity, producing newsprint at 12 mills in North America and South Korea (Resolute Forest Products 2015). In April 2009 the company filed for creditor protection in both the United States and Canada, with a debt of US $6 billion, but it emerged from creditor protection in December 2010 (Wikipedia 2015a).

In 2011, Resolute announced that Bowater Mersey faced "unprecedented production costs" that required labor concessions, power cost reductions, and restructured costs of fiber. According to company spokesman Seth Kursman, the Bowater newsprint mill was the least profitable among the 18 company-owned or -operated pulp and paper mills and the 24 wood products mills in Canada, the United States, and South Korea. Kursman reported that the electricity expense at Mersey was the highest of any area in which the company operates a mill, and the average fiber cost of $150 per ton compared to the $88 cost per ton in the United States was an important factor. AbitibiBowater wanted to reduce labor costs from $97 to $80 per metric ton and manufacturing costs from $537 to $480 per metric ton, to cut total costs between $4 and $14 million (Zaccagna 2011).

That same year, the Bowater mill requested a special five-year discount rate for electricity, and while Bowater officials would not disclose whether the mill would close if the reduced rate wasn't approved, Bowater Mersey CEO Brad Pelley said, "The probability of us continuing operations is improved if we are granted the tariff" (CBC News 2011, p. 1). Paul Quinn, a forestry analyst at RBC Capital Markets, said, "The cost savings will not be easy, particularly on the labor and energy side, but are necessary at a time of declining demand for newsprint in North America" (Zaccagna 2011, p. A:1).

The Announcement to Close the Mill

On June 15, 2012, Resolute Forest Products announced Bowater Mersey would be idled indefinitely the next day, and the mill, timberland, and power plant (called the Brooklyn Power Corporation and owned by Resolute) would be for sale. Within six months, the government of Nova Scotia had purchased all shares of Bowater Mersey for CA $1 from Resolute and the Washington Post Company. In this arrangement, the provincial government acquired the Bowater Mersey assets, consisting of 555,000 acres of forest, the Brooklyn pulp and paper mill, a deep-water terminal at Brooklyn, and the power plant. The provincial government also acquired Resolute's liabilities, including $20 million in debt, a $120 million pension liability for workers, and environmental liabilities for the pulp mill site. The provincial government simultaneously sold the Brooklyn Power Corporation for $25 million to the Nova Scotia Power Corporation. Within a few days of establishing ownership, the provincial government announced that the Brooklyn mill would be decommissioned and the site would become a forest industry research facility focusing on biomass energy, renamed Renova Scotia Bioenergy Inc.

Prior to the mill shutdown announcement, Darrell Dexter, the Nova Scotia premier, announced a $25 million forgivable loan to the company in $5 million annual installments. The $25 million was to keep the mill's paper machines operating, make efficiency improvements, and upgrade the power plant. In addition to the provincial loan, union mill workers had voted to cut 110 jobs to save the mill by reducing labor costs. According to the *Globe and Mail* (2012b, p. A:1), "The lifeline thrown to the company in December by the province was valued at a total of $50 million. In addition to the $25 million forgivable loan, the province also spent $23.75 million to buy about 10,120 hectares of woodland from the company. Another $1.5 million was offered over three years to train workers. So far, $605,000 has been spent on training to improve safety, efficiency, and production, said a spokeswoman with the Department of Economic Development."

The CBC noted that amid the struggling forestry industry in Nova Scotia, the NewPage Port Hawkesbury paper mill had shut down in 2011, then resumed operations 13 months later after the province announced a $124.5 million aid package, which allowed Port Hawkesbury Paper to employ half the workers it once did. Then, Nova Scotians experienced the shutdown of the Minas Basin Pulp and Power Company in Hantsport in mid-December 2012, which displaced 135 workers (Jackson 2012). Citing marketplace challenges, increased competition from newer and more efficient mills, and rising operating costs, Minas Basin owners recognized that the mill was too small to achieve long-term sustainability and did not seek support from the provincial government (*Pulp and Paper Canada Daily News* 2012).

In mid-January 2014, Resolute announced the mothballing of one of the last paper machines at the Fort Francis mill; the machine was expected to remain out of action at least through the first quarter. The decision to temporarily shutter the mill was based on softening demand for the high-quality printing paper produced at the mill. Resolute was adamant that the shutdown was not permanent (Hale 2014).

Following the shaky recovery of the NewPage Port Hawkesbury mill, the *Kenora Daily Miner* reported, "A panel examining options for southwestern Nova Scotia's economy had recommended the province acquire the lands as part of a broader plan to revive the region's economy. There had been concerns that if Nova Scotia didn't purchase the land, it would be purchased by foreign interests that would export the wood" (Hale 2014, p. A:1).

The Closure of the Bowater Mersey Mill at Brooklyn

About 320 employees were terminated when the Brooklyn newsprint mill was closed (Jackson 2012). The mill, which can no longer be used to make paper, will be transformed into a forest industry research facility, providing few opportunities for reemployment for area mill workers (Reuters 2012). Papermakers made up nearly half of the mill labor force; the balance was composed of trades personnel or transportation workers (Figure 9.4). Among those with seniority, the great majority of Bowater workers were over 45: 40 percent of the workers were between 45 and 49, another 29 percent were between 50 and 54, and 4 percent were 55 or older. Thus, 73 percent were over the age of 45. Few of the Bowater workforce were younger workers: only five workers (3 percent) were between ages 20 and 24, 12 workers (8 percent) were between ages 25 and 34, and another nine (9 percent) were between ages 35 and 39.

Creating an Economic Development Assessment

Because of the number of Bowater Mersey employees who would lose their jobs when the mill and other Resolute forestry operations closed, the province stepped up efforts to fast-track economic development opportunities in the region by establishing a Transition Advisory

Figure 9.4 Bowater Workforce (from seniority at the time of closure)

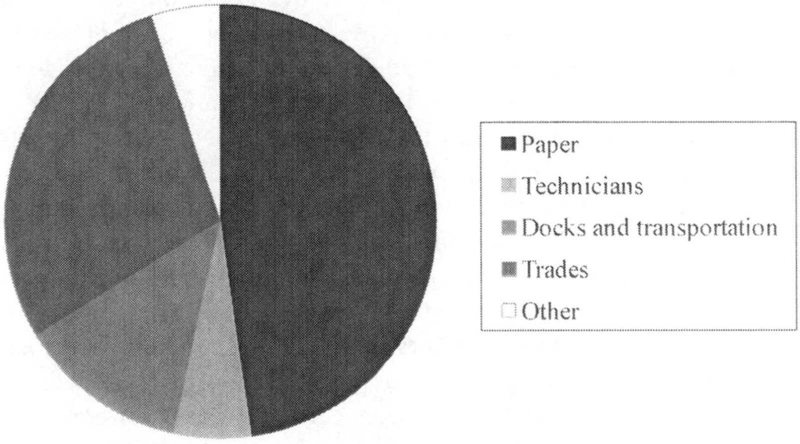

- Paper
- Technicians
- Docks and transportation
- Trades
- Other

SOURCE: Municipality of the Region of Queens, Nova Scotia.

Team. The team recognized that it was a challenging time for the community because of the immediate, permanent loss of jobs in the paper mill and sawmill, but also because of uncertainty over the future of forestry throughout southwest Nova Scotia.

The province was concerned about the viability of the aging community. The team operated for six months, hosting public discussions and sessions for former Bowater mill workers with officials from the Department of Labour and the Supervisor of Pensions Office, who responded to their pension concerns. The focus was on future growth opportunities for the area, but separate breakout meetings at these events allowed participants to raise the concerns of displaced mill workers, woodlot owners, truckers, and forestry contractors. The Transition Advisory Team received input from 75 individuals and community groups and met with 67 individuals at 23 team meetings but felt the absence of youth and young adult views. To remedy this, the team worked with several junior and senior high schools to engage youth in the planning process.

In Lunenburg and Queens counties, 75 percent of the labor force worked in sectors other than manufacturing. The Transition Advisory Team's report notes, "It is clear that the overwhelming preference of the community is for the province to take ownership and control of the Bowater-Resolute lands, thereby supporting essential jobs that contribute to the economy and facilitating innovation in the forestry sector." Thus, the team's mission was to focus on development of small to medium-sized local businesses, "rather than on attracting big industry from outside" (Nova Scotia Transition Advisory Team 2012, p. 12).

The team report also notes that "the full impact of the Bowater Mersey Paper Company shutdown has not yet been felt by the community. The first, most direct impact was the shutdown of the paper mill in Liverpool, where more than 300 people lost their jobs. The second round of impacts were felt when the Oakhill sawmill in Dayspring ceased operations. The third round of impacts will be felt when the severance pay of the displaced workers is all paid out. And the final round of impacts are being felt gradually as wood prices are depressed, harvesters lose the market for their wood, and sawmills have fewer markets for their chips" (Nova Scotia Transition Advisory Team 2012, p. 14). The report proposed planning for other communities relying heavily on a few larger employers: "The province needs to consider where the next crisis might occur and assist those communities in putting together the strategies and plans to respond to this type of crisis well in advance of any major changes in local circumstances" (p. 16).

PROGRAMS TO ASSIST DISLOCATED MERSEY WORKERS

Programs available through Employment Nova Scotia include the following four. In all four programs, the applicant must receive an employment assessment and develop a Return to Work Action Plan with a case manager as part of the application.

1) Skills Development is an employment program that provides financial assistance to eligible individuals to help them acquire the full-time skills training they need to obtain work. Components include the following:

   - Full-time training exists, and EI benefits continue until the end of the benefit period, after which living expenses may be received.

   - If the displaced worker is not receiving EI benefits, financial assistance for living expenses may be available.

   - Temporary financial assistance may be provided for dependent care, tuition, books, disability needs, transportation, and accommodation.

   - Provincial assistance could last up to three years, depending on the participant's Return to Work Action Plan.

2) START is a program encouraging employers to hire Nova Scotians into jobs requiring work experience or apprenticeship.[5] Financial incentives are provided to employers willing to hire.

3) Self Employment assists unemployed, eligible individuals in starting businesses. Entrepreneurial support (information, coaching, mentoring, and access to specific training) may be available, for a maximum of 40 weeks.

4) Job Creation Partnerships (JCPs) enables participants to acquire work experience that assists them in finding full-time employment; maximum duration is for 52 consecutive weeks.

Ongoing Programs

Employment Nova Scotia set up career resource centers in Liverpool and Bridgewater, with on-site career specialists providing information on pensions, pharmaceutical care, apprenticeship, adult education, Nova Scotia Community College (NSCC) programs, and government training programs and services. Career resource center staff work to match displaced workers with employment opportunities.

By March 2014, 81 displaced Bowater workers had used the services. The Department of Labour and Advanced Education (LAE) has worked closely with the displaced workers and their families in transition planning, while Employment Nova Scotia (ENS) works with the local NSCC campus to consider options when several clients are interested in training in a common field.

Economic development is an essential component during a community transition period following the economic restructuring of a major employer. Based on a model developed in British Columbia, a Community Development Tool Kit is available to assist local government in adjustment planning. Included in this model is significant and long-term financial assistance to rural regions.

A Bowater Response Strategic Plan was created to do the following:

- Help displaced Bowater workers transition to new careers
- Minimize the impact on communities and local businesses
- Work with Resolute and the CEP union to establish a Joint Action Team to address issues of concern for those displaced
- Help former Bowater employees understand and receive their severance, benefits, and pensions
- Provide support to families as they adjust to job loss

Certain programs have been established to help workers transition to new careers:

- Career counseling has helped displaced workers identify new career paths and related training needs.
- Group counseling for union members has been established.
- Job search clubs have been started.
- Trades and career information sessions have been created.

Efforts to create policy change were initiated to facilitate retraining and job search by waiving the usual three-month job search period, evaluating the feasibility of training for out-of-province employment, and allowing workers receiving severance to receive training supports.

To spearhead government efforts, three project teams were established: 1) the Community Adjustment Team coordinates efforts among government and local leaders, 2) the Economic Development Team coordinates economic development efforts, and 3) the Forestry Team addresses issues associated with the forestry supply chain.

In addition to these project teams, a Transition Advisory Committee was established to help identify and resolve community issues.

Ramifications of the Bowater Mersey Closure

Attributing the loss of revenue to less usage by its top two electricity customers, the privately owned Nova Scotia Power requested a rate hike to help absorb fixed costs. Since its rates were already among the highest in the country, the provincial power company appeared to have limited support for the $3.50 monthly increase (Taber 2012).

When the NewPage paper mill in Cape Breton, struggling with rising shipping and electricity costs, announced it would shut down in September 2011, Nova Scotia's premier, Darrell Dexter, said the provincial government was willing to help market the NewPage products (Canadian Press 2011).

In a December 2011 interview, AbitibiBowater CEO Richard Garneau said that 2009 demand for company products had been 24 million tons but that in 2011 it was going to be 13 million tons, so "don't expect that we're going to continue to do business as usual" (Marotte 2011, p. A:1). The firm was exploring producing biofuel from wood waste and developing engineered wood products as value-added products.

THE CANADIAN LABOR MARKET

Between 1980 and 1990, 2,200 jobs were lost in Port Alberni's forest industry, mostly from MacMillan Bloedel mill closures (Wood 1991). Another 1,300 positions were lost between 1991 and 1993, which translates to a payroll reduction of $58.5 million. Such job loss was ascribed to the need to increase productivity and lower production costs—largely through substituting capital investment for employment, reducing wood usage, and lowering chemical-use processes.

The recession of the early 1990s hit Canadian manufacturing hard: even after a full economic recovery, more than 575,000 Canadian workers had been displaced from their jobs (Silver, Shields, and Wilson 2005). Yet as part of a continuing retrenchment from neoliberal policies, EI eligibility became more restrictive, declining to half of what it had been prior to 1990. Most of the downsizing occurred in Quebec and Ontario, and hardest hit was manufacturing, construction, and retail. More than 635,000 workers lost their jobs between 1993 and 2001, and those 25–34 years old were the most vulnerable. Because chances for reemployment decline as the length of joblessness increases—referred to as a "scarring effect" —after two years, only about three-quarters of those displaced in the 1990–1991 recession had found work. "For the remaining quarter of these workers," write Silver, Shields, and Wilson, "job restructuring created a path away from full-time employment to one of labour market detachment and exclusion" (p. 794). From the 1980s to the mid-1990s, part-time work became more prevalent—particularly among women—making up almost 20 percent of all employment. But, as Silver, Shields, and Wilson point out, "Workers who have not found stable work at 18 months (after displacement) face a high likelihood of long-term unemployment or contingent employment. They also face severe economic hardship as employment benefits expire" (p. 797).

In short, Silver, Shields, and Wilson (2005, p. 798) note that "only half (49.8 percent) of those Canadians who held a full-time job and lost that job to restructuring during the 1990s were able to find full-time jobs that lasted more than one year. The other half were unemployed, moved out of the labour market, worked in unstable full-time jobs, in part-time, and other forms of contingent work." Part-time work and self-employment, they note, do not lead to full-time paid work and employment stability for most structurally unemployed full-time workers, nor does "being compelled to take the first job that comes along, regardless of its quality" (p. 799).

Being unemployed not only keeps dislocated workers at a distance from colleagues, clients, and customers, but those displaced tend to withdraw, thus accepting and internalizing a norm of social distance between those who are "not in the system" (i.e., not employed) and those who are employed. Displacement disrupts career paths for younger workers and retirement plans for older ones. Thus, the distress of losing a job affects job losers above and beyond the loss of income.

The Scarring of Unemployment: What Are the Effects of Job Loss?

Once displaced workers find new employment, there may be an increased sense of labor insecurity, particularly if they have accepted employment at a lower wage than what they previously earned. Jobless applicants for available positions are carefully screened and tend to be given closer scrutiny than those applicants who are already employed. Scarring includes the loss of firm-specific human capital, and, if unemployment persists, general skills may also deteriorate (Arulampalam, Gregg, and Gregory 2001). As Young (2012) states, "UI supports people's spending and consumption, but it does little to support their identity, sense of purpose or self-regard."

Shaw (1986, p. 380), notes that Canada's largest job creation program—the Canada Works Program—has as its major aim to "reinforce income protection in places particularly hard hit by long-duration unemployment" but has more recently diverted its resources into training programs. Carrington and Zaman (1994) and others report that displaced workers may find new employment, but often at reduced wages. For example, Morissette, Qiu, and Chan (2013) find that high-seniority displaced Canadian workers had earnings losses of between 10 and 18 percent five years after their dislocation.

One former mill employee at the Grand Falls–Windsor mill, which closed in March 2009, said he was appreciative of the provincial government assistance: officials did a good job, he said, of establishing programs for workers to go back to school to get training in various fields, and paying 100 percent of their tuition (Hickey 2012).

The mill closing was financially difficult for many workers, with 90 percent of the breadwinners "working back and forth through Alberta." However, it was also a hardship interpersonally—for most of them, the mill represented the biggest and best portion of their social life. "They looked forward to going in there, seeing their buddies, and now that part of their life is gone, and they're home; they haven't developed social skills" (Hickey 2012, p. A:1).

U.S. UNEMPLOYMENT INSURANCE CHARACTERISTICS

The U.S. unemployment insurance system is an experience-rated payroll tax and, according to Brechling and Laurence (1995), is unique in the world. In essence, employers creating layoffs that are temporary and recurrent are charged the costs of those layoffs. The layoffs do not always lead to permanent employment changes, but employers that terminate workers in a major displacement or closure (and thus create permanent employment change) are also charged the payroll tax. In the United States, UI exists to help ease the financial pain of job loss, but it is not designed to replace earnings, nor to be sufficient to reduce job search efforts.

Canada-U.S. Unemployment Income Differences

Green and Riddell (1993) note three differences in UI between the United States and Canada: 1) since 1972, UI benefits, relative to average earnings, have been higher in Canada than in the United States; 2) average duration of UI claims has also been higher in Canada; and 3) "an unemployed worker is . . . three times more likely to receive UI in Canada than in the United States" (p. S114).

Moorthy's (1990) research supports the view that when Canada had a larger unemployment rate than the United States, it could be partly attributed to the accelerated labor-force participation of Canadian women, but also to a more liberal UI benefits program—i.e., benefits were provided to those who were truly displaced, but also to those who left their jobs and to some who had reentered the labor force. Canada continued to make UI payments beyond 26 weeks "easily available" in the 1980s when the United States did not. Overall, the gap in UI payments between the two countries increased in the 1980s. Canadians also have a higher job-leaver rate—which may indicate that Canadians are more willing to be unemployed than U.S. residents.

One significant difference between the Canadian and U.S. systems is the subsidies the province is willing to contribute to retain a paper mill. An example would be the Port Hawkesbury paper mill in Nova Scotia, where the new owner purchased the mill in 2013 and received a $124 million provincial government subsidy package (Beswick 2013).

SUMMARY

A comparison of Canadian and U.S. labor force characteristics and policies is not an unusual undertaking for North American social scientists. Canada has a long history of providing assistance to displaced workers, and we looked at their efforts to assist displaced Bowater Mersey mill workers in 2012 to see whether Canada has remained a model of assistance.

The Bowater Mersey and Verso Sartell mills were closed within a few weeks of each other, during the slow recovery from the Great Recession. Canada's economic recovery appeared to happen earlier than that of other G-7 countries, as it has added one million new jobs since 2009. However, Nova Scotia, home to the Bowater Mersey mill, had the smallest recovery of any province.

While Canada's unemployment rate exceeded that of the United States from 1980 until 2008, the tables have turned, and the U.S. unemployment rate now exceeds that of Canada. We note that definitions become important in providing some understanding of societal approaches and programs. While the U.S. makes a distinction between active and passive job seekers, Canada does not. And whereas unemployment insurance is viewed as a social safety net in Canada, in the United States it exists to ease the loss of work but is not designed to replace earnings or be large enough to minimize job search efforts.

Silver, Shields, and Wilson (2005) note that even two years after job loss, many Canadian job losers were not fully integrated into the labor force. Some found work that didn't last very long, while others found only part-time work, a difficulty for displaced U.S. workers too.

The paper industry in both countries is experiencing decreased demand for paper products, shutdown of several paper mills each year, turnover in corporate ownership, and both expansion abroad and the acquisition of Canadian mills by foreign owners.

Resolute Forest Products sold the Bowater Mersey property to the government of Nova Scotia for a token amount, and the province assumed substantial debt and pension liability. Of the 320 employees terminated at Bowater Mersey, 73 percent were older than 45.

The province became an active agent in providing assistance by establishing a Transition Advisory Team for the benefit of the community at large, as well as skills development programs for those displaced. Other programs utilized inducements to encourage employers to hire those displaced, facilitated self-employment, formed Job Creation Partnerships, and established career resource centers and economic development programs. A Bowater Response Strategic Plan, involving Resolute and the CEP union, assisted the dislocated workers.

Significant societal and cultural differences are reflected in a U.S.-Canada comparison of efforts for displaced workers, but Canadian efforts to assist those confronted with job loss in a way that displays sensitivity to individual and family needs contains lessons worthy of consideration by U.S. policymakers.

Notes

1. Batt served as a special assistant to the U.S. Secretary of Labor, developing programs for federal economic assistance to areas of severe unemployment.
2. Along with Canada, the G-7 countries include the United States, the United Kingdom, Germany, France, Italy, and Japan.
3. The long-term unemployment rate is the share of the labor force that has been unemployed for at least 27 weeks.
4. The difficulties and promises of the paper industry in Canada appear to be much the same as in the United States, including mill closures. Recent closures, affecting several provinces, include the following:
   - The Minas Basin Pulp and Power containerboard mill in Hantsport, Nova Scotia, closed in December 2012, affecting 135 employees. It cited market challenges; increased competition from newer, more efficient mills; and rising operating costs.
   - The 2008 closure of the Dalhousie, New Brunswick, AbitibiBowater mill affected 300-plus employees.
   - The Fraser Papers pulp mill in Thurso, Quebec, closed in May 2009, terminating 300 employees. The company cited challenges from American wood pulp subsidies, U.S. import duties, and the global economic slowdown.
   - The Tembec paper mill closure in 2009 terminated 300 workers in Powerview–Pine Falls, Manitoba.
   - The 2005 AbitibiBowater pulp and paper mill closed in Kenora, Ontario.
   - The March 2009 closure at the AbitibiBowater mill in Grand Falls–Windsor, New Brunswick, displaced 450 mill workers and 250 additional workers in paper-associated jobs (Hickey 2012).
5. The START program expired at the end of March 2014.

10

The Future of Economic Displacement for Papermakers

Unemployment figures are creeping down . . . but the jobs being created aren't like those we've lost. While two-thirds of the jobs lost during the recession were middle-income jobs, about half of those created since have been in low-wage sectors like tourism, hospitality, and retail sales. What's more, a greater proportion of them are temp positions than in recoveries past.
—Rana Foroohar (2014, p. 34).

ADVICE TO A JOB LOSER

"Ask Matt," a weekly column in the *Minneapolis Star Tribune*, recently addressed the question, "I lost my job. It was a total shock. Now what?" (Krumrie 2014). The response emphasized three points: job losers need to 1) use existing networking connections, including relatives, to let people know they are looking for work; 2) update their resume to emphasize leadership skills, performance levels, special assignments, and to cite any awards or training; and 3) stay positive and aggressive.

The question "Now what?" after job loss is step one for all displaced workers. Further consolidation and job loss within the paper industry remain all but certain: "There's no possible way that all the paper machines that are operating today will operate in two years," said one industry insider. "In fact, closures are desperately needed right now" (Schmid 2014).

Acquisitions have brought this on, but also the loss of foreign markets, increased competition from Asia and South America, and the continuing conversion from paper to electronic means in the United States. Furthermore, retiring older paper machines increases the prospect of worker dislocation, since building a new paper mill in the United States has been a rare event over the past 30 years.

While our analysis points out differences in how displaced workers cope with their job loss, our literature review shows that coping styles are related to workers' resources and needs, which vary according to age. Policymakers and community residents tend to focus on retraining and reemployment for those displaced, suggesting that one model fits all. What we find is that older workers often make a reasonable adjustment to job loss without the same kind of retooling that is needed by younger workers. Current programming policy for displacement does not take this into account, as recognized by Rook, Dooley, and Catalano:

> Suppose an elderly worker, without modern work skills, is laid off in a terminal plant closure. If the region is experiencing massive unemployment, the prospects that this individual will ever be recalled may be vanishingly small. In such a situation, active coping efforts that are appropriate for some younger workers (e.g., enrolling in classes to learn job interviewing skills and résumé preparation) may only produce repeated humiliations for the displaced older worker and a measurable decline in psychological well-being. A few such individuals may adapt successfully on their own, but research has yet to identify how this adaptation may be optimized.
>
> We largely lack intervention mechanisms that can be tailored suitably to the person's age, cohort, and economic prospects, and the daunting complexity of developing cost-effective interventions is apt to discourage many researchers and service providers. But such efforts to develop interventions assume great urgency at a time when deep recessions appear to be beyond political control. (1991b, p. 171)

Allenspach (2013, p. A:1) interviewed Lyle Fleck, a former United Steel Workers Local 274 president, who started working at the Sartell mill in 1981. He said the adjustment was hard on older workers: "Since the blowup, I've seen some people go through very hard times, dealing with some bad issues. Some have gone to work at mills in Becker or Duluth, or they've moved to the Dakotas and found something else. But when you're talking about 300 or 400 people, you're always going to have some who are going to have trouble. You can't find work that comes close to paying what you were making, and, when you're not working, you feel like a failure. What's next? You're 59. Are you going to go back to school?"

Verso Job Loss

The October 2011 downsizing announcements at Bucksport, Maine, and Sartell, Minnesota, and the subsequent closure of the Sartell mill, were essentially a way for Verso to reduce costs and production simultaneously. Data analysis indicates that among all Verso job losers, those displaced in the closure of the Sartell mill were the most significantly impacted and the most upset. We found that the job loss impacts on mental and emotional health for Sartell workers were negative, for both those downsized and those displaced at the shutdown of the Sartell mill, but that the mental health impacts were particularly hard on those Sartell workers who became job losers when the mill was closed.

Respondents displaced from the Sartell mill also had the strongest negative response to job loss of the three samples: only 19 percent considered their job loss good for themselves, and only 20 percent considered it good for their families. Thirty-two percent of those downsized from Sartell viewed job loss as good for themselves, and 31 percent viewed it as good for their families, while 60 percent of the Verso workers downsized from Bucksport reported that their job loss was good for themselves, and the same percentage reported that it was good for their families. We speculated that those Sartell workers displaced at the mill shutdown were most upset with their job loss because they had survived the earlier downsizing and were now—after all—losing their jobs. It was also these displaced workers from Sartell who had the highest percentage of respondents who had expected to retire from their mill positions (63 percent), but now they, too, were to be job losers.

Adding to this keen disappointment, Sartell workers were not provided with an early retirement option, but at the time of job loss, early retirement was a real option for a number of Bucksport respondents. Forty-five percent of the Bucksport respondents claimed to be retired, whereas only 20 percent of the Sartell respondents did.

The "Now what?" question in the "Ask Matt" column needs to be asked for Verso workers, with the following information as backdrop:

- The average age of workers in the three samples of dislocated papermakers was 55 years, with variation of a year downward for those downsized from Sartell, a year upward for those displaced when the Sartell mill was closed, and right on age 55 for those downsized from Bucksport. While age could well be a factor in reemployment, another element in the mix was the difficult economy in the slow recovery during the postrecession period.

• Most workers had been employed at their respective paper mill for a good number of years—averaging 22 years at Bucksport, 25 years for those downsized at Sartell, and 29 years for those terminated at the closure of the Sartell mill.

• With the exception of the temporary workers at Bucksport, most Verso production workers earned $25–$40 per hour and had health benefits through the company, for which their contribution was 20 percent of the cost. Long-term workers could have as much as six weeks of paid vacation. At the Bucksport mill, there were 40 temporary workers, who were paid considerably less than the pay scale for permanent workers. Independent of which mill one worked at, or whether one was a temporary or permanent worker, job loss has both emotional and financial ramifications.

• The Bucksport downsizing differed from that at Sartell in two significant ways: 1) downsized Sartell workers had 60 days to be looking for work and exploring options, while Bucksport workers had the disadvantage of being released almost immediately; and 2) the Bucksport announcement included an early retirement option, with the expectation that many—if not most—of the 125 workers who were to be terminated would be able to stay on because more senior employees were leaving. The early retirement option thus provided a significant employment option for those workers who were not as close to retirement. Transfer was not an option for production or maintenance workers at either the Bucksport or Sartell mill.

• Most displaced workers (86 percent) were either married or had a partner.

"Now what?" receives a different response when one is a year or two from retirement and the company provides an option for early retirement. Those long-term employees who had been receiving good wages and benefits who didn't have options to take early retirement or transfer would have a different array—and a reduced range—of options.

Employment Options Are Limited

While some dislocated paper workers will find replacement work in the paper industry, most terminated paper workers will not. In part this is because many workers do not want to relocate, and some will accept other jobs or be forced to accept part-time work. Some will remain unemployed. Boak (2014) finds that of those who have been unemployed for more than six months, only 11 percent will regain steady full-time work. Thus, many of the long-term unemployed stop looking for work, some are able to retire, and others are able to claim federal disability benefits or are helped with side jobs and assistance from friends and family. "The number of people unemployed for more than six months has tripled since the recession began at the end of 2007," says Boak (p. D:2). "It peaked at 6.77 million in early 2010 and has declined to a still-high level as more unemployed workers have ended their job hunts and are no longer counted as unemployed." One poll finds that 47 percent of unemployed Americans have given up looking for work (Hsu 2014). Nearly half of the unemployed who were contacted by the poll hadn't been on a job interview within the past month, and for those unemployed for more than two years, the percentage increases to 71 percent. Most of our Verso respondents (66 percent) reported they didn't plan to go back to school, and 44 percent said they would not relocate. It is true that employment options are limited for displaced workers, and they appear even more limited for jobless older workers. That being said, displaced workers who have quit looking for work, or who won't relocate, further hamper their chances at finding reemployment.

Karren and Sherman (2012) suggest that unemployment discrimination is an "add-on" stigma for those displaced, primarily for those who are older and for those who are unemployed for long periods of time. For those who are unemployed for long durations, concerns about an individual's work ethic could suggest character flaws to the mind of the interviewer, who may fault the applicant for being long-term unemployed. Indeed, it is possible to read too much into a given situation.

Paper Mill Closures in the United States Continue

In February 2014, International Paper planned to lay off up to 700 workers and permanently close its Courtland, Alabama, mill the next month, affecting 1,096 workers and about 5,400 related jobs in logging and forestry (McDonough 2014a). Continuing paper mill closures from 2011 to 2013 are identified in Figure 10.1.

In Maine and Minnesota, as well as other states, the problem of restructuring the pulp and paper industry presents a continuing difficulty when paper machines are retired or a mill closes. For example, in Maine in 2014, Great Northern Paper closed its East Millinocket mill, and Old Town Fuel and Fiber terminated its pulp operation. Job displacement in the pulp and paper industry calls for additional programmatic assistance. Fortunately, WIA provides job-search assistance, training, and other supports for those who lose jobs because of staff reductions or closures, but there continues to be a great need.

Figure 10.1 Mill Curtailments and Closures, 1989–2013

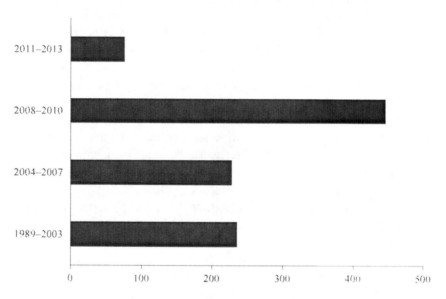

NOTE: Mill closures from 2011 to 2013 have been added to the earlier mill changes depicted in Figure 2.1. Only North and South Dakota, Utah, and Nevada have avoided job loss impacts for mill workers. Earl Gustafson of the Wisconsin Paper Council notes that while closures and shutdowns occur, some closed mills are purchased and reopened.
SOURCE: Pulp and Paperworkers' Resource Council (2014).

Wisconsin publishing-grade paper mills have been closing at the rate of one a year since 2006 (Schmid 2012a). With the loss of 300–600 jobs from each closing, the impacts are not unlike those dark days of Michigan's automaker closures. About 12,500 workers are employed in Wisconsin's paper and pulp operations, so the industry is important to the state.

With increased competition, the U.S. paper industry continues to be confronted by several conditions that are likely to reduce employment options. The paper industry is recognized as a mature industry that faces environmental demands in the production process, as well as predictions of increasing decline in paper use. Efforts to reduce production in a flooded market will require that pulp and paper producers assess their alternatives.

ASSISTANCE TO DISPLACED INDIVIDUALS

The media continue to announce mill closures and job losses, such as the 700–800 jobs General Mills announced on September 30, 2014. This follows the closure of plants in Lodi, California, and Methuen, Massachusetts, which displaced 430 and 144 workers, respectively (Hughlett 2014). Fortunately, there has also been good news: Minnesota recently received $17.5 million in workforce training grants "aimed at underemployed and unemployed workers and those negatively impacted by foreign trade. The focus is on higher-skilled jobs that typically pay much more than $10 an hour" (DePass 2014a, D:2).

Unemployment Insurance

Generally, with unemployment insurance (UI), states provide cash benefits to unemployed workers for up to 26 weeks. When the unemployment rate is sufficiently high in a given state, the federal or state extended benefit program provides additional weeks. Through an Emergency Unemployment Compensation program, unemployed workers who have exhausted regular UI benefits may get further payments.

Retraining

According to SBETC, 134 former Verso Sartell employees have received retraining. Seventy of the 86 people who left SBETC programming have jobs, and those 70 people—whose average Verso wage was nearly $32 an hour— are now making $28 an hour. In Bucksport, nine displaced workers were involved in training programs, while 65 workers signed up for the Trade Adjustment Assistance program, with 46 attending workshops on resume writing and interviewing skills and 48 attending workshops related to job search.

"The 134 people who received training also benefited from the federal Trade Adjustment Assistance program, which paid for education and made them eligible for extended unemployment benefits," Allenspach (2013) reports. "Another 80 former Verso workers aged 50 and older received a state Reemployment Trade Assistance supplement of 50 percent of the wage difference between the jobs the people left behind and what they're able to get in new employment. The benefit can mean up to $10,000 in the first two years."

Temporary Work Assignments

Some displaced workers accept temporary assignments, hoping that the temp position turns into a permanent full-time position—a chance to get noticed, if you will. "Alternative work arrangements"—temp agencies, part-time and self-employed contractors, freelancers and on-call workers—now constitute 35 percent of the current workforce, and they will likely reach 40 percent (60 million people) by 2020. The growth spurt in "just-in-time labor" is due in part to companies not wanting to commit to full-time hiring until a more complete economic recovery is evident, but such arrangements also free the employer from paying benefits such as Social Security, Medicare, and UI, which are covered by staffing agencies. Additionally, Allen (2014a) maintains that "in the most recent recession, repeated rounds of bruising layoffs were emotionally draining, sapping company morale" (p. D:5). Using temp workers lets the employer avoid that cycle.

Assistance to Firms to Employ Those Displaced

During the early 1980s, Minnesota created the Minnesota Employ-ment and Economic Development (MEED) Wage Subsidy Program, which, as Root and Park (2009, p. 196) note, "provided private sector employers up to $4 per hour in wages and $1 per hour in benefits for a six-month period for hiring an applicant who was unemployed and either ineligible for or had exhausted their UI benefits or workers com-pensation." Employers were given an incentive to continue employment beyond the six-month period, but if the employee was not kept on after the six months, they were obliged to repay a portion of the subsidy. The state legislature failed to fund the program in 1985, and efforts to assist firms to hire the unemployed in peak periods of high unemployment have not been rekindled. Given the slow recovery from the Great Recession, a revision of the MEED Wage Subsidy Program could be reconsidered.

Displaced paper workers willing to relocate may find employment with another papermaker, and we suggested that Bucksport job losers may have easier access to paper mill reemployment simply because there are more paper mills in Maine. Other mill workers, including those in the trades, may find the transition to other work without the need to relocate. But essentially, many displaced paper mill workers are in manufacturing-related jobs, which is not currently a growth industry.

Finding work locally is one difficulty, but finding work with com-parable pay and benefits is something else entirely. Geographical con-centration of dislocated workers from a mill that may have been the community's dominant employer means that they are not only compet-ing for jobs with friends and neighbors but also with former coworkers.

Targeted Assistance

Direct assistance to dislocated workers takes the form of job search or retraining. Indirect assistance could also be targeted to firms to enable them to exploit new technologies—in paper mill research it could include biomass fuel production. Ideally it would lead to new products or technology and increased employment opportunities. START was a program used in Nova Scotia that encouraged employers, through financial incentives, to hire unemployed residents needing work or an apprenticeship. The Canadian Employment Insurance system, as noted in the previous chapter, paid for maternity and parental leave as well as illness coverage.

Assisting Communities

Assisting the community where many workers have lost their jobs is another plausible form of assistance. Redevelopment or conversion of the worksite, or some other form of community assistance, might be considered, although U.S. examples are uncommon. However, our Canadian chapter illustrated that community involvement was an important part of the Bowater-Mersey closure. And while the provincial government acquisition of the paper mill assets could be viewed as atypical, that would also be true for the earlier provincial offer of a $25 million forgivable loan to keep the paper mill operating. In the Bowater-Mersey closure, the viability of the community was of concern—including growth opportunities for the community, the inclusion of area residents on the Transition Advisory Team, and the emphasis on development of small- to medium-sized local businesses.

Direct Assistance to Displaced Workers

Funding may be available to dislocated U.S. workers who are veterans or who have a reasonably short-term period before they qualify for Social Security. Dislocated workers who are as much as two years short of retirement may qualify for supplemental funding by volunteering for specific tasks within the community on a nearly full-time basis. As noted in Chapter 9, jobless Canadians in high unemployment areas were able to apply for a "regional extended benefit" provision. Additional Canadian programs noted earlier include assistance for self-employment, as well as Job Creation Partnerships, both of which appear to fit the U.S. culture and could easily be adapted here.

VERSO ADVOCACY FOR THE PULP AND PAPER INDUSTRY

To its credit, Verso has been proactive in advocating for a sustainable and thriving pulp and paper industry in Maine. Although still a relatively new company in Maine,[1] Verso is advocating for the paper industry as a whole, since it believes that pulp and paper, as the state's largest manufacturing segment and second-ranking export, make up an industry that Maine cannot afford to lose. Paper companies represent more than 20 percent of all foreign exports, pay the highest manufacturing wages, and spend nearly $900 million annually on goods and services within the state. The Maine paper industry accounts for one of every six manufacturing jobs, and paper mills make up 60–80 percent of the local tax base. A company publication notes that, despite there being fewer mills and workers, Maine produces more paper than it ever has. Challenges to be addressed include high energy costs, transportation, and an inconsistent regulatory environment (Verso 2009).

Issues Confronting the Pulp and Paper Industry in Maine

Energy. Energy costs have increased considerably since 1990, and the cost for energy in Maine is much higher than the U.S. average. Verso uses a mix of fuels in papermaking, generating hydropower, and looks for ways to conserve, improve efficiency, and reduce greenhouse gas emissions. The company wants state assistance to support a Maine liquified natural gas terminal to increase the supply of natural gas and not load further regulations or costs onto Maine's electric rates.

Sustainability. Even in Maine, which is 90 percent forested, sustainability is an issue. Maintaining a balance between growth and tree removal will sustain Maine's paper industry and satisfy client demands for fiber to come from a forest certified as sustainable by an independent party. While it is incumbent upon Verso to use trees, water, energy, and chemicals as efficiently as possible, Maine can ensure that all wood harvested—for lumber, pulp and paper, biofuel, or other industrial purposes—comes from sustainably managed forests, and it can develop public policy to assure that any new energy strategy that includes greater use of wood as a biofuel in mills carefully evaluates the potential environmental and economic consequences (Verso 2009).

Workforce. The issue here is that the current workforce is older and that "young people have grown up knowing little about the paper industry except cutbacks, layoffs, and mill closings" (Verso 2009, p. 9).

While Verso supports summer programs, scholarships, and apprentice-ships, the state's role could be to help guidance counselors and others encourage career exploration in the industry, and to cooperate with pulp and paper companies to promote living and working in rural Maine.

Environmental regulations. These are important in maintaining Maine's dominant pulp and paper industry. Verso, as part of a commit-ment to reducing its environmental footprint, says that it has reduced air emissions by 74 percent since 2000 at the Bucksport mill, and that it has similarly reduced nitrogen oxide emissions, sulfur dioxide emissions, landfill sludge, and 99 percent of the pollutants discharged at its water treatment plant. It says it has undertaken a similar effort at the Andro-scoggin Mill. The company seeks what it describes as "consistent" interpretation and application of environmental laws and regulations.

Transportation. Verso names this as a key issue in helping Maine mills remain competitive. Because rail transportation is more efficient than trucks for moving rolls of paper, Verso would like Maine to recog-nize reliable rail service as a major economic development issue.

GETTING PAST THE GREAT RECESSION IN MINNESOTA

The difficulty in getting past the Great Recession continued well into 2014. Minnesota shed over 4,000 jobs in April of that year—the fourth consecutive month of subpar job growth (Belz 2014e). Even so, Minnesota's unemployment rate improved in April, moving downward to 4.7 percent—the lowest rate since September 2007. And in June, 8,500 jobs were added, pushing it down further, to 4.5 percent (Belz 2014d). But even with an unemployment rate more than 1.5 percent below the national average of 6.1 percent, there were 136,000 Min-nesotans who remained unemployed in July 2014.[2] But the lackluster recovery included a slow reduction nationally in the number of part-time workers (Kanell 2014): 26.3 million Americans work part-time, and nearly 30 percent of these, or 7.4 million, are part-timers because they can't find full-time employment. The Labor Department reported a national unemployment rate of 6.1 percent, the best reading since

September 2008 (Lee and Hsu 2014), with the job market hitting its stride by recording the fifth consecutive month with over 200,000 new employees.

The Great Recession eliminated manufacturing jobs across the Upper Midwest, and Minnesota struggled with a slow recovery. In 2014 Minnesota still had 23,100 fewer manufacturing jobs than it did at the prerecession peak. Even though in overall employment numbers it had recovered all the jobs it had lost, those jobs were made up primarily in the service economy; construction and manufacturing employment were still way down from prerecession levels (Belz 2014c). And while more job openings have been created in Minnesota, average weekly wages have barely increased—they are less than 1 percent higher. But surrounding states may be even worse off: in a nine-state survey, Minnesota had the highest rating in manufacturing recovery over the past three years (DePass 2014b).

By July 2014, the number of U.S. residents who said they were not looking for a job because they did not think they could find one had fallen by 351,000 from the previous year (Belz 2014a). However, wages have remained low in the postrecession recovery because millions remain out of work, whether on the rolls or not (Rugaber 2014).

The St. Cloud Area

While job gains are uneven throughout the state, St. Cloud has recently been booming, adding 4,003 jobs in the 12 months beginning in May of 2013, a 3.9 percent annual growth rate (Belz 2014b). This came despite a loss of 68 jobs when work was transferred to a new factory in Alabama (Ramstad 2014). Other layoffs in the area included 100 jobs at Hutchinson Technology, which has terminated nearly 60 percent of its 5,400 employees since 2006 (Alexander 2014). These conditions made it harder for displaced paper workers to find new jobs.

National Emergency Grants

The Minnesota Dislocated Worker (DW) Program receives National Emergency Grants (NEGs) from the U.S. Department of Labor to temporarily expand services in response to natural disasters and large job-loss situations. Minnesota received six NEGs in Fiscal 2011, three NEGs in Fiscal 2012, and four NEGs in Fiscal 2013. In Fiscal 2011, the state program served the largest number of displaced workers (3,631) and helped almost twice as many customers (17,000) as the Work Investment Act (WIA) Dislocated Worker Program, the American Recovery and Reinvestment Act (ARRA), and NEGs combined (Minnesota DEED 2011). It served 13,000 and 12,000 customers the following two years, again roughly twice as many as the other agencies combined.

Neither the Experience of Unemployment Nor the Length of Unemployment Is Uniform

Even displaced workers from the same facility have vastly different experiences. We note that some of the Sartell workers have responded rather well, even though their health care costs are more than they want to pay. They have taken work that, although not at the same pay level they had received at Verso, is full-time work that occupies them, and that they are making the best of. Unemployment among married couples has been concentrated on husbands rather than wives (Boushey 2011) and has particularly increased among husbands in older couples. Job loss among older workers finds them with concerns about retirement and the task of finding new employment.

Plausible Helpful Changes for Displaced Workers

Unemployment Insurance. UI is the primary safety net for laid-off workers, replacing part of a worker's lost income during periods of unemployment. However, laid-off part-time workers have a harder time qualifying for UI benefits than unemployed full-time workers because of UI eligibility restrictions. In 2001, Minnesota became one of 12 states with favorable UI policies for part-time workers, although still not equitable with those for full-time workers. Maine changed its UI policy to include part-time workers in 2003 (McHugh, Segal, and Wenger 2002). In our view, unemployment insurance should be extended to laid-off part-time workers in all states. But beyond that, a top policy priority should be to create access to well-paying jobs for those seeking full-time work, including older, displaced paper workers (Boushey 2011).

Good employment options. While we support extending UI for those workers who have part-time jobs, what would be preferable would be good-paying full-time jobs for those seeking full-time work. Displaced workers, papermakers and others, including older workers, should have access to good jobs. Boushey (2011) maintains that "having access to good jobs must be a top policy priority," and we concur.

60 days' notice. Because job loss has such a large impact on the individual worker and his or her family, it makes sense for *all* full-time workers to have 60 days' notice or 60 days' compensation after getting a downsizing/displacement notice. We believe this policy should be effected, independent of the number or percentage of employees downsized or displaced, or the number of workers in the labor force where the displacement occurs.

Further education and training. Individual workers and their employers should be encouraged to seek means of continuing the workers' education and advancing their knowledge. Employers could support individual initiatives but also be facilitators in creating programs and support to make the education or training happen. Expanding worker skills and advancing their knowledge will maximize opportunities if displacement should occur.

Unemployment discrimination. Older displaced workers have difficulty obtaining employment and therefore may be unemployed for an extended period. Equating the length of their unemployment with a personal flaw in these workers is an example of unemployment discrimination and should be discouraged.

Reduce barriers for the long-term unemployed. Those who have been looking for work for six months or more are considered long-term unemployed. Their numbers rose from 16.6 percent of unemployed in 1982 to 43.0 percent in 2010 (Boushey 2011). We support programs that reduce employment barriers for the long-term unemployed.

Help older displaced spouses locate employment. The share of married couples who have one spouse employed and one unemployed has increased most among couples where the older spouse is between the ages of 55 and 64. They have an especially difficult time finding replacement work. We encourage support for dislocated worker families, regardless of which spouse has suffered job loss (Boushey 2011).

SUMMARY

Analysts predict there will be continuing worker dislocation and consolidation in the paper industry for three reasons: 1) the current paper surplus in the United States, 2) the continuing retirement of existing paper machines, and 3) the process of paper manufacturers buying other paper producers, which frequently leads to mill closures. If future displaced workers are like those in the Verso Bucksport downsizing, the Sartell downsizing, or the Sartell shutdown, then programs need to be considered for two broad categories: 1) younger workers who can benefit from retraining and 2) older workers who prefer to bypass retraining options and find reemployment. The latter have the most difficulty finding new work and will need help locating that work, or placement in subsidized employment programs. One effort that had considerable merit was the MEED Wage Subsidy Program, which was tried for a period in the early 1980s.

Some displaced workers—like those terminated from Sartell in the mill shutdown—will need assistance in minimizing the mental health impacts of job loss. Among the suggestions noted above, clearly 60 days' wages or 60 days' notification of displacement should start the process. During those 60 days, those to be displaced could receive counseling and job search assistance, or, if an immediate employment option became available, they could be promptly released from their commitment to complete their soon-to-be-lost employment.

Notes

1. Verso's first full year as a company was 2007; it operated two mills in Maine (at Bucksport and Jay) with 1,600 employees, which had formerly belonged to the International Paper Company.
2. That 6.1 percent was the lowest rate since September 2008. Still, an unemployment rate of 6 percent is historically high—the rate was between 4 and 5 percent in the months before the Great Recession. Moreover, low-paying sectors lead the employment gains, adding only six cents to the average hourly wage. House and Leubsdorf (2014) suggest unemployment might be more accurately measured using a broader gauge, which would include discouraged job seekers as well as people working part-time because they can't find full-time work. If that were the measurement for U.S. unemployment, the rate would be 12.1 percent, down from 14.2 percent a year earlier.

11

Epilogue

The Verso Paper Corporation announced on Monday that it would acquire NewPage Holdings, a specialty paper company that emerged from bankruptcy in 2012, in a deal valued at $1.4 billion.
—Rachel Abrams, *New York Times* (2014, p. B:1)

Given the industry pressures from Asia and South America, as well as the decline in print media and increased use of online formatting in the United States, the question of whether Verso's acquisition of NewPage was a reasonable business decision needs to be raised. David J. Paterson, Verso's president, argued that "as a larger, more efficient organization with a sustainable capital structure, we will be better positioned to compete effectively" (Abrams 2014, p. B:1). The interest Verso had in acquiring NewPage, rumored among Sartell paper workers for some time, came to the fore when NewPage was in bankruptcy, from September 2011 to December 2012.

Nine months after the acquisition, Verso officials released an October 1, 2014, statement that stunned Bucksport workers: the mill could not be made profitable and would close by December 1, 61 days later. Layoffs began December 1 for the 570 Bucksport employees. The Verso announcement also came as a surprise to John Williams, president of the Maine Pulp and Paper Association, as there had been no effort to effect changes at the mill. Employees were not asked to suggest ways to reduce costs, an approach sometimes used to avert downsizing or closure decisions. Officials said one reason for the closure was "how long the merger with NewPage was taking" (WCSH-TV 2014).

The Bucksport announcement came one week after Great Northern Paper (with idled mills in Millinocket and East Millinocket, Maine) filed for Chapter 7 bankruptcy, which allowed it to liquidate assets to pay off more than 1,000 creditors on liabilities of over $50 million (Bell 2014). Verso-Bucksport was the third Maine paper mill to close in 2014: Great Northern had closed the East Millinocket mill in February, and Old Town Fuel and Fiber had shut down its pulp operation in August, terminating 180 workers (Hoey 2014). As a result of these and similar events, Maine's paper industry, which had employed more than 12,000 workers in 2000, shrank to only 7,000 by 2015.

The histories of Verso and NewPage reflect recent industrial shifts and uncertainties. While both produce coated paper, Verso is half the size of NewPage in both sales and output. With the Sartell mill's closure, Verso has three mills. Owned by Apollo Management, a New York private equity firm, Verso was created in a spin-off from International Paper in 2006. NewPage originated as Consolidated Papers, founded in 1902 in Wisconsin Rapids, Wisconsin, by the Mead family, sold to Finnish papermaker Stora Enso Oyj in 2000 and then to Cerberus Capital Management, another New York private equity firm, in 2007, when it became NewPage. The Verso-NewPage transaction had to go through a lengthy antitrust review, which anticipated the sale of one of the mills as a condition of approval: officials were concerned that too many mills in North America already produced too much coated publishing paper (Schmid 2014). U.S. demand for coated paper peaked at 13.75 million tons in 2006. Since then, tablet computers, e-readers, and mill closures have reduced production to roughly 7 million tons. China overtook the United States in 2009 as the world's largest paper producer; one can buy its imported paper products in Madison or Eau Claire for less than one would spend on paper manufactured in Wisconsin (Schmid 2012b).

THE VERSO ACQUISITION

The buyout was initially viewed as joining the three Verso mills (Table 11.1) with eight NewPage mills in six states (Table 11.2). Then Verso announced the Bucksport closure, and a month later NewPage announced it would sell its Rumford, Maine, and Biron, Wisconsin, mills to Catalyst Paper, contingent upon its acquisition by Verso. Thus, the two Verso mills are joined by six remaining NewPage mills for a total of eight paper mills under the Verso banner: two each in Michigan and Wisconsin and one each in Maine, Maryland, Minnesota, and Kentucky. Verso acquired NewPage for $1.4 billion. Subsequently, Catalyst paid $74 million to NewPage for the Rumford and Biron mills (Richardson 2014d).

Table 11.1   Verso Mill Operations When the Company Acquired NewPage

	Quinnesec, MI	Jay, ME	Bucksport, ME
Year established	1985	1965	1930
Employees as of 12/31/2013	475	840	570
Product categories	Coated freesheet	Coated freesheet and groundwood	Coated groundwood and specialty
Capacity total (total tons per year) for 2013	425,000	635,000	405,000

SOURCE: Verso Corporation.

At the announcement of the planned NewPage acquisition, Verso chief financial officer Robert Mundy said layoffs were not expected "at this time" (Abrams 2014). A New York corporate management lawyer noted that neither company had discussed closing mills during negotiations, and that "the possibility of the merged company closing mills in the future was not likely" (Canning 2014).

At acquisition, Verso said it would save $175 million during the first 18 months from administrative efficiencies and by buying needed raw materials—wood, pulp, and chemicals—in bulk (Richardson 2014c). Part of that savings would accrue because the Verso Jay mill and the NewPage Rumford mill—only 24 miles apart—were no longer competing on wood purchases. However, when the Rumford mill was sold to Catalyst, the competition resumed. Indeed, some costs would increase. U.S. Forest Service timber sales decreased in President Obama's 2014 budget proposal (Johnson 2013b), meaning less raw material for mills. Too, more houses were being constructed, further increasing the demand for wood and hence the cost of making paper.

The Rumford Mill

Even before it was sold to Catalyst, the Rumford mill made the news earlier that November when it announced that in February it would indefinitely idle one of its paper machines and lay off 18 salaried and 110–120 hourly workers. Union leadership at the Rumford mill had not anticipated any change in the announced layoffs from the Verso pur-

Table 11.2 NewPage Mill Operations When Verso Acquired NewPage

	Wickliffe, KY	Rumford, ME	Luke, MD	Escanaba, MI	Duluth, MN	Biron, WI	Stevens Point, WI	Wisconsin Rapids, WI
Year established	1970	1901	1888	1911	1987	1892	1919	1904
Employees as of 12/31/2013	439	808	819	943	287	412	239	977
Product categories	Coated freesheet, uncoated, specialty	Coated freesheet and groundwood	Coated Freesheet	Coated freesheet and groundwood, uncoated, specialty	Super-calendered	Coated groundwood	Specialty	Coated freesheet
Capacity total (total tons per year) for 2013	285,000	565,000	480,000	785,000	270,000	370,000	185,000	560,000

SOURCE: Verso Corporation.

chase of the NewPage chain of mills (Richardson 2014b). The Rumford mill is unionized, while the Verso mill in Jay, nearby, is nonunion.[1]

Financial Impacts of the Bucksport Closure for Verso

An analyst at Moody's Investors Service suggests the Bucksport mill shutdown was a "smart move," as it will conserve cash and improve Verso's long-term financial picture; at the moment, he says, Verso is on the edge of default (Richardson 2014d). Moody's downgraded Verso's bond rating last June from B3 to Caa3, based on its view that Verso's debt obligations are "judged to be of poor standing and are subject to very high credit risk." If the merger with NewPage were to prove unsuccessful, Verso would be headed for bankruptcy, the Moody's analyst said (Richardson 2014c).

Not only would the Bucksport closure save money, it would also help the remaining coated-paper mills by reducing supply—decreasing Verso's capacity to produce coated paper by 28 percent and North American coated capacity by 10 percent. Coated paper production is expected to decline by about 6 percent a year (Richardson 2014a). While Moody's Investors Service had a gloomy view of Verso's future, at least one wood science professor at the University of Maine was more optimistic. Professor Robert Rice viewed the struggles to achieve sales of coated paper as primarily a condition of the Great Recession; he envisions a stable market for coated paper as the economy recovers (Richardson 2014c).

"Unemployment is often only the most immediate and dramatic cost of displacement among middle-aged men," write Parnes and King (1977, p. 95). "Even after they find other work, many individuals continue to suffer the consequences of displacement through less attractive occupational assignments, lower earnings and, perhaps, some damage to physical and mental well-being." Upon the announcement of the Bucksport shutdown, local seniors anticipated a tax hike that, with their fixed incomes, would make living in Bucksport difficult. Local business owners anticipated loss of business and began thinking about staff cuts. Local impacts were on the minds of many Bucksport residents because taxes on the Bucksport mill made up 47 percent of town revenue (Hoey 2014). Out-of-state paper companies advertised for Bucksport workers who would be dismissed December 1 (Eichacker 2014)—among them Flambeau River Papers (Wisconsin) and Gorham Paper and Tissue (New Hampshire), looking to fill positions such as mechanical engineer, process engineer, paper machine manager, general laborers, and journeymen.

The sale of the Rumford and Biron NewPage mills (both producing coated papers) to Catalyst was likely to speed up the Department of Justice antitrust review (CBPIS 2014b). Indeed, a paper industry analyst expected that the U.S. Department of Justice would "require the new Verso to shed some mills before approval to lessen the company's domination of the coated paper market" (Richardson 2014c, p. 5).

One observer believed that the Bucksport closure announcement was both an attempt to appease the U.S. Department of Justice and a convenient cover to close a mill and reduce product.[2]

Anticipating the Bucksport Closure and Seeking Alternatives

Both of Maine's U.S. senators, Susan Collins and Angus King, were critical of Verso for not providing more notice of the closure. They released a statement that said, "Given the harm its decisions will cause more than 500 workers and their families, it would have been helpful if the company had worked more closely with the workers, community, and the state to identify ways to lessen this blow" (Hoey 2014, p. 7).

While Verso adhered to the mandatory 60-day Worker Adjustment and Retraining Notification (WARN) window prior to shutdown when it made the announcement that it would close the Bucksport facility, there were additional approaches it could have applied, which have been used in shutdowns—including some in pre-WARN years when no advance notice was required. The Greencastle, Indiana, worker terminations serve as an illustration of the possibilities.

IBM Closure in Greencastle, Indiana

In November 1986, IBM announced the closure of its Indiana parts-distribution center, which employed 985 workers. It offered all employees transfers to other IBM operations. IBM, which had been in Greencastle for 33 years, would begin the facility phase-down within 30 days. In announcing the closure, IBM offered to donate the 350,000-square-foot facility and its 234 acres of property to the city, plus provide $1.5 million to help offset the loss of tax revenue. In addition, IBM said it would assign an executive to work full-time with the city to locate a new employer for the site.

The IBM spokesman said the company would pay moving expenses for employees who relocated, and if they could not sell their homes, IBM would purchase them. Those who did not relocate would be eligible for up to $5,000 from IBM for retraining expenses, and the company would operate an outplacement service to help them find new jobs. If an employee found a job in a city some distance away, IBM would pay the increased costs of commuting for one year. Those resigning would receive twice the normal separation allowance, up to a maximum of two years' worth of pay. IBM would continue current levels of corporate and employee United Way contributions for three years (Schoch 1986, pp. 1, 10).

Of the 985 IBM employees at Greencastle, approximately 400 retired, 500 relocated, and fewer than 50 resigned. Within 18 months, a plastic injection molding company had built a 200,000-square-foot facility on the former IBM grounds for 200 employees; another 100,000-square-foot facility had been built for 260 workers manufacturing seat covers; and a distributor of women's apparel had created 300 more jobs in the former IBM facility. In 1988, three other employers brought 250 positions to Greencastle. The local paper's editor trumpeted the news about the flock of arrivals (Bernsee 1989). Gutchess (1985) gives multiple examples of each of six strategies to assist displaced workers and maximize employment security in a community: 1) guarantees and other no-layoff policies, 2) employment buffering strategies, 3) voluntary workforce reductions, 4) worker-oriented adjustment strategies, 5) easing the adjustment to technological change, and 6) job replacement strategies. Regarding the last, she says, a company uses its funds and expertise to help new enterprises start up in its old location, providing jobs for either its own laid-off employees or others in the community.

Ways for a Company to Provide Help for Displaced Workers

"Beyond the economic impact," writes Minchin (2006, p. 45), "the plant closure also caused severe psychological and emotional problems for many workers, who compared the loss of their jobs to the death of a close relative." Assistance from the company and state or federal programs can relieve workers and their families from bearing the brunt of job loss. This help, Minchin says, can include the following six measures:

1) After the announcement of closure, some workers will be able to find reemployment quickly, but in order to receive separation pay (or some other company benefit) they will be tied to work until the closure. For some, the new job will no longer be available to them if they are unable to start work immediately. Companies could help workers obtain reemployment by having a flexible time for release rather than requiring all workers to remain until the actual closure. Staggering their terminations is also helpful when large numbers of employees will be terminated, since most local labor markets cannot handle the release of a large number of workers at one time.

2) Was career counseling available during the last 60 days of operation at the Bucksport mill? If not, it could have been useful for those interested in retraining. For dislocated workers wishing to remain in the paper industry, assistance in making contacts with other companies could be provided, along with letters of recommendation.

3) Did Verso provide assistance to those who would retire at the closure? Were Verso Bucksport human resources staff available to provide information on insurance, financial management, or retirement options to employees? All of these matters could potentially be useful to those anticipating retirement.

4) Counseling on a host of topics, including maximizing prospects for employment, retirement options, obtaining unemployment benefits, and the need for support while seeking employment, could be offered in the weeks preceding job loss. While this might come most easily from the company's human resources personnel, it could also be provided by contracting with consultants, or in cooperation with local union leaders.

5) Extending the length of time between the closure announcement and the actual day of shutdown beyond the 60-day minimum required by law could allow workers to get certification training, complete a General Educational Development (GED) certification, and learn interviewing skills.

6) A mill in financial difficulties can involve managers and work-ers in taking the initiative to become problem solvers to avoid closure (Sirkin and Stalk 1990). Verso did not involve its Bucksport employees in problem solving, possibly because the company may have been more interested in closing the mill.

These are all steps companies can take so as not to leave communi-ties and workers in the lurch. The lack of employer involvement, prior to termination, in helping employees facing dislocation is a missed opportunity for all involved.

Notes

1. While the Androscoggin Mill in Jay is currently nonunion, it was, until 1988, Local 14 of the United Paperworkers International Union. The mill site in Jay has been the site of environmental activism, with environmental issues becoming integrated into other union issues. According to Brucher (2011, p. 109),

> United Paperworkers International Union Local 14 and International Brotherhood of Firemen and Oilers Local 246 went on strike at the Andro-scoggin Mill in a refusal to grant International Paper concessions on wages, work rules, and outsourcing. In the end, however, the strike was about more than economic issues. Union members exposed both International Paper's poor environmental record and the state's inability to regulate the mill. This message found resonance in the community as the mill continued to illegally pollute the region's air and water. The worst occurrence, the 5 February 1988 chlorine dioxide gas leak, spurred the formation of Citizens Against Poison.

> The town of Jay has used a local environmental control law to push for pen-alties against International Paper, including a 1993 violation of its air emissions permit, for which the company incurred a $394,000 penalty.

> Minchin (2004) goes into more detail about the 1987 strike at Jay, Maine; Lock Haven, Pennsylvania; and De Pere, Wisconsin.

2. John Schmid, e-mail message to authors, November 15, 2014.

Appendix A
2012 Confidential Survey of Workers Formerly Employed by Verso in Bucksport, Maine, and Sartell, Minnesota

This questionnaire is part of a study to find out more about the adjustment needs of workers in the paper industry where a downsizing and job termination has occurred. We are assessing the needs of workers from two Verso facilities in Minnesota and Maine where job loss took place at nearly the same time. While we want to know how we—as neighbors and citizens—can minimize the problems faced by dislocated workers, regardless of age, we are also interested in any unique adjustment needs of paper mill workers. We ask for your help in providing information that will help us learn more, and thus, ultimately, be able to help others who might be confronted with economic dislocation.

We have the support of labor and state offices in both Minnesota and Maine to help us contact you, and this questionnaire is being mailed by one of those organizations. While they support our research, they do not provide funding. Other funding allows us to pay you the enclosed $10 for your participation, which is a token of our appreciation. And if you are interested in the results, we will send you a summary of what we learn; just check the box at the bottom of the page.

We ask that you provide your name and address below, then complete the balance of the questionnaire and return it in the enclosed stamped addressed envelope. Note that all information you provide is confidential. Any questions that don't apply to you/your situation, or that you don't want to answer, just leave blank. There are no right or wrong answers; we are interested in your response.

Whether you live in Maine or Minnesota, we suspect you're aware of the many paper mill closures or personnel reductions that have taken place in recent years. As researchers, we are hopeful that our analysis of the information that you help provide will be useful to those in the paper industry who might be displaced in the future, or useful for any displaced workers. The purpose of this study is to learn more about the adjustment to job termination after an extended recession. Of particular interest to us is (1) your attachment to your present home and locale, and (2) your interest in retraining or continuing education.

Since you may have worked at the paper mill prior to the Verso acquisition, we want you to know that we're interested in your experience at the Bucksport or Sartell mill you worked in, regardless of whether it was owned by Verso or not when you started there.

Do not be put off by the number of questions; most questions can be answered by putting a circle around the number of the answer that best fits you/ your situation. If you need more space for those few questions that request that you write something, please use the back of the page. If you have questions, let us know; contact information and some information about the researchers is available at the end of the questionnaire. Thanks again.

IF NEEDED, PLEASE TELL US HOW TO REACH YOU:

Name:_____Address:_____

City, State, & Zip:_____Phone or email: _____

☐ **YES, send me a summary of the results!**

_____

FIRST, SOME QUESTIONS ABOUT YOU:
[1] Your gender: *(Circle one number.)* 1. Female   2. Male

[2] What is your marital status? *(Circle one number.)*
   1. Married
   2. Living with significant other/partner
   3. Divorced or separated
   4. Widowed
   5. Single, never married

[3] And what is the highest level that you completed in school? *(Circle one number.)*
   1. Less than a high school diploma
   2. High school diploma
   3. Some college/associate's degree or technical college degree
   4. College degree
   5. Graduate or professional training

[4] What is your age, please?   _____ years

[5] Are you presently *(Circle the number of one response, please.)*
  1. employed full-time   5. in a training/education program
  2. employed part-time   6. unemployed, looking for work
  3. retired   7. unemployed, not looking for work
  4. unable to work at present

[6] Are you renting, or do you own your home?   1. Renting   2. Own

HERE ARE SOME QUESTIONS ABOUT YOUR VERSO POSITION AND WORK:
[7] What was your job at the mill? *(i.e., operator, secretary, engineer)* _____
_____

[8] When was your last day of work at Verso? *(month/day/year)*_____

[9] How many years did you work at the paper mill? _____years

[10] Prior to this downsizing, were you ever laid off and recalled back to work at the Verso paper mill? *(Circle one number.)*   1. Yes   2. No

[11] IF YES TO QUESTION 10, How many times: 1   2   3   4 ___(other)

[12] How was it that you applied for a job at the paper mill? *(Circle one number.)*
    1. I saw an ad in the paper.
    2. Some friends told me they were hiring.
    3. Someone from my family (father, mother, brother, sister) already worked there.
    4. My training/experience was applicable to the work they did, so I applied.
    5. An extended family member worked there and encouraged me to apply.
    6. Other; please specify:_____

AND SOME QUESTIONS ABOUT RETRAINING OR EDUCATION YOU'RE INTERESTED IN:

[13] After your job at Verso ended, did you attend a training or education program to obtain new skills or help you get a new job? (1) Yes   (2) No

[14] What additional training/education do you need/want so you could obtain the work you want to do?_____
_____

[15] What would you need to be able to enter a training program? *(Check all that you would need.)*

___Paid tuition   ___Free child care
___Tuition plus stipend for books ___A means of transportation
   and equipment   ___Spouse to get a better job
___ None of the above

[16] Do you think it is necessary to upgrade your skills to get a job?
   1. Yes   2. No

ADJUSTING TO JOB LOSS:
[17] In a few words, how are things going for you now?_____
_____
_____
_____
_____

SINCE YOU LEFT VERSO, IF YOU ARE WORKING OR LOOKING FOR WORK:
[18] Between the time Verso laid you off and now, how many weeks altogether were you totally unemployed and looking for work? _____ weeks

[19] Have you had more than one job since leaving Verso? 1. Yes   2. No

[20] IF YES TO QUESTION 19: How many jobs have you had? 1 2 3 4+

[21] How long did it take you to find your first job after you left Verso?
_____weeks

[22] If you are presently employed, did you have a new job lined up by the time you separated from Verso?   1. Yes   2. No

[23] IF YES TO QUESTION 22, How did you locate this position? *(Circle the numbers of all that apply.)*
   1. Asked friends, neighbors, others about work possibilities.
   2. Looked in newspapers.
   3. Sent out resumes to several companies.
   4. Talked to people at the Workforce Center.
   5. Applied for jobs at places I thought I might like to work.
   6. Other; please specify:_____

[24] Have you received unemployment compensation after leaving Verso?
  1. Yes 2. No

[25] IF YES TO QUESTION 24: How many weeks of UC benefits did you draw?
  1. About _____weeks   2. I'm still receiving UC.

[26] IF YOU ARE RETIRED: When Verso downsized, did you retire earlier than you had planned to?   1. Yes   2. No

[27] IF MARRIED OR WITH SIGNIFICANT OTHER: As a result of losing your Verso job, did your spouse/significant other change his or her employment?
  1. My spouse/significant other was not working and did not start to work after the downsizing at Verso.
  2. My spouse/sig. other was not working but took a job after the downsizing.
  3. My spouse/sig. other was already working and continued to work at the same job after the Verso downsizing.
  4. My spouse/sig. other was already working but began to work more hours at his or her job after the Verso downsizing.
  5. My spouse/sig. other was already working but changed jobs to get more hours or higher pay after the Verso downsizing.
  6. My spouse/sig. other was already working and took a second job after the Verso downsizing.

HERE ARE SOME QUESTIONS ABOUT RELATIONSHIPS AND HOW THEY MIGHT HAVE CHANGED SINCE YOUR JOB LOSS. FOR EACH QUESTION, CIRCLE THE NUMBER OF THE ANSWER THAT FITS BEST.
[28] How has the loss of your job affected your relationship with your spouse/sig. other?
  1. I have grown closer to my spouse/significant other since the downsizing.
  2. My relationship with my spouse/significant other has not changed.
  3. My spouse/significant other and I have had some difficulties since my job loss.

[29] And how has the loss of your job affected your relations with other family members?
  1. I have grown closer to my family since the downsizing.
  2. My relationship with my family has not changed since the downsizing.
  3. I have become more distant from my family since the downsizing.

[30] Sometimes displaced workers believe prospective employers have treated them differently from other applicants. Do you believe this is true for you?
1. Yes   2. No   3. Unsure
4. Don't know because I am not applying for work

[31] IF YES TO Q. 30: Which of the following do you believe influences such treatment? *(Circle the numbers of all that apply.)*

1. Having worked at Verso   5. My union membership
2. Being an older worker   6. Being a displaced worker
3. My education level   7. Other; specify:_____
4. Earning higher wages

NOW, SOME QUESTIONS ABOUT WHERE YOU LIVE:
[32] What is the population of the community in which you live (or, if you live in the country, the community with which you most closely identify)? Approximately_____ people

[33] How long have you lived in this community? _____ years

[34] How far from your residence is it (one way) to the Verso plant? _____ miles

[35] Since the Verso downsizing, have you sold your home?   1. Yes   2. No

[36] Has your family discussed whether you should sell your home?
1. Yes   2. No

[37] Have you tried to sell your home?   1. Yes   2. No

[38] If the economy were different, would you be interested in moving?
1. Yes   2. No

[39] Have you moved since you left Verso?   1. Yes   2. No

[40] IF you have moved, why did you move? *(Check all that apply.)*
__ To be closer to family members   __ To be closer to better schools
__ To be closer to my new work   __ We were in foreclosure
__ To reduce my housing costs   __ House/apt was too large
__ Medical reasons forced relocation   __ House/apt was too small
__ I moved to a warmer climate   __ We moved to a newer home
__ Other; please specify:_____

ISSUES:

[41] What problems are you facing, or what concerns do you have at the moment? _____

_____

[42] Is there anything you expect will be a problem for you in the next 2–3 years?_____

_____

[43] Now, some months after you left Verso, how is it for you financially?
   1. No problem; I/we have retirement income.
   2. No problem, since I have found other work.
   3. It's not major, but my present income is not the same as when I was at Verso.
   4. We have to budget pretty closely to make it each month.
   5. My finances are a major problem, and my family is really struggling.
   6. We expect that we will have to apply for some kind of assistance.
   7. We are receiving some kind of assistance—i.e., fuel assistance or food stamps.

[44] How about unemployment in your area—are there good-paying jobs that you would like to have that are available in your area?   1. Yes   2. No

[45] Have you visited a Workforce Center to look for work?   1. Yes   2. No

[46] IF NO TO Q. 45: Why not?
1. I'm retired.   4. I'm waiting for a good job to come along.
2. I have been sick.   5. I'm caring for a sick family member.
3. I'm helping with child care.   6. Other:_____

IMPACTS OF THE JOB LOSS FOR YOU AND YOUR FAMILY:
[47] Has the loss of your job at Verso affected your physical health?
(Check one.)
__ Yes, I have serious health problems.
__ Yes, I have slight health problems.
__ There is no change in my physical health.
__ My health has improved some.
__ I have had considerable improvement in my health since leaving the mill.

[48] Looking back, how do you think the loss of your job at Verso affected your overall mental and emotional health? Losing my Verso job: *(Check one.)*
__ Greatly harmed my overall mental and emotional health
__ Slightly harmed my overall mental and emotional health
__ Had no real effect on my overall mental and emotional health
__ Slightly improved my overall mental and emotional health
__ Greatly improved my overall mental and emotional health

[49] From your experience, what are the three major adjustments you have had to make since leaving the paper mill?_____
_____
_____
_____

[50] If you are not working now, check the answer(s) that best fit(s) your situation:
__ I am not able to work.   __ I have given up looking for
__ I have retired.   a decent-paying position.
__ I am actively looking for work.   __ Other:_____

[51] If you have been looking for work, why do you think it is that you haven't found work? *(Check all that apply.)*
__ I think my age is against me.
__ I have rejected work because of low wages or poor work conditions.
__ My resume or interview skills need to be improved.
__ I am between jobs at the moment.
__ Finding a good fit with the right job just takes time.
__ I was retired, but now I want to work again.
__ Other; please specify:_____

[52] Since your downsizing, have you or your family done any of the following? *(Circle the numbers of all that apply.)*
   1. Obtained extra paid work
   2. Cut back on expenses generally
   3. Borrowed money from relatives
   4. Cut back on how often we eat out
   5. Pawned items
   6. Taken out a loan
   7. Not used medical services as much as needed
   8. Let some needed home repairs go
   9. Cashed in some pension/stocks

10. Cut back on driving to save money
11. Cut back on going out to movies
12. Other; please specify:_____

_____

[53] Regarding your job loss at Verso, would you say the downsizing was generally good for you or generally bad? 1. Generally good. 2. Generally bad.

[54] Then, regarding your family and the Verso downsizing, would you say the downsizing was generally good for your family or generally bad for your family?
    1. Generally good.   2. Generally bad.

[55] Please indicate why you answered as you did to the two previous questions. _____

[56] Did you ever expect that you would leave Verso through separation rather than normal retirement? *(Circle one answer.)*
    1. No, I had planned to retire from Verso.
    2. It was a possibility that Verso would have a downsizing, but I didn't think I would get caught in it.
    3. Yes, I worried about job loss from Verso a good deal.
    4. Yes, but I didn't worry about it.

[57] Has your union been helpful to you since you left Verso? *(Circle one number, please.)*
    1. No, because I haven't needed help.
    2. Yes, when I have needed help.
    3. No, not when I've needed help.
    4. No, because I've not been a union member.

[58] What could the company or the union have done to better prepare you for job loss? *(Check all that apply.)*
    __1. Provide a job club to network and help me find a job.
    __2. Offer classes on money management.
    __3. Offer classes on money management for retirement.
    __4. Offer classes to upgrade skills.
    __5. Offer classes on running your own business.
    __6. Other, please specify_____

[59] Thinking back to the time when you left Verso, which of the following reflect your feelings at that time? *(Check all that apply.)*
___1. I didn't know where to find another good job.
___2. I was upset because I had expected to retire from Verso.
___3. I was concerned about my finances, bills, etc.
___4. I was upset over the loss of fringe benefits.
___5. I was very depressed.
___6. I was relieved.
___7. I wasn't particularly concerned.
___8. I was expecting to retire then, so it was fine.
___9. Other; please specify:_____

Do you Strongly Agree, Agree, Disagree, or Strongly Disagree with the following statements? *(Circle your response for each question, nos. 60–66.)*

[60] My social life is great.   SA   A   D   SD

[61] I feel kind of worthless.   SA   A   D   SD

[62] Life goes on after Verso, and it's better!   SA   A   D   SD

[63] Since I left Verso I have missed mortgage or rent payments.
                                                                          SA   A   D   SD
[64] Since Verso I have cut back on what I buy because of limited income.
                                                                          SA   A   D   SD

[65] Over the past six months I have postponed medical or dental care because of the cost.   SA   A   D   SD

[66] Losing the Verso job was due to circumstances or factors beyond my control.   SA   A   D   SD

[67] Taking everything into account, how satisfied are you with what you are presently doing compared to working at Verso? *(Circle one.)*
    1. Very satisfied   2. Satisfied   3. Dissatisfied   4. Very dissatisfied

[68] Are you now employed part-time or full-time?
    1. Part-time 2. Full-time 3. Neither

[69] If it were a possibility, and an opportunity to go back to work at Verso came up, would you return to work there? 1. Yes 2. No

THANK YOU FOR COMPLETING THIS QUESTIONNAIRE. PLEASE CALL US OR WRITE TO US IF THERE ARE OTHER JOB LOSS CONCERNS YOU WOULD LIKE TO DISCUSS.

Dr. Rosemarie Park, 612-625-6267 (parkx002@umn.edu)
Dr. Ken Root, 763-588-4589 (kenroot@msn.com)

Dr. Park is an associate professor in organizational leadership, policy, and development at the University of Minnesota in Minneapolis, where her primary teaching and research interests are continuing education and retraining issues.

Dr. Root is a retired professor of sociology from Luther College, Decorah, Iowa. In 2008, he and Dr. Park wrote *Forced Out: Older Workers Confront Job Loss* (First Forum Press), which was based on their three-year study of adjustment to job loss by displaced older defense industry production workers.

Appendix B
2012 Confidential Survey of Workers Displaced after the Fire at the Sartell Paper Mill

As you may know, my research colleague and I are involved in a study of the impacts of job loss for Verso workers who were downsized from the Sartell, Minnesota, and Bucksport, Maine, plants. You may know about our research because each Sartell and Bucksport worker displaced prior to the fire was given $10 along with our request to complete a job loss questionnaire. That research was ongoing at the time of the fire at the Sartell plant. With a brief delay after the fire, Verso decision makers decided to close the Sartell facility, and you and 250+ others were without work. Because we were already involved in a study of job loss among paper-mill employees, we wanted to extend our research to you and others who lost their jobs in the shutdown. Our problem was that we didn't have funding to include all those displaced.

We have recently been successful in getting funding for 100 of the Sartell employees who were displaced from work when the paper mill closed. You are one of the 100, and your name was randomly drawn from the entire roster. From this sample of 100, we will generalize our findings to the entire workforce that was terminated after the fire. Thus, your views and responses to questions reflect your situation, but are viewed as similar to those who were not drawn in the sample. This questionnaire is part of a study to find out about the adjustment needs of workers in the paper industry where a downsizing and job termination has occurred, particularly the adjustment to job termination after an extended recession. While we want to know how we—as neighbors and citizens—can minimize the problems faced by dislocated workers, regardless of age, we are also interested in any unique needs of paper mill workers. We ask for your help in providing the information that will help us learn more, and thus, ultimately, help others who might be confronted with economic dislocation. We ask that you complete and return the enclosed questionnaire.

We have the support of labor and DEED to help us contact you, and this questionnaire is being mailed by one of those organizations. While they support our research, they do not provide funding. Other funding allows us to pay you the enclosed $10 for your participation, which is a token of our appreciation. If you are interested in the results, we will send you a summary of what we learn; just check the box at the bottom of this page.

We ask that you provide your name and address below, then complete the questionnaire and return it in the enclosed stamped addressed envelope. Note that all information you provide is confidential. Any questions that don't apply to you/your situation, or that you don't want to answer, just leave blank. There are no right or wrong answers; we are interested in your response.

DO NOT BE PUT OFF BY THE NUMBER OF QUESTIONS, most questions can be answered by putting a circle around the number of the answer that best fits you/your situation. If you need more space for those few questions that request that you write something, please use the back of a page. If you have questions, let us know; contact information and some information about the researchers is available at the end of the questionnaire. THANK YOU!

IF NEEDED, PLEASE TELL US HOW TO REACH YOU:

Name: _____. Address: _____.

City, State, & Zip: _____.

Phone or email: _____.

☐ **YES, send me a summary of the results!**

Note

1. Since this questionnaire was almost identical to the one in Appendix A, we have not reprinted the actual questionnaire; just the cover letter (above). This questionnaire, which was sent to Sartell workers terminated in the closure of the mill, has the same questions (in the same order) as our questionnaire to those downsized from Sartell and Bucksport. The only difference is the wording of the question germane to the situation. For example, in the questionnaire to those displaced from Bucksport and Sartell we asked (Q10): "Prior to this downsizing, were you ever laid off and recalled back to work at the Verso paper mill?" while Q10 for those terminated at the Sartell closure was, "Prior to the mill closure, were you ever laid off from the paper mill and recalled back to work?"

Appendix C
Methodological Considerations

In an effort to determine factors that account for differences in mill worker response to the impact of job loss for themselves and their families, we created a number of additional partial tables, based on more complete tables in Chapter 4. To aid in determining specific influences, we ran cross-tabulations between only two sets of data from these complete tables. For instance, using Table 4.5 (reproduced here as Appendix Table C.1), we compared only the frequencies of the data sets from the Sartell and Bucksport downsizings, then the data sets for the Bucksport downsizing and those terminated in the Sartell shutdown, and finally the comparison of those downsized from Sartell with the Sartell respondents who were terminated at the mill closure. Chi square was calculated for each table to determine whether the distributions we were observing were likely to occur by chance, and if so, Somer's d, as the measure of association, was also calculated. We show only those partial tables where the chi square value was significantly different from chance and Somer's d was strong.

Table C.1 Financial Situation for Dislocated Paper Workers after Job Loss (%)

	Sartell downsized	Bucksport downsized	Terminated Sartell workers at closure
Finances are not a problem.	12	33	16
Present income is less than at Verso.	31	34	42
We have to budget closely each month.	34	21	30
Finances were a major problem/ currently receiving assistance/ or will soon apply for assistance.	24	11	12
N	89	61	64

NOTE: Columns may not sum to 100 because of rounding. Chi-square = 16.32 with 6 degrees of freedom. P is significant at < 0.01. Somers' d = −0.12.

Several variables were considered. The first was the respondents' financial situation (Table C.1), where, of the three tables that were broken out of this complete table, only the partial one comparing the downsized Sartell and downsized Bucksport data (Table C.2) was significant (chi-square = 14.26 with 3 degrees of freedom and a Somers' d value of −0.25); hence, the other two partial tables are not shown. Other partial tables included in this appendix break down the variables of health impacts, job loss impacts for the displaced worker, and job loss impacts for the worker's family. In all of the partial tables where the displaced Sartell workers were compared with those from Sartell who became job losers in the mill shutdown, there were no statistically significant differences (thus, these partial tables are also not included here), providing support for the view that the Sartell workers were much alike, regardless of when they lost their jobs. In all of the other tables, however, there were statistically significant differences, at least at the 0.01 level, and more often at the 0.001 level, with sufficiently strong measures of association.

Table C.2 indicates that the difference between those downsized from Sartell and Bucksport is significant, with Bucksport respondents much less likely to indicate finances were a problem after job loss.

Table C.2 Financial Situation for Downsized Sartell and Bucksport Workers after Job Loss

Financial situation	Sartell downsized		Bucksport downsized	
	n	%	n	%
Finances are not a problem.	11	12	20	33
Present income is less than at Verso.	28	31	21	34
We have to budget closely each month.	30	34	13	21
Finances were a major problem/ currently receiving assistance/ or will soon apply for assistance.	21	24	7	11
N	90	101	61	99

NOTE: Columns may not sum to 100 percent because of rounding. Chi-square = 14.26 with 3 degrees of freedom. P is significant at 0.01. Somers' d = −0.25.

Tables C.3 and C.4, which are broken out of Table 4.6, reiterate that the job loss impacts of mental and emotional health for Sartell workers were negative for both those downsized and those displaced at the shutdown of the Sartell mill. The mental health impacts were particularly hard on those Sartell workers who became job losers when the mill was closed.

Table C.3 Assessment of Whether Job Loss Has Affected Overall Mental and Emotional Health for Downsized Sartell and Bucksport Respondents Only

Health impacts	Sartell downsized		Bucksport downsized	
	n	%	*n*	%
Harmed mental and emotional health	45	49	18	28
No real effect	27	29	20	31
Improved my mental and emotional health	20	22	26	41
N	92	100	64	100

NOTE: Chi-square = 11.52 with 2 degrees of freedom. P is significant at 0.01. Somers' d = 0.22.

Table C.4 Assessment of Whether Job Loss Has Affected Overall Mental and Emotional Health for Terminated Sartell and Bucksport Respondents Only

Health impacts	Terminated Sartell workers at shutdown		Bucksport downsized	
	n	%	*n*	%
Harmed mental and emotional health	39	59	18	28
No real effect	16	24	20	31
Improved my mental and emotional health	11	17	26	41
N	66	100	64	100

NOTE: Chi-square = 21.86 with 2 degrees of freedom. P is significant at 0.001. Somers' d = −0.31.

While Sartell and Bucksport respondents differed in their responses as to whether their downsizing was good or bad for themselves, and for their families, it is the difference between the workers displaced by the Sartell shutdown and the workers downsized at Bucksport that is the largest. Comparison of Sartell respondents between Tables C.5 and C.6, and between Tables C.7 and C.8, confirms that the displaced workers from Sartell had the strongest negative response to job loss of the three samples.

Table C.5 Respondents' Views about Whether Their Downsizing Was Generally Good or Generally Bad for Themselves—Downsized Sartell and Bucksport Respondents Only

Was job loss good or bad for me?	Sartell downsized		Bucksport downsized	
	n	%	n	%
Job loss was "good"	30	32	36	60
Job loss was "bad"	60	67	24	40
N	90	99	60	100

NOTE: Columns may not sum to 100 percent because of rounding. Chi-square = 10.38 with 1 degree of freedom. P is significant at 0.01. Somers' d = −0.26.

Table C.6 Respondents' Views about Whether Their Job Loss Was Generally Good or Bad for Themselves—Terminated Sartell and Downsized Bucksport Respondents Only

Was job loss good or bad for me?	Terminated Sartell workers at shutdown		Bucksport downsized	
	n	%	n	%
Job loss was "good"	13	19	36	60
Job loss was "bad"	48	81	24	40
N	61	100	60	100

NOTE: Chi-square = 18.78 with 1 degree of freedom. P is significant at 0.001. Somers' d = 0.39.

Table C.7 Respondents' Views about Whether Their Downsizing Was Generally Good or Generally Bad for Their Families—Downsized Sartell and Bucksport Respondents Only

Was job loss good or bad for my family?	Sartell downsized		Bucksport downsized	
	n	%	n	%
Job loss was "good"	28	31	34	60
Job loss was "bad"	61	68	23	40
N	89	99	57	100

NOTE: Columns may not sum to 100 percent because of rounding. Chi-square = 11.30 with 1 degree of freedom. P is significant at 0.001. Somers' d = −0.28.

Table C.8 Respondents' Views about Whether Their Downsizing Was Generally Good or Bad for Their Families—Terminated Sartell and Downsized Bucksport Respondents Only

Was job loss good or bad for my family?	Terminated Sartell workers at shutdown		Bucksport downsized	
	n	%	*n*	%
Job loss was "good"	12	20	34	60
Job loss was "bad"	49	80	23	40
N	61	100	57	100

NOTE: Chi-square = 19.79 with 1 degree of freedom. P is significant at 0.001. Somers' d = 0.41.

Several plausible explanations could account for the noted differences, including the following:

1) The number of retirements differs between the Bucksport and Sartell samples, with 26 Bucksport respondents reporting they were retired, while 18 from Sartell made that statement (45 percent versus 20 percent of the samples). Retirement could account for finances not being a problem for the Bucksport respondents, whereas a displaced Sartell worker could be near retirement age but not be retired—simply looking for work.

2) While actual retirements constitute one component, it is also worth considering the data indicating respondent expectations of retirement from their Verso mill position. For those displaced from Sartell at the shutdown, 63 percent had expected to retire from Verso, which was also the view shared by 45 percent of those downsized from Sartell but only 25 percent of those downsized from Bucksport. In essence, Bucksport workers were working at the mill but didn't expect to do it for a lifelong period. It is certainly a possibility that the perception of displacement difficulties could be influenced by the desire or interest in keeping the mill job.

3) The potential for new employment could be a consideration, since we know that the majority of those who had already moved by the time of our data collection (13 of 16) were from Sartell. Furthermore, there are many more paper mills in Maine than in Minnesota (42 pulp and paper mills in Maine compared to four in Minnesota), and the opportunity for work in the same field might be a greater possibility for Bucksport workers than for any of the Sartell workers, although it might also require relocation (CPBIS 2015).

4)   The fact is that the completion rate for Bucksport respondents is the lowest of the three mill samples of displaced workers, and the possibility of response bias should be considered.

Appendix D
2013 Letter to Married Couples Formerly Employed by Verso in Sartell, Minnesota

To: Six Identified Couples

October 12, 2013

From: Ken Root

As you may know (or recall), all the workers in the Verso downsizing at Sartell and Bucksport, and a sample of 100 workers involved in the closure of the Sartell facility, have been asked to participate in a survey. The goal of that project is to assess the impact of job loss for paper mill workers, particularly after an extended recession. That project continues, and some of you who are receiving this letter have been involved by completing a mailed questionnaire.

This letter is to describe a bit more of our project and ask for your involvement—whether you have completed our questionnaire or not. The good news is that based on our earlier publications, the Upjohn Institute for Employment Research (in Kalamazoo, MI) is interested in publishing our book about this downsizing and closure. We are pleased with that prospect. I believe this is the first large study of job loss among paper mill workers, although there have been numerous paper mill shutdowns.

While there are [two] researchers involved in this study, and we are each responsible for providing leadership in creating initial drafts of various chapters, I proposed that we have a chapter where both the husband and wife are now without work as a result of the Verso downsizing and Sartell mill shutdown. It turns out that all the displaced married couples were employed at Sartell; none at Bucksport. As a job loss researcher, I know—as you know—that when an adult family member loses a job, there can be some difficult days, and sometimes those days stretch into weeks or months. However, what we don't know much about are the stresses and strains in a family when the two adults both lose their jobs, nor how those couples work through that stress. Thus, I'm interested in interviewing each couple listed above if you will let me. I think this can be done in 1–1 ½ hours in your home, or elsewhere if needed. We have funding to pay each couple a total of $50 for your time and your willingness to speak frankly about job loss issues and how you have resolved them. Whatever is ultimately written about your situation will have your approval before publication. If desired, fictitious names may be used.

I'm not sure I have all the married couples from the Sartell mill. If you know of others, please let me know who they are, and I will also contact them. And, at the moment, I don't have an address for Joe and Mary Smith—can anyone provide help?

Because I'm interested in interviewing you about the pressures of job loss when both major incomes are threatened by job loss, I will be contacting you by email or phone in the next few days to see if you are agreeable to set up an appointment. Thanks very much for considering this request.

References

Abrams, Rachel. 2014. "Verso Paper to Buy NewPage Holdings." *New York Times*, January 6. http://dealbook.nytimes.com/2014/01/06/verso-paper-to -buy-newpage-holdings/?_r=0 (accessed July 8, 2015).

Adams, Jeff, Herb N. Kessel, and Fred Maher. 1990. *The Goodyear Plant Closing: A Case Study of Worker Readjustment in Vermont*. Prepared for the Vermont Department of Employment and Training. Colchester, VT: Saint Michael's College, Center for Social Science Research.

Alexander, Steve. 2014. "Hutchinson Technology Sets More Layoffs; the Firm Will Cut 100 of Its 2,500 Jobs amid a Troubled Disk-Drive Market." *Minneapolis Star Tribune*, May 22, D:2.

Allen, Brad. 2014a. "A Job Just Ain't What It Used to Be." *Minneapolis Star Tribune*, May 25, D:5.

———. 2014b. "Rewriting Their Career Scripts." *Minneapolis Star Tribune*, July 6, D:5.

Allenspach, Kevin. 2012. "Investigations Continue at Verso Paper." *St. Cloud Times*, June 7, A:1. http://bangordailynews.com/2012/06/07/business/ officials-investigating-fire-at-minn-verso-mill-that-killed-1-and-injured -4/?ref=search (accessed October 12, 2015).

———. 2013. "Life after Verso Closure Tough for Some Workers." *St. Cloud Times*, November 3, A:1. http://insurancenewsnet.com/oarticle/2013/11/03/ Life-after-Verso-closure-tough-for-some-workers-%5BSt-Cloud-Times -Minn%5D-a-414933.html (accessed July 8, 2015).

Amano, Robert A., and R. Tiff Macklem. 1998. "Unemployment Persistence and Costly Adjustment of Labour: A Canada-U.S. Comparison." *Canadian Public Policy* 24(S1): S138–S151.

Anderson, Christopher J., and Jonas Pontusson. 2007. "Workers, Worries, and Welfare States: Social Protection and Job Insecurity in 15 OECD Countries." *European Journal of Political Research* 46(2): 211–235.

Arulampalam, Wiji, Paul Gregg, and Mary Gregory. 2001. "Unemployment Scarring." *Economic Journal* 111(475): F577–F584.

Associated Press. 2013a. "Half of Older Workers Say They're Delaying Retirement, Poll Finds." *Minneapolis Star Tribune*, October 15, A:4.

———. 2013b. "Potential Buyer of Brainerd Paper Mill Drops Out." *Minneapolis Star Tribune*, October 15. http://www.startribune.com/ printarticle/?id=227907021 (accessed June 30, 2015).

Attewell, Paul. 1999. "The Impact of Family on Job Displacement and Recovery." *Annals of the American Academy of Political and Social Science* 562(1): 66–82.

Austin, Anna. 2008. "Reinventing the Mill." *Biomass* 2(12): 22–26. http://
biomassmagazine.com/articles/2221/reinventing-the-mill (accessed June
25, 2015).

Baker, Michael, Miles Corak, and Andrew Heisz. 1998. "The Labour Market Dynamics of Unemployment Rates in Canada and the United States."
Canadian Public Policy 24(Suppl. 1): S72–S89.

Baker, Peter. 2014. "Long-Term Jobless Will Get New Help." *Minneapolis
Star Tribune*, February 1, A:1, A:10.

Batt, William L. Jr. 1983. "Canada's Good Example with Displaced Workers."
Harvard Business Review 61(4): 6–22.

Bay-Lake Regional Planning Commission, Central Upper Peninsula Plan-
ning and Development (CUPPAD) Regional Commission, and Northwest
Regional Planning Commission. 1999. *A Profile of the Paper Industry in
Wisconsin and Upper Michigan*. Washington, DC: U.S. Department of
Commerce, Economic Development Administration.

Bell, Tom. 2014. "Bankruptcy Filing Appears to End Era in Maine Paper-
making." *Portland Press Herald*, September 23. http://www.centralmaine
.com/2014/09/23/great-northern-paper-files-for-bankruptcy/ (accessed September 2, 2015).

Beller, Andrea H. 1982. "Occupational Segregation by Sex: Determinants and
Changes." *Journal of Human Resources* 17(3): 371–392.

Belz, Adam. 2013. "Cloquet Mill Turns Its Focus to Textiles." *Minneapolis Star Tribune*, November 1, D:1–D:2. http://www.highbeam.com/doc/
1G1-347988225.html (accessed August 26, 2015).

———. 2014a. "Fewer U.S. Job Seekers Giving Up the Search." *Minneapolis
Star Tribune*, July 4, D:1–D:2.

———. 2014b. "May Job Gains Best Yet This Year." *Minneapolis Star Tribune*, June 20, A:1, A:9.

———. 2014c. "Minnesota's Scars Still Show Despite Job Surge." *Minneapolis Star Tribune*, June 22, D:1, D:8.

———. 2014d. "State Gained 8,500 Jobs in June." *Minneapolis Star Tribune*,
July 18, D:1–D:2.

———. 2014e. "State Shed 4,200 Jobs in April." *Minneapolis Star Tribune*,
May 16, D:1–D:2.

Bernsee, Eric. 1989. "It's Greencastle, Putnam County . . . with Six New Industries in Three Years, Area No Longer State's Best-Kept Secret." *Greencastle
Banner Graphic*, September 12, A:1, A:12.

Beswick, Aaron. 2013. "For Sale: Well-Used Paper Maker." *Halifax Chronicle
Herald*, November 27. http://thechronicleherald.ca/novascotia/1170406
-for-sale-well-used-paper-maker (accessed August 13, 2015).

Boak, Josh. 2014. "Just 11% of U.S. Long-Term Unemployed Find Jobs." *Minneapolis Star Tribune*, March 21, D:2.

Boushey, Heather. 2011. *Not Working: Unemployment among Married Couples. Unemployment Continues to Plague Families in Today's Tough Job Market*. Washington, DC: Center for American Progress. www .americanprogress.org/issues/labor/report/2011/05/06/9620/not-working -unemployment (accessed August 4, 2015).

Brainerd Dispatch. 2002. "From Northwest Paper Co. to Sappi Ltd." June 21, A:1.

Brechling, Frank, and Louise Laurence. 1995. *Permanent Job Loss and the U.S. System of Financing Unemployment Insurance*. Kalamazoo, MI: W.E. Upjohn Institute for Employment Research.

Brown, S. Kathi. 2006. *Attitudes toward Work and Job Security*. AARP Strategic Issues Research. Washington, DC: American Association of Retired Persons. http://assets.aarp.org/rgcenter/econ/work_2006.pdf (accessed June 26, 2015).

Brucher, William. 2011. "From the Picket Line to the Playground: Labor, Environmental Activism, and the International Paper Strike in Jay, Maine." *Labor History* 52(1): 95–116.

Bureau of Labor Statistics (BLS). 2003. *Local Area Unemployment Statistics: Alternative Measures of Labor Underutilization for States, 2003*. Washington, DC: Bureau of Labor Statistics. http://data.bls.gov/cgi-bin/print.pl/lau/stalt03.htm (accessed October 29, 2015).

———. 2009. *Local Area Unemployment Statistics*: *Alternative Measures of Labor Underutilization for States, 2009*. Washington, DC: Bureau of Labor Statistics. http://data.bls.gov/cgi-bin/print.pl/lau/stalt09q4.htm (accessed August 18, 2015).

———. 2011. *Local Area Unemployment Statistics: Alternative Measures of Labor Underutilization for States, 2011*. http://data.bls.gov/cgi-bin/print.pl/lau/stalt11q4.htm (accessed October 29, 2015).

———. 2013. *Current Employment Statistics—CES (National). Archived Current Employment Statistics Monthly Highlights*. Washington, DC: Bureau of Labor Statistics. http://www.bls.gov/ces/ceshilightsarch.htm (accessed October 20, 2015).

———. 2014. *Local Area Unemployment Statistics: Alternative Measures of Labor Underutilization for States, Third Quarter of 2013 through Second Quarter of 2014 Averages*. Washington, DC: Bureau of Labor Statistics. http://data.bls.gov/cgi-bin/print.pl/lau/stalt.htm (accessed October 29, 2015).

———. 2015a. *Databases, Tables, and Calculators by Subject: Mass Layoff Statistics*. Washington, DC: Bureau of Labor Statistics. http://data.bls.gov/

timeseries/MLUMS00NN0015003?data_tool=XGtable (accessed October 4, 2015).

———. 2015b. *Mass Layoff Statistics*. Washington, DC: Bureau of Labor Statistics. http://www.bls.gov/mls/ (accessed October 27, 2015).

———. 2015c. *Databases, Tables, and Calculators by Subject: Quarterly Census of Employment and Wages*. Washington, DC: Bureau of Labor Statistics. http://data.bls.gov/timeseries/ENUUS000205322?data_tool=XGtable (accessed November 16, 2015).

Burgard, Sarah A., Jennie E. Brand, and James S. House. 2007. "Toward a Better Estimation of the Effect of Job Loss on Health." *Journal of Health and Social Behavior* 48 (4): 369–384.

———. 2009. "Perceived Job Insecurity and Worker Health in the United States." *Social Science and Medicine* 69(5): 777–785.

Burtless, Gary. 1998. "Relative Unemployment in Canada and the United States: An Assessment." *Canadian Public Policy* 24(Suppl. 1): S254–S263.

Business Wire. 2011. "Verso Paper Corp. Announces Permanent Shutdown of Three Paper Machines." Business Wire, October 11. http://www.business wire.com/news/home/20111011005480/en/Verso-Paper-Corp.-Announces -Permanent-Shutdown-Paper#.VZQnu0bQO_s (accessed July 1, 2015).

Canadian Press. 2011. "Nova Scotia Will Help Market NewPage Paper Mill Products, Premier Says." *Globe and Mail*, August 23. http://www.theglobe andmail.com/news/national/nova-scotia-will-help-market-newpage-paper -mill-products-premier-says/article4200180/ (accessed August 13, 2015).

Canning, Rob. 2014. "Verso Paper Buys NewPage, Paper Mill Closings Unlikely." WKMS Radio and Associated Press, January 6. http://wkms.org/ post/verso-paper-buys-newpage-paper-mill-closings-unlikely (accessed September 2, 2015).

Card, David E., and W. Craig Riddell. 1993. "A Comparative Analysis of Unemployment in Canada and the United States." In *Small Differences That Matter: Labor Markets and Income Maintenance in Canada and the United States*, David Card and Richard B. Freeman, eds. Chicago: University of Chicago Press, pp. 149–189.

Carnevale, Anthony P., Nicole Smith, and Jeff Strohl. 2015. *Help Wanted: Projections of Jobs and Education Requirements through 2018*. Technical summary. Washington, DC: Georgetown University, Center on Education and the Workforce. https://cew.georgetown.edu/wp-content/uploads/help _wanted_technical_appx.pdf (accessed August 11, 2015).

Carrington, William J., and Asad Zaman. 1994. "Interindustry Variation in the Costs of Job Displacement." *Journal of Labor Economics* 12(2): 243–275.

CBC News. 2011. "Bowater Mill Requests Discount on Power." CBC News,

October   24.   http://www.cbc.ca/news/canada/nova-scotia/bowater-mill
-requests-discount-on-power-1.1054394 (accessed August 13, 2015).

Center for Paper Business and Industry Studies (CPBIS). 2012. "Adapting to
the New Reality: Fluff Pulp." *Newsletter of the Center for Paper Business
and Industry Studies* 12(5): 1–2.

———. 2013a. "Statistics Corner: Third Quarter 2013 Financial Results."
Newsletter of the Center for Paper Business and Industry Studies 13(9):
8–9.

———. 2013b. "Trend Indicators from Industry Intelligence Inc." *Newsletter
of the Center for Paper Business and Industry Studies* 13(8): 1.

———. 2014a. "Trend Indicators from Industry Intelligence Inc." *Newsletter
of the Center for Paper Business and Industry Studies* 14(1): 2–3.

———. 2014b. "Trend Indicators from Industry Intelligence Inc." *Newsletter
of the Center for Paper Business and Industry Studies* 14(8): 2–4.

———. 2015. *Mills Online*. Atlanta, GA: Center for Paper Business and Industry Studies. http://www.cpbis.gatech.edu/data/mills-online-new (accessed
November 13, 2015).

Center for Workforce Research and Information. 2015a. *Labor Market Area
Definitions*. Augusta, ME: Center for Workforce Research and Information. www.maine.gov/labor/cwri/LMADefinitions.html (accessed August
6, 2015).

———. 2015b. *Demographics of Employment and Unemployment in Maine:
Table: Labor Force Participation and Employment Status by Age and Gender, 2000–2014*. Augusta, ME: Center for Workforce Research and Information. http://www.maine.gov/labor/cwri/cps.html (accessed November
18, 2015).

Chan, Sewin, and Ann Huff Stevens. 2001. "Job Loss and Employment Patterns of Older Workers." *Journal of Labor Economics* 19(2): 484–521.

Christensen, Laurits Rolf, and Richard E. Caves. 1997. "Cheap Talk and
Investment Rivalry in the Pulp and Paper Industry." *Journal of Industrial
Economics* 45(1): 47–73.

Cooper, David. 2014. "Long-Term Unemployment Far Exceeds Pre-Great
Recession Levels in Virtually Every State." Economic Snapshot. Washington, DC: Economic Policy Institute. http://www.epi.org/publication/long
-term-unemployment-record-levels-virtually/ (accessed August 11, 2015).

Corak, Miles. 2012. "The Gap between U.S. and Canadian Unemployment
Rates Is Bigger than It Appears." *Economics for Public Policy* (blog), May
4.   http://milescorak.com/2012/05/04/the-gap-between-us-and-canadian
-unemployment-rates-is-bigger-than-it-appears (accessed August 13, 2015).

Cottell, Philip L. 1974. *Occupational Choice and Employment Stability among*

Forest Workers. Bulletin No. 82. New Haven, CT: Yale University School of Forestry and Environmental Studies.

Davis, Steven J., and Till von Wachter. 2011. "Recessions and the Costs of Job Loss." Milton Friedman Institute Working Paper No. 2011-009. Chicago: University of Chicago. https://econresearch.uchicago.edu/sites/econ research.uchicago.edu/files/BFI_2011-009.pdf (accessed June 26, 2015).

Department of Finance Canada. 2014. *Jobs Report: The State of the Canadian Labour Market.* Ottawa, Canada: Department of Finance Canada.

DePass, Dee. 2013. "$2 Billion Sale Puts Boise's International Falls Plant at Risk." *Minneapolis Star Tribune,* September 17, D:1–D:2. http://www .startribune.com/2-billion-sale-puts-boise-s-international-falls-plant-at -risk/223964661/ (accessed June 26, 2015).

———. 2014a. "State Receives Federal Training Grant." *Minneapolis Star Tribune,* September 30, D:2.

———. 2014b. "State's Factories in High Gear." *Minneapolis Star Tribune,* July 2, D:1–D:2.

Eaton, Adrienne E., and Jill Kriesky. 1994. "Collective Bargaining in the Paper Industry: Developments since 1979." In *Contemporary Collective Bargaining in the Private Sector,* Paula B. Voos, ed. Madison, WI: Industrial Relations Research Association, pp. 25–62.

Eder, Steve. 2008. "WARN Act Falls Short as Jobs Vanish." *Toledo Blade,* December 22. http://www.toledoblade.com/business/2008/12/22/WARN -Act-falls-short-as-jobs-vanish.html (accessed July 13, 2015).

Eichacker, Charles. 2014. "Out-of-State Paper Companies Target Verso Workers." *Ellsworth American,* November 12. http://www.ellsworthamerican .com/featured/state-paper-companies-target-verso-workers (accessed September 2, 2015).

Farber, Henry S. 2011. "Job Loss in the Great Recession: Historical Perspective from the Displaced Workers Survey, 1984–2010." IZA Discussion Paper No. 5696. Bonn, Germany: Institute for the Study of Labor.

Feyder, Susan. 2012. "Cloquet Paper Mill Plans Switcheroo." *Minneapolis Star Tribune,* March 12. http://www.paperadvance.com/news/industry -news/652-cloquet-paper-mill-plans-switcheroo.html (accessed June 26, 2015).

FileUnemployment.org. 2015. *Unemployment Benefits Comparison by State.* Washington, DC: FileUnemployment.org. http://fileunemployment.org/ unemployment-benefits-comparison-by-state (accessed November 6, 2015).

Foroohar, Rana. 2014. "The Flat-Paycheck Recovery." *Time* 183(1): 34.

Forster, Julie. 2011. "Stacking Up Temporary Jobs Has Become a Long-Term Situation for Many Workers." *St. Paul Pioneer Press,* December 24. http:// www.twincities.com/ci_19610933 (accessed August 18, 2015).

Frey, Dianne. 1986. "A Survey of Sole Parent Workforce Barriers." Discussion Paper No. 12. Canberra, Australia: Department of Social Security.

Fryer, David, and Peter Warr. 1984. "Unemployment and Cognitive Difficulties." *British Journal of Clinical Psychology* 23(1): 67–69.

Gabriel, Jackie. 2014. "Small Town Resilience through Industrial Restructuring in America's Heartland: Muscatine, Iowa, Five Years after the Grain Processing Corporation Lockout." Paper presented at the seventy-seventh annual meeting of the Midwest Sociological Society, held in Omaha, NE, April 3–6.

Getman, Julius. 1998. *The Betrayal of Local 14: Paperworkers, Politics, and Permanent Replacements.* Ithaca, NY: ILR Press.

Giebelhaus, August, and Steven Usselman. 2005. *Policy, Organization, and Innovation in American Pulp and Paper since 1914: Historical Perspectives on Contemporary Problems.* Final Report for Center for Paper Business and Industry Studies. Atlanta, GA: Georgia Institute of Technology.

Globe and Mail. 2012a. "AbitibiBowater Shareholders Approve New Resolute Forest Products Name." *Globe and Mail,* May 23. http://www.theglobe andmail.com/globe-investor/abitibibowater-shareholders-approve-new -resolute-forest-products-name/article4204061/ (accessed July 8, 2015).

———. 2012b. "Bowater Mill Closing Indefinitely in Nova Scotia." *Globe and Mail,* June 15. http://www.theglobeandmail.com/report-on -business/bowater-mill-closing-indefinitely-in-nova-scotia/article4265759/ (accessed August 13, 2015).

Gowan, Mary A. 2012. "Employability, Well-Being, and Job Satisfaction Following a Job Loss." *Journal of Managerial Psychology* 27(8): 780–798.

Graffagna, David. 1993. *On Compensation: Employer Experience in Work Force Reductions.* Lincolnshire, IL: Hewitt Associates.

Grass, Eric, and Roger Hayter. 1989. "Employment Change during Recession: The Experience of Forest Product Manufacturing Plants in British Columbia, 1981–1985." *Canadian Geographer* 33(3): 240–252.

Gray, David, and Gilles Grenier. 1998. "Jobless Durations of Displaced Workers: A Comparison of Canada and the United States." *Canadian Public Policy* 24(Suppl. 1): S152–S169.

Grayson, J. Paul. 1985. "The Closure of a Factory and Its Impact on Health." *International Journal of Health Services* 15(1): 69–93.

Greater St. Cloud Development Corporation. 2014. *Workforce Data.* St. Cloud, MN: Greater St. Cloud Development Corporation. http://greaterstcloud .com/businesses/saint-cloud-mn-workforce-climate/ (accessed August 11, 2015).

Green, David A., and W. Craig Riddell. 1993. "The Economic Effects of Unemployment Insurance in Canada: An Empirical Analysis of UI Disentitlement." *Journal of Labor Economics* 11(1, Part 2): S96–S147.

Greenstone, Michael, and Adam Looney. 2011. *Unemployment and Earnings Losses: The Long-Term Impacts of the Great Recession on American Workers*. Hamilton Project. Washington, DC: Brookings Institution. http://www.hamiltonproject.org/files/downloads_and_links/110411_jobs_green stone_looney.pdf (accessed July 9, 2015).

Gutchess, Jocelyn F. 1985. *Employment Security in Action: Strategies That Work*. New York: Pergamon Press.

Hale, Alan S. 2014. "Shutdown at Fort Frances Paper Mill Puts 150 Jobs in Jeopardy." *Kenora Daily Miner and News*, January 15. http://www.kenora dailyminerandnews.com/2014/01/15/shutdown-at-fort-frances-paper-mill -puts-150-jobs-in-jeopardy (accessed June 26, 2015).

Harry, Jan A., and Marika Tiggemann. 1992. "The Psychological Impact of Work Re-Entry Training for Female Sole Parents." *Australian Journal of Social Issues* 27(2): 75–91.

Helliwell, John F. 1998. "The Unemployment Gap: Results, New Questions, and Policy Implications." *Canadian Public Policy* 24(Suppl. 1): S264–S270.

Hickey, Sue. 2012. "Former Mill Worker Reflects on Closure after Three Years." *Telegram*, March 29. www.thetelegram.com/News/Local/2012 -03-29/article-2942197/Former-mill-worker-reflects (accessed August 13, 2015).

High, Steven, and David W. Lewis. 2007. *Corporate Wasteland: The Landscape and Memory of Deindustrialization*. Ithaca, NY: ILR Press.

Hoey, Dennis. 2014. "Another Blow to Maine's Paper Industry: Verso Paper to Close Bucksport Mill Dec. 1, Displacing More than 500 Workers." *Portland Press Herald*, October 1. http://www.pressherald.com/2014/10/01/ verso-paper-to-close-bucksport-mill-displacing-500 (accessed September 2, 2015).

Holland, Craig. 2008. *A Skills Transferability Analysis to Support Reemployment and Retraining Plans Prepared for the Former Workers of Fraser Paper*. Augusta, ME: Maine Department of Labor, Center for Workforce Research and Information.

House, Jonathan, and Ben Leubsdorf. 2014. "The Job Picture Is Improving, but with Caveats." The Aggregator. *Minneapolis Star Tribune*, July 6, D:8.

Hsu, Tiffany. 2014. "Poll: Many Jobless Americans Are Not Looking for Work." *Minneapolis Star Tribune*, May 25, D:3.

Hughlett, Mike. 2014. "General Mills to Cut 700 More Jobs." *Minneapolis Star Tribune*, September 30, D:1–D:2.

Hunter, Helen. 1955. Innovation, Competition, and Locational Changes in the Pulp and Paper Industry: 1880–1950." *Land Economics* 31(4): 314–327.

Jackson, David. 2012. "Province Buys Bowater Lands." *Halifax Chronicle Herald*, December 10. http://thechronicleherald.ca/novascotia/237791 -province-buys-bowater-lands (accessed August 13, 2015).

Jensen, Karl P. 1999. "Fast Track Installation Brings New PM Online in Seven Months: Oconto Falls Mill Returns to Its Roots with Tissue PM Installation." *Pulp and Paper* 73(1): 78. www.risiinfo.com/db_area/archive/p_p _mag/1999/9901/focus3.htm (accessed October 30, 2015).

Jin, Robert L., Chandrakant P. Shah, and Tomislav J. Svoboda. 1997. "The Impact of Unemployment on Health: A Review of the Evidence." *Journal of Public Health Policy* 18(3): 275–301.

Johnson, Joe. 2013. *The State of Working Maine in 2013*. Augusta, ME: Maine Center for Economic Policy. http://www.mecep.org/wp-content/ uploads/2013/11/State_of_Working_Maine_2013_fullreport_11-25-2013 _Joel_FINAL-3.pdf (accessed August 11, 2015).

Johnson, Joel. 2014. "41,600 Mainers Are Working Part-Time Because of the Bad Economy." *Maine Center for Economic Policy Blog*, January 31. http:// blog.mecep.org/2014/01/41600-mainers-are-working-part-time-because -of-the-bad-economy (accessed August 6, 2015).

Johnson, Kirk. 2013b. "A Mill's Fate Weighs Heavy on a Washington Timber Town." *New York Times*, April 15, A:10.

Joint Economic Committee Democratic Staff (JEC). 2013. "Women in Manufacturing." U.S. Congress. Joint Economic Committee. 113th Cong., 1st sess., pp. 1–7.

Jones, Charisse. 2009. "Sour U.S. Economy Has Put 40% of Americans on Edge." *USA Today*, March 13, A:1. http://usatoday30.usatoday.com/print edition/news/20090313/1amoneyworries13_cv.art.htm (accessed July 9, 2015).

Jones, Jeffrey M. 2012. *Benefit Reductions Remain Top Worry for American Workers*. Gallup.com, August 22. http://www.gallup.com/poll/156821/ benefit-reductions-remain-top-worry-american-workers.aspx (accessed October 30, 2015).

Jones, Stephen R. G., and W. Craig Riddell. 1998. "Gross Flows of Labour in Canada and the United States." *Canadian Public Policy* 24(Suppl. 1): S103–S120.

Kanell, Michael. 2014. "Part-Time Ranks Are Falling, but Only Slowly." *Minneapolis Star Tribune*, May 7, D:1–D:2.

Karren, Ronald, and Kim Sherman. 2012. "Layoffs and Unemployment Discrimination: A New Stigma." *Journal of Managerial Psychology* 27(8): 848–863.

Kessel, Herbert, and Frederick Maher. 1991. *Worker Readjustment to G.E. Layoffs*. Prepared for the Vermont Department of Employment and Training. Colchester, VT: Saint Michael's College, Center for Social Science Research.

Kletzer, Lori G. 2000. Trade and Job Loss in U.S. Manufacturing, 1979–1994. In *The Impact of International Trade on Wages*, Robert C. Feenstra, ed. Chicago: University of Chicago Press, pp. 349–396.

Kolberg, William H., ed. 1983. *The Dislocated Worker: Preparing America's Workforce for New Jobs*. Cabin John, MD: Seven Locks Press.

Krueger, Alan B., Judd Cramer, and David Cho. 2014. "Are the Long-Term Unemployed on the Margins of the Labor Market?" *Brookings Papers on Economic Activity* 2014(Spring): 229–299.

Krumrie, Matt. 2014. "Ask Matt: I Lost My Job. Now What?" Ask Matt, *Minneapolis Star Tribune*, August 3, K:5.

Kuhn, Peter, and A. Leslie Robb. 1998. "Shifting Skill Demand and the Canada-U.S. Unemployment Gap: Evidence from Prime-Age Men." *Canadian Public Policy* 24(Suppl. 1): S170–S191.

Leana, Carrie R., and Daniel C. Feldman. 1995. "Finding New Jobs after a Plant Closing: Antecedents and Outcomes of the Occurrence and Quality of Reemployment." *Human Relations* 48(12): 1381–1401.

Lee, Don, and Tiffany Hsu. 2014. "Finally, Big Gains in Hiring Are Back." *Minneapolis Star Tribune*, July 4, A:1, A:5.

Lee, Marlene A., and Nadwa Mossaad. 2010. *Assessing Comparability of Available Data on Characteristics of the Science, Technology, Engineering, and Mathematics Workforce: Canada, United Kingdom, and United States*. Washington, DC: Population Reference Bureau. http://www.prb.org/pdf10/comparability-stem.pdf (accessed August 13, 2015).

Leighton, Julia L., Melissa R. Roderick, and Nancy Folbre. 1981. *Pick Up Your Tools and Leave, the Mill Is Down: Plant Closings in Maine, 1971—1981*. Brunswick, ME: Bowdoin College, Department of Economics.

Levine, Judith A. 2009. "It's a Man's Job, or So They Say: The Maintenance of Sex Segregation in a Manufacturing Plant." *Sociological Quarterly* 50(2): 257–282.

Lippman, Daniel. 2013. "A Long View on Employment—Where Growth Is Coming." *Minneapolis Star Tribune*, September 15, D:6.

Little, Craig B. 1976. "Technical-Professional Unemployment: Middle-Class Adaptability to Personal Crisis." *Sociological Quarterly* 17(2): 262–274.

Loveland, George. 2005. *Under the Workers' Caps: From Champion Mill to Blue Ridge Paper*. Knoxville, TN: University of Tennessee Press.

Luo, Michael. 2010. "At Closing Plant, Ordeal Included Heart Attacks." *New York Times*, February 24. www.nytimes.com/2010/02/25/us/25stress.html?ref=todayspaper&pagewanted=print (accessed June 26, 2015).

Lupo, Crystal, and Conner Bailey. 2011. "Corporate Structure and Community

Size: Factors Affecting Occupational Community within the Pulp and Paper Industry." *Society and Natural Resources* 24(5): 425–438.

Lusardi, Annamaria. 2012. "Numeracy, Financial Literacy, and Financial Decision-Making." *Numeracy* 5(1): 1–12. http://scholarcommons.usf.edu/ numeracy/vol5/iss1/art2/ (accessed November 30, 2015).

MacDougall, Ian, ed. 2009. "Through the Mill: Personal Recollections by Veteran Men and Women Penicuik Paper Mill Workers." *Journal of the Edinburgh Bibliographical Society* 4(2009): 97–99.

Maine Pulp and Paper Association. 2013a. *Facts about Maine's Pulp and Paper Industry*. Augusta, ME: Maine Pulp and Paper Association. http:// www.pulpandpaper.org/ (accessed June 30, 2015).

———. 2013b. *History of Papermaking*. Augusta, ME: Maine Pulp and Paper Association. http://www.pulpandpaper.org/history.shtml (accessed June 29, 2015).

Mainecareercenter.com. 2013. *Workforce Investment Act*. Augusta, ME: maine careercenter.com. http://www.mainecareercenter.com/services-programs/ training/workforce/index.shtml (accessed July 13, 2015).

Maine.gov. 2015a. *Special Programs for Laid-Off Workers*. Augusta, ME: maine.gov. http://www.maine.gov/labor/unemployment/specialprograms .html#federal (accessed July 13, 2015).

———. 2015b. *Top 25 Private Employers in Maine by Average Monthly Employment by County (4th quarter 2014)*. Augusta, ME: maine.gov. http://www .maine.gov/labor/cwri/publications/pdf/MaineCountyTop25Employers.pdf (accessed July 13, 2015).

Marcotty, Josephine. 2013. "Forests in State Give Way to Farmland; Some See the Trend as a Threat to Water Quality and Wildlife." *Minneapolis Star Tribune*, October 26, A:1, A:7.

Marohn, Kirsti. 2012. "Paper Mill Industry throughout State Undergoes Changes." *St. Cloud Times*, August 3, A:1.

Marotte, Bertrand. 2011. "AbitibiBowater: From Behemoth to Lean and Green." *Globe and Mail*, December 26. http://www.theglobeandmail.com/ report-on-business/industry-news/energy-and-resources/abitibibowater -from-behemoth-to-lean-and-green/article1357415/ (accessed June 30, 2015).

Mawhiney, Anne-Marie, and Jan Lewis. 1999. "Local Service Providers' Perceptions of the Effects of Mass Layoffs." In *Boom Town Blues. Elliot Lake: Collapse and Revival in a Single Industry Community*, Anne-Marie Mawhiney and Jane Pitblado, eds. Toronto: Dundurn, pp. 170–187.

Mawhiney, Anne-Marie, and Jane Pitblado, eds. 1999. *Boom Town Blues. Elliot Lake: Collapse and Revival in a Single-Industry Community*. Toronto: Dundurn.

Mayberry, Dan. 2005. "Shocked, Only Not: False-Positive Cases of Employment Decline." Federal Reserve Bank of Minneapolis *Fedgazette* 2005(November): 8.

McCarthy, Patrick. 2014. "Productivity in the Pulp and Paper Industry." *Newsletter of the Center for Paper Business and Industry Studies* 14(4): 1–2.

McCubbin, Hamilton I., and Joan M. Patterson. 1981. "Family Stress and Adaptation to Crises: A Double ABCX Model of Family Behavior." Paper presented at the annual meeting of the National Council on Family Relations, held in Milwaukee, WI, October 13–17.

McDonough, Tom. 2014a. "Trend Indicators from Industry Intelligence Inc." *Newsletter of the Center for Paper Business and Industry Studies* 13(10): 2.

———. 2014b. "Statistics Corner: Employment in Pulp, Paper, and Board Mills." *Newsletter of the Center for Paper Business and Industry Studies* 14(1): 2.

McHugh, Rick, Nancy E. Segal, and Jeffrey B. Wenger. 2002. *Laid Off and Left Out—Part-Time Workers and Unemployment Insurance Eligibility: How States Treat Part-Time Workers and Why UI Programs Should Include Them*. New York: National Employment Law Project.

Miller, Claire Cain. 2012. "Google Deal Gives Publishers a Choice: Digitize or Not." *New York Times*, October 4. http://www.nytimes.com/2012/10/05/technology/google-and-publishers-settle-over-digital-books.html (accessed June 30, 2015).

Miller, Paul W. 1997. "The Burden of Unemployment on Family Units: An Overview." *Australian Economic Review* 30(1): 16–30.

Mills, Glenn. 2013. "Maine's Workforce Challenges." PowerPoint Presentation to State Workforce Investment Board. Augusta, ME: Center for Workforce Research and Information.

Minchin, Timothy J. 2004. "'It Tears the Heart Right Out of You': Memories of Striker Replacement at International Paper Company in De Pere, Wisconsin, 1987–88." *Oral History Review* 31(2): 1–27.

———. 2006. "'Just Like a Death': The Closing of the International Paper Company Mill in Mobile, Alabama, and the Deindustrialization of the South, 2000–2005." *Alabama Review* 59(1): 44–77.

Minimum-Wage.org. 2015. *Maine Minimum Wage 2014, 2015*. Washington, DC: Minimum-Wage.org. http://www.minimum-wage.org/states.asp?state=Maine (accessed August 11, 2015).

Minnesota Department of Employment and Economic Development (Minnesota DEED). 2011. *Minnesota Dislocated Worker Program State Fiscal Year 2011 Annual Report: Supporting Dislocated Workers through Economic Recovery*. St. Paul, MN: Minnesota Department of Employment and Economic Development.

————. 2012. *Minnesota Dislocated Worker Program State Fiscal Year 2012 Annual Report: Supporting Our Workforce, Strengthening Our Economy.* St. Paul, MN: Minnesota Department of Employment and Economic Development.

Moorthy, Vivek. 1990. "Unemployment in Canada and the United States: The Role of Unemployment Insurance Benefits." Federal Reserve Bank of New York *Quarterly Review* 14(Winter): 48–61.

Morissette, René, Hanqing Qiu, and Ping Ching Winnie Chan. 2013. "The Risk and Cost of Job Loss in Canada, 1978–2008." *Canadian Journal of Economics* 46(4): 1480–1509.

Mui, Ylan Q. 2014. "More American Workers Are Stuck in Part-Time Jobs." *Minneapolis Star Tribune*, July 3, D:1–D:2.

Nedelkoska, Ljubica, and Frank Neffke. 2011. "Skill Shortage and Skill Redundancy: Asymmetry in the Transferability of Skills." Paper presented at the Dynamics of Institutions and Markets in Europe (DIME) Final Conference, held in Maastricht, Netherlands, April 6–8.

Neitzert, Monica, Anne-Marie Mawhiney, and Elaine Porter. 1999. "Life after Layoff: Women in a Remote Single-Industry Community." In *Boom Town Blues. Elliot Lake: Collapse and Revival in a Single Industry Community*, Anne-Marie Mawhiney and Jane Pitblado, eds. Toronto: Dundurn, pp. 53–74.

Neuwirth, Robert, and Jim Rosenberg. 1998. "Bowater Shuts Pulp Mill, Sells Land; Abitibi Buys Stone Mill." *Editor and Publisher* 131(43): 38. http:// eds.b.ebscohost.com.ezproxy.hclib.org/ehost/delivery?sid=c4b71601-1aa9 -4ec1-a000-7f98f (accessed June 26, 2015).

New York Times. 1986. "Maine Town Divided by Bitter Strike." *New York Times*, December 27. http://www.nytimes.com/1986/12/28/us/maine -town-divided-by-bitter-strike.html (accessed June 30, 2015).

Newman, Betsy K. 1995. "Career Change for Those over 40: Critical Issues and Insights." *Career Development Quarterly* 44(1): 64–66.

Northrup, Herbert R. 1969. *The Negro in the Paper Industry.* Philadelphia: University of Pennsylvania Press.

Nova Scotia Transition Advisory Team. 2012. *Our Community, Our Future.* Final Report. Halifax, Nova Scotia: Government of Nova Scotia Transition Advisory Team.

Oklahoma Employment Security Commission. 2008. *National Emergency Grant (NEG).* Oklahoma City, OK: Oklahoma Employment Security Commission. http://www.ok.gov/oesc_web/Services/Workforce_Services/ Assistance_Programs/National_Emergency_Grant_%28NEG%29.html (accessed October 21, 2015).

Opidee, Ioanna. 2012. "The State of Magazine Paper in 2012: Closures, Con-

solidations, and Waning Demand for Print Lead to Market Volatility." *Folio*
41(1): 10. www.foliomag.com/2012/state-magazine-paper-2012 (accessed
June 26, 2015).

Ortiz, Susan Y., and Vincent J. Roscigno. 2009. "Discrimination, Women, and
Work: Processes and Variations by Race and Class." *Sociological Quarterly*
50(2): 336–359.

Osborn, William C. 1974. *The Paper Plantation: Ralph Nader's Study Group
Report on the Pulp and Paper Industry in Maine*. New York: Grossman.

Oyebode, A. Taiwo, Linda F. Cantley, Martin D. Slade, Keshia M. Pollack,
Sally Vegso, Martha G. Fiellin, and Mark R. Cullen. 2009. "Sex Differences in Injury Patterns among Workers in Heavy Manufacturing." *American Journal of Epidemiology* 169(2): 161–166.

Padavic, Irene. 1991. "The Re-Creation of Gender in a Male Workplace." *Sym-
bolic Interaction* 14(3): 279–294.

Parker, Kim, and Eileen Patten. 2013. "The Sandwich Generation: Rising Financial Burdens for Middle-Aged Americans." Social and Demographic Trends
Series. Washington, DC: Pew Research Center. www.pewsocialtrends
.org/2013/01/30/the-sandwich-generation/ (accessed July 14, 2015).

Parks, James. 2009. "Women Workers: The Hidden Casualties of Manufacturing Job Loss." *Demos: An Equal Say and an Equal Chance for All* (AFL-
CIO blog), September 23. http://www.demos.org/news/women-workers
-hidden-casualties-manufacturing-job-loss (accessed July 14, 2015).

Parnes, Herbert S., Mary G. Gagen, and Randall H. King. 1981. "The Incidence
and Impact of Job Loss among Long-Service Workers." In *Work and Retirement: A Longitudinal Study of Men*, Herbert S. Parnes, ed. Cambridge, MA:
MIT Press, pp. 67–93.

Parnes, Herbert S., and Randall H. King. 1977. "Middle-Aged Job Losers."
Industrial Gerontology 4(2): 77–95.

Payne, Roy, Peter Warr, and Jean Hartley. 1984. "Social Class and Psychological Ill-Health during Unemployment." *Sociology of Health and Illness* 6(2):
152–174.

Pesendorfer, Martin. 2003. "Horizontal Mergers in the Paper Industry." *RAND
Journal of Economics* 34(3): 495–515.

Poletaev, Maxim, and Chris Robinson. 2008. "Human Capital Specificity: Evidence from the Dictionary of Occupational Titles and Displaced Worker
Surveys, 1984–2000." CIBC Working Paper No. 2008-3. London, Ontario,
Canada: University of Western Ontario. http://economics.uwo.ca/cibc/
workingpapers_docs/wp2008/Poletaev_Robinson03.pdf (accessed July 9,
2015).

Portis, Bernard, and Michel G. Suys. 1970. *The Effect of Advance Notice in a
Plant Shutdown: A Study of the Closing of the Kelvinator Plant in London,*

Ontario. London, Ontario, Canada: University of Western Ontario, School of Business Administration.

Prasad, Eswar, and Alun Thomas. 1998. "Labour Market Adjustment in Canada and the United States." *Canadian Public Policy* 24(Suppl. 1): S121–S137.

Pulp and Paper Canada Daily News. 2012. "Minas Basin Closing Mill; Cannot Achieve Long Term Sustainability." *Pulp and Paper Canada Daily News,* Nov. 5. http://www.pulpandpapercanada.com/news/minas-basin-closing -mill-cannot-achieve-long-term-sustainability/1001820259/?&er=NA (accessed August 13, 2015).

Pulp and Paperworkers' Resource Council. 2014. *Mill Curtailments and Closures Map.* McGehee, AZ: Pulp and Paperworkers' Resource Council. www.pprc.info/html/millclosures.htm (accessed October 4, 2015).

Pursell, Donald E., and William D. Torrence. 1978. "Age and Reactions to Unemployment: An Empirical Examination of Job Search Methods and Postunemployment Earnings." In *Proceedings of the Thirty-First Annual Meeting of the Industrial Relations Research Association,* B. D. Dennis, ed. Madison, WI: Industrial Relations Research Association, pp. 141–148.

Quinn, Peggy. 1999. "Bringing People through Life Transitions." In *Boom Town Blues. Elliot Lake: Collapse and Revival in a Single-Industry Community,* Anne-Marie Mawhiney and Jane Pitblado, eds. Toronto: Dundurn, pp. 39–41.

Ramstad, Evan. 2014. "Remington Will Close Rifle Plant in St. Cloud; 68 Jobs to Be Lost." *Minneapolis Star Tribune,* May 20, D:1–D:2.

Rayman, Paula. 1987. "Women and Unemployment." *Social Research* 54(2): 355–376.

Reliable Plant. 2007. "Women Hit Hard by Manufacturing Job Loss in Canada." *Reliable Plant,* March 8. http://ftp.reliableplant.com/Read/5172/women-hit-hard-by-manufacturing-job-loss-in-canada (accessed July 14, 2014).

Reskin, Barbara. 1993. "Sex Segregation in the Workplace." *Annual Review of Sociology* 19(1993): 241–270.

Resolute Forest Products. 2014. *SEC Filings, Item 2: Management's Discussion and Analysis of Financial Condition and Results of Operations.* Form 10-K, March 3. Montreal, Quebec: Resolute Forest Products.

———. 2015. *Newsprint.* Montreal, Quebec, Canada: Resolute Forest Products. http://www.resolutefp.com/Products/Newsprint (accessed August 12, 2015).

Reuters. 2012. "Resolute Forest Products Inc. Completes Sale of Bowater Mersey Paper Company Limited." Reuters, December 10. http://paper -products.capitallink.com/company/news.html?ticker=RFP (accessed August 13, 2015).

Richardson, Whit. 2014a. "Analyst: Mill Closure Boosts Verso's Finances." *Portland Press Herald*, October 8. http://www.centralmaine.com/2014/10/08/analyst-mill-closure-boosts-versos-finances/ (accessed November 30, 2015).

———. 2014b. "Rumford Paper Mill Union Leader: Verso Takeover Won't Stop February Layoffs but Does Offer Hope." *Bangor Daily News*, January 6. http://bangordailynews.com/2014/01/06/business/rumford-paper-mill-union-leader-verso- (accessed September 2, 2015).

———. 2014c. "Verso-NewPage Merger Could Bring Upheaval before Prosperity for Maine Mills, Say Experts." *Bangor Daily News*, January 26. http://bangordailynews.com/2014/01/26/business/verso-newpage-merger-could-bring-upheaval (accessed November 30, 2015).

———. 2014d. "Verso Paper to Acquire NewPage for $1.4 Billion." *Bangor Daily News*, January 6. http://bangordailynews.com/2014/01/06/business/verso-paper-to-purchase-new-page-for- (accessed September 2, 2015).

Rieland, Don. 2011. "'Where Are the Jobs?' . . . Blame the Tech Boom." Commentary. Ferndale, WA: Buy American 1st. www.buyamerican1st.com/tag/pulp-mill-closure (accessed June 26, 2015).

Robertson, Tom. 2013. "Boise Mill Layoff of 265 Workers 'Devastating.'" Minnesota Public Radio News, May 2.
http://www.mprnews.org/story/2013/05/02/regional/boise-mill-international-falls (accessed June 26, 2015).

Rondon, Michael. 2013. "Paper Industry Begins to Stabilize: Things Are Beginning to Stabilize after Years of Wild Swings." *Folio*, February 1. www.foliomag.com/2013/paper-industry-begins-stabilize (accessed June 26, 2015).

Rones, Philip L., and Diane E. Herz. 1992. *Older Workers in the Labor Market.* A Report from the Congressional Research Service to the Chairman of the Select Committee on Aging. U.S. Congress. House of Representatives. 102nd Cong., 2nd sess. Washington, DC: U.S. Government Printing Office.

Rook, Karen, David Dooley, and Ralph Catalano. 1991a. "Age Differences in Workers' Efforts to Cope with Economic Distress." In *The Social Context of Coping*, John Eckenrode, ed. Plenum Series on Stress and Coping. New York: Plenum Press, pp. 79–105.

———. 1991b. "Stress Transmission: The Effects of Husbands' Job Stressors on the Emotional Health of Their Wives." *Journal of Marriage and the Family* 53(1): 165–177.

Root, Kenneth A. 1977. "Workers and Their Families in a Plant Shutdown." Paper presented at the annual meeting of the American Sociological Association, held in Chicago, IL, September 5–9.

Root, Kenneth A., and Roger Mayland. 1978. "The Plant's Closing; What Are We Going to Do? Worker and Family Response to Job Displacement."

Paper presented at the annual meeting of the National Council on Family Relations, held in Philadelphia, PA, October 19–22.

Root, Kenneth A., and Rosemarie J. Park. 2009. *Forced Out: Older Workers Confront Job Loss*. Boulder, CO: Lynne Rienner Publishers.

———. 2016. *Surviving Job Loss: Papermakers in Maine and Minnesota*. Kalamazoo, MI: W.E. Upjohn Institute for Employment Research.

Root, Kenneth A., Steven A. Root, and Louise A. Sundin. 2007. "Public School Teachers Join the Ranks of Dislocated Workers." In *Research in the Sociology of Work*. Vol. 17, *Workplace Temporalities*, Beth A. Rubin, ed. Bingley, UK: Emerald Group, pp. 465–496.

Rosenfeld, Rachel A. 1983. "Sex Segregation and Sectors: An Analysis of Gender Differences in Returns from Employer Changes." *American Sociological Review* 48(5): 637–655.

Rosenfeld, Rachel A., and Kenneth I. Spenner. 1992. "Occupational Sex Segregation and Women's Early Career Job Shifts." *Work and Occupations* 19(4): 424–449.

Roth, Louise Marie. 2002. "Selling Women Short: A Research Note on Gender Differences in Compensation on Wall Street." In *Workplace/Women's Place: An Anthology*, Paula J. Dubeck and Dana Dunn, eds. 2nd ed. Los Angeles: Roxbury Publishing, pp. 207–216.

Rugaber, Christopher S. 2014. "Recession Lingers in Wages." *Minneapolis Star Tribune*, September 9, D:3.

Rugaber, Christopher S., and Paul Wiseman. 2013. "Women Regain All Jobs Lost in Recession; Minnesota Was a Bright Spot, with Recovery Also Benefiting Men." *Minneapolis Star Tribune*, September 13, A:1.

Sartell Newsleader. 2011. "Verso Plans to Lay Off 175 Employees." *Sartell Newsleader*, October 13, A:1.

Schafer, Lee. 2014. "Lying to Get a Job Is a Sign of the Times." *Minneapolis Star Tribune*, February 5, D:1.

Schmenner, Roger W. 1982. *Making Business Location Decisions*. Englewood Cliffs, NJ: Prentice Hall.

Schmid, John. 2012a. "Bankrolled and Bioengineered, China Supplants Wisconsin's Paper Industry." *Milwaukee Journal Sentinel*, December 11. http://www.jsonline.com/business/bankrolled-and-bioengineered-china -supplants-wisconsins-paper-industry-183049221.html (accessed September 4, 2015).

———. 2012b. "Wisconsin's Place in Paper Industry under Siege." *Milwaukee Journal Sentinel*, December 8. http://www.jsonline.com/business/paper -industry-digital-china-wisconsin-182612951.html (accessed September 2, 2015).

———. 2014. "Wisconsin's Paper Industry Braces for Uncertainty." *Milwau-

kee Journal Sentinel, June 7. http://www.jsonline.com/business/wisconsins
-paper-industry-braces-for-uncertainty-b99284187z1-262261441.html
(accessed September 2, 2015).

Schoch, Eric B. 1986. "IBM Will Close Plant in Indiana." *Indianapolis Star*, November 12, A:1, A:10.

Seewald, Nancy, and Esther D'Amico. 2009. "Reshuffling the Paper Chemical Stack." *Chemical Week* 171(4): 22–23. http://www.chemweek.com/sections/cover_story/Reshuffling-the-Paper-Chemical-Stack_16922.html (accessed June 26, 2015).

Sentementes, Gus G. 2010. "Recession Takes Psychological Toll: Layoffs, Workplace Uncertainty Can Aggravate Mental Problems." *Baltimore Sun*, May 31. http://www.lacanadaonline.com/sports/sns-health-workers-mental -health,0,1878055.story?page=2 (accessed June 26, 2015).

Shaw, James B., and Elain Barrett-Power. 1997. "A Conceptual Framework for Assessing Organization, Work Group, and Individual Effectiveness during and after Downsizing." *Human Relations* 50(2): 109–127.

Shaw, R. Paul. 1986. "Unemployment and Low Family Incomes in Canada." *Canadian Public Policy* 12(2): 368–386.

Sheikh, Munir A. 1998. "Structural and Macro Policy and the Canada-U.S. Unemployment Rate Gap." *Canadian Public Policy* 24(Suppl. 1): S271–S276.

Shultz, George P., and Arnold R. Weber. 1964. "The Fort Worth Project of the Armour Automation Committee." *Monthly Labor Review* 87(1): 53–57.

———. 1966. *Strategies for the Displaced Worker: Confronting Economic Change*. New York: Harper and Row.

Silver, Susan, John Shields, and Sue Wilson. 2005. "Restructuring of Full-Time Workers: A Case of Transitional Dislocation or Social Exclusion in Canada? Lessons from the 1990s." *Social Policy and Administration* 39(7): 786–801.

Sirkin, Harold L., and George Stalk Jr. 1990. "Fix the Process, Not the Problem." *Harvard Business Review* 68(4): 26–33.

Smith, Suzanna. 1991. "Women's Reactions to Job Loss: The Moral Dilemmas of a Plant Closing." *Agriculture and Human Values* 8(3): 35–46.

Sobel, David, and Susan Meurer. 1994. *Working at Inglis: The Life and Death of a Canadian Factory*. Toronto: James Lorimer.

Stassen-Berger, Rachel E. 2014. "Deadlock on Minimum Wage Loosening: If the House and Senate Can Work out Details, Minnesota Is Set to Increase Its Minimum Wage from One of the Nation's Lowest to One of the Highest This Year." *Minneapolis Star Tribune*, March 4, A:1, A:7.

Stephens, Melvin Jr. 2003. "Job Loss Expectations, Realizations, and Household Consumption Behavior." NBER Working Paper No. 9508. Cambridge,

MA: National Bureau of Economic Research. http://www.nber.org/papers/ w9508 (accessed November 17, 2015).

Stern, James L. 1969. "Evolution of Private Manpower Planning in Armour's Plant Closings." *Monthly Labor Review* 92(12): 21–28.

Stevens, Joe B. 1978. *The Oregon Wood Products Labor Force: Job Rationing and Worker Adaptation in a Declining Industry.* Oregon State University Agricultural Experiment Station Special Report No. 529. Corvallis, OR: Oregon State University, Department of Agricultural and Resource Economics.

Storer, Paul A., and Marc A. Van Audenrode. 1998. "Exploring the Links between Wage Inequality and Unemployment: A Comparison of Canada and the U.S." *Canadian Public Policy* 24(Suppl. 1): S233–S253.

Strom, Sara. 2003. "Unemployment and Families: A Review of Research." *Social Service Review* 77(3): 399–430.

Sullivan, Daniel G., and Till von Wachter. 2009. "Job Displacement and Mortality: An Analysis Using Administrative Data." *Quarterly Journal of Economics* 124(3): 1265–1306.

Svensen, Erling, Gunnar Neset, and Hege R. Eriksen. 2007. "Factors Associated with a Positive Attitude towards Change among Employees during the Early Phase of a Downsizing Process." *Scandinavian Journal of Psychology* 48(2): 153–159.

Sweeney, Brendan, and John Holmes. 2013. "Problematizing Labour's Agency: Rescaling Collective Bargaining in British Columbia Pulp and Paper Mills." *Antipode* 45(1): 218–237.

Taber, Jane. 2012. "Mill Closings Prompt Nova Scotia Power Company to Seek Higher Rates." *Globe and Mail*, May 9. http://www.theglobeandmail .com/news/national/mill-closings-prompt-nova-scotia-power-company-to -seek-higher-rates/article4105833/ (accessed August 13, 2015).

Thayer, Gail. 2002. *Maine's Unemployment Compensation System and the Full-Time Work Requirement.* Hallowell, ME: Maine Women's Policy Center.

TheLedger.com. 2015a. *Maine—Historical Changes.* Lakeland, FL: Ledger Media Group. http://www.ledgerdata.com/unemployment/history/maine/ (accessed October 26, 2015).

———. 2015b. *Minnesota—Historical Changes.* Lakeland, FL: Ledger Media Group. http://www.ledgerdata.com/unemployment/history/minnesota/ (accessed October 26, 2015).

Theshastamill.com. 2015. *Mill Closure and Aftermath.* Anderson, CA: Theshastamill.com. http://www.theshastamill.com/Post%20Closure/index .html (accessed June 30, 2015).

Thiess, Rebecca. 2011. "The Great Recession's Long Tail: Third Anniversary Underscores Severity of Labor Market Woes." EPI Briefing Paper No. 294. Washington, DC: Economic Policy Institute.

Thomas, L. Eugene, Esther McCabe, and Jane E. Berry. 1980. "Unemployment and Family Stress: A Reassessment." *Family Relations* 29(4): 517–524.

Thorp, Ben, Harry Seamans, Harry Cullinan, Masood Akhtar, Pat McCarthy, Keith Van Scotter, and Russell Wanke. 2014. "Pulp and Paper Innovations: Our Capital Intensive Industry Has Seen Some Remarkable Innovations and Achievements over the Past 30 Years." *Paper360°* 2014(July/ August): 12–16, 36. http://www.nxtbook.com/naylor/PPIS/PPIS0414/index.php?startid=12 (accessed June 26, 2015).

Tosti-Kharas, Jennifer. 2012. "Continued Organizational Identification Following Involuntary Job Loss." *Journal of Managerial Psychology* 27(8): 829–847.

Townsend, Alan, and Francis Peck. 1985. "An Approach to the Analysis of Redundancies in the UK (post-1976): Some Methodological Problems and Policy Implications." In *Politics and Method: Contrasting Studies in Industrial Geography*, Doreen Massey and Richard Meegan, eds. New York: Methuen, pp. 64–87.

Turkington, Carol. 1986. "Farm Women and Stress." American Psychological Association *Monitor on Psychology* 17(6): 18–19.

University of Maine. 2013. *Eastern Fine Paper Company Oral History Project*. Orono, ME: University of Maine, Maine Folklife Center. https://umaine.edu/folklife/research-and-exhibits/research/eastern-fine-paper-company-oral-history-project/ (accessed July 9, 2015).

U.S. Census Bureau. 2015. *Census of Population and Housing*. Washington, DC: U.S. Census Bureau. http://www.census.gov/prod/www/decennial.html (accessed October 27, 2015).

U.S. Department of Labor (USDOL). 1971. "The Employment Problems of Older Workers." Prepared for the White House Conference on Aging, November 29. Bureau of Labor Statistics Bulletin No. 1721. Washington, DC: U.S. Department of Labor.

———. 2015a. *Comparison of State Unemployment Laws*. Washington, DC: U.S. Department of Labor, Employment and Training Administration. http://www.unemploymentinsurance.doleta.gov/unemploy/comparison2012.asp (accessed November 6, 2015).

———. 2015b. *The Worker Adjustment and Retraining Notification Act: A Guide to Advance Notice of Closings and Layoffs*. Washington, DC: U.S. Department of Labor, Employment and Training Administration. http://www.doleta.gov/programs/factsht/warn.htm (accessed August 12, 2015).

Verso Corporation (Verso). 2009. *Maine on Paper: An Industry We Can't Afford*

to Lose. Memphis, TN: Verso Paper Corporation. http://www.nipimpressions
.org/photos/File206.pdf (accessed September 4, 2015).

von Wachter, Till, and Elizabeth Weber Handwerker. 2009. "Variation in the
Cost of Job Loss by Worker Skill: Evidence Using Matched Data from California, 1991–2000." Mimeo, Columbia University.

Voydanoff, Patricia. 1983a. "Unemployment: Family Strategies for Adaptation." In *Stress and the Family*. Vol. 2, *Coping with Catastrophe*, Charles
R. Figley and Hamilton I. McCubbin, eds. New York: Brunner/Mazel, pp.
90–102.

———. 1983b. "Unemployment and Family Stress." In *Research on the Inter-
weave of Social Roles*. Vol. 3, *Jobs and Families*, Helena Znaniecka Lopata
and Joseph H. Pleck, eds. Greenwich, CT: JAI Press, pp. 239–250.

Warnactlaw.com. 2012. *Maine Revised Statutes*. Washington, DC: Warnact-
law.com. http://www.warnactlaw.com/pdfs/me_rev_stat_tit_26_625b.pdf
(accessed July 13, 2015).

Warr, Peter. 1987. *Work, Unemployment, and Mental Health*. Oxford: Claren-
don Press.

Warr, Peter, and Paul Jackson. 1983. "Self-Esteem and Unemployment among
Young Workers." *Le Travail Humain* 46(2): 355–366.

Warr, Peter, Paul Jackson, and Michael Banks. 1988. "Unemployment and
Mental Health: Some British Studies." *Journal of Social Issues* 44(4):
47–68.

WCSH-TV. 2014. "Catalyst Intends to Buy Rumford Paper Mill from New-
Page." WCSH-TV, October 30. Portland, ME: WCSH-TV. http://www
.wcsh6.com/story/news/local/2014/10/30/cataylst-rumford-paper-newpage
-purchase/18209821/ (accessed September 2, 2015).

White, Nathan. 2008. "Canadian Town Troubled by Paper Mill Closure." Man-
ufacturing.net, January 31. Madison, WI: Manufacturing.net.

Wiercinski, Susan. 2012. "In the Paper Market, the More Things Change, the
More They Stay the Same—at Least for Now." Sheridan blog entry, February 9. http://www.sheridan.com/blog/paper-market-more-things-change
-more-they-stay-same-least-now (accessed June 26, 2015).

Wikipedia. 2014a. *Pulp and Paper Industry in the United States*. San Francisco,
CA: Wikipedia. https://en.wikipedia.org/wiki/Pulp_and_paper_industry
_in_the_United_States (accessed June 30, 2015).

———. 2014b. *Verso Paper Sartell Mill*. San Francisco, CA: Wikipedia.
https://en.wikipedia.org/wiki/Verso_Paper_Sartell_Mill (accessed June 30,
2015).

———. 2015a. *Resolute Forest Products*. San Francisco, CA: Wikipedia.
http://en.wikipedia.org/wiki/AbitibiBowater (accessed August 12, 2015).

———. 2015b. *Unemployment Benefits*. San Francisco, CA: Wikipedia.

https://en.wikipedia.org/wiki/Unemployment_benefits (accessed August 12, 2015).

———. 2015c. *Worker Adjustment and Retraining Notification Act*. San Francisco, CA: Wikipedia. https://en.wikipedia.org/wiki/Worker_Adjustment _and_Retraining_Notification_Act (accessed August 12, 2015).

———. 2015d. *Workforce Investment Act of 1998*. San Francisco, CA: Wikipedia. https://en.wikipedia.org/wiki/Workforce_Investment_Act_of_1998 (accessed August 25, 2015).

Wilkinson, Derek, and David Robinson. 1999. "Search, Succour, and Success: Looking for Jobs from Elliot Lake." In *Boom Town Blues. Elliot Lake: Collapse and Revival in a Single-Industry Community*, Anne-Marie Mawhiney and Jane Pitblado, eds. Toronto: Dundurn, pp. 75–88.

Wirtz, Ronald A. 2005. "Company Mass Layoffs: The 'Other' Job Shock." Federal Reserve Bank of Minneapolis *Fedgazette* 2005(November): 10.

Wood, Robert S. 1991. *An Analysis of the Forest Industry Employment Situation in Port Alberni*. Victoria, BC: Ministry of Forests.

Wright, Barry, and Julian Barling. 1998. "'The Executioners' Song': Listening to Downsizers Reflect on Their Experiences." *Canadian Journal of Administrative Sciences* 15(4): 339–354.

Young, Cristobal. 2012. "Losing a Job: The Nonpecuniary Cost of Unemployment in the United States." *Social Forces* 91(2): 609–634.

Zaccagna, Remo. 2011. "'Window of Opportunity' Open for Bowater Mill." *Halifax Chronicle Herald*, November 3. http://thechronicleherald.ca/business/29197-window-opportunity-open-bowater-mill (accessed August 13, 2015).

Zagorsky, Jay L. 1993. "Job Vacancies in the United States and Canada." *Journal of Economic and Social Measurement* 19(4): 305–319.

———. 1996. "The Effect of Definitional Differences on U.S. and Canadian Unemployment Rates." *Canadian Business Economics* 4(2): 13–21.

Zavala, Kathy. 2013. *Stearns-Benton Customized Response to Verso Paper Mill Layoffs*. St. Cloud, MN: Stearns-Benton Employment and Training Council. http://www.mwca-mn.org/Best_Practices/2013/Layoff%20Customized %20Response-%20Stearns-Benton.pdf (accessed July 10, 2015).

Ziewitz, Kathryn, and June Wiaz. 2004. *Green Empire: The St. Joe Company and the Remaking of Florida's Panhandle*. Gainesville, FL: University Press of Florida.

Authors

Kenneth A. Root is a professor emeritus of sociology at Luther College in Decorah, Iowa. He now resides in Minneapolis, Minnesota. This is his second book with Rosemarie Park. Their first, *Forced Out: Older Workers Confront Job Loss*, followed the experiences of 173 factory workers from their first reactions at being laid off to more studied reflections years later. It was published in 2009 by Lynne Rienner Publishers in Boulder, Colorado, as a FirstForum Press book. Root earned a bachelor's degree from St. Olaf College and a master's and doctorate from the University of Iowa, as well as a master's in social work from the University of Wisconsin–Madison. A past president of the Iowa Sociological Association, he serves as a research consultant focusing on the issues of dislocated workers.

Rosemarie J. Park is an associate professor of education in the Department of Organization, Leadership Policy, and Development at the University of Minnesota's College of Education and Human Development. She earned a doctorate in education from Harvard University. Her areas of interest include adult literacy education, plain language in law and government, educational needs of the workforce, and blended learning. She was trained as an elementary teacher in Great Britain and has taught in elementary schools and adult literacy settings in both Great Britain and the United States. Park has published in such journals as *Reading Research Quarterly, Adult Literacy and Basic Education*, and *Clarity*. Other publications include a previous book with Kenneth A. Root, *Forced Out: Older Workers Confront Job Loss*, published in 2009 by Lynne Rienner Publishers in Boulder, Colorado.

Index

The italic letters *f, n,* or *t* following a page number indicate a figure, note, or table on that page. Double letters mean more than one such item on a single page.

About the Institute

The W.E. Upjohn Institute for Employment Research is a nonprofit research organization devoted to finding and promoting solutions to employment-related problems at the national, state, and local levels. It is an activity of the W.E. Upjohn Unemployment Trustee Corporation, which was established in 1932 to administer a fund set aside by Dr. W.E. Upjohn, founder of The Upjohn Company, to seek ways to counteract the loss of employment income during economic downturns.

The Institute is funded largely by income from the W.E. Upjohn Unemployment Trust, supplemented by outside grants, contracts, and sales of publications. Activities of the Institute comprise the following elements: 1) a research program conducted by a resident staff of professional social scientists; 2) a competitive grant program, which expands and complements the internal research program by providing financial support to researchers outside the Institute; 3) a publications program, which provides the major vehicle for disseminating the research of staff and grantees, as well as other selected works in the field; and 4) an Employment Management Services division, which manages most of the publicly funded employment and training programs in the local area.

The broad objectives of the Institute's research, grant, and publication programs are to 1) promote scholarship and experimentation on issues of public and private employment and unemployment policy, and 2) make knowledge and scholarship relevant and useful to policymakers in their pursuit of solutions to employment and unemployment problems.

Current areas of concentration for these programs include causes, consequences, and measures to alleviate unemployment; social insurance and income maintenance programs; compensation; workforce quality; work arrangements; family labor issues; labor-management relations; and regional economic development and local labor markets.

CPSIA information can be obtained at www.ICGtesting.com
Printed in the USA
LVOW08s0511050216

473691LV00003B/4/P